This Is What A Feminist Slut Looks Like

Perspectives on the SlutWalk Movement

edited by

Alyssa Teekah, Erika Jane Scholz, May Friedman,
and Andrea O'Reilly

DEMETER

DEMETER PRESS

The publisher gratefully acknowledges the the financial assistance of the Government of Canada through the Canada Book Fund.

Canada

Demeter Press
140 Holland Street West
P. O. Box 13022
Bradford, ON L3Z 2Y5
Tel: (905) 775-9089
Email: info@demeterpress.org
Website: www.demeterpress.org

Demeter Press logo based on the sculpture "Demeter" by Maria-Luise Bodirsky <www.keramik-atelier.bodirsky.de>

Front cover artwork: Pomona Lake <hello@pomonalake.ca>

Printed and Bound in Canada

Library and Archives Canada Cataloguing in Publication

This is what a feminist slut looks like : perspectives on the slutwalk movement / edited by Alyssa Teekah, Erika Jane Scholz, May Friedman and Andrea O'Reilly.

Includes bibliographical references.
ISBN 978-1-926452-15-9 (paperback)

1. Feminism. 2. Feminists. I. O'Reilly, Andrea, 1961–, author, editor II. Friedman, May, 1975–, author, editor III. Teekah, Alyssa, 1988–, author, editor IV. Scholz, Erika Jane, 1983– author, editor

HQ1155.T55 2015   305.42   C2015-901677-0

*For all those who have been shamed and blamed,
and in solidarity with all those who take action
against sexual violence.*

Table of Contents

CONTENTS

Acknowledgements

Dedicated to my parents, the original authors of the book on supporting your child. They are my best friends and my fiercest fans, from marching on that April day to creating Facebook accounts just to comment and debate people on the Slutwalk Facebook group.

To my "adopted" sister Raisa with whom I've shared many ups and downs through our sometimes paralleled, sometimes diverging, sometimes weaving paths on the journey of feminist and personal understanding.

To Tara Atluri, one of the fiercest women I have had the pleasure of learning from, who helped me to see the fiery, passionate dimensions of political engagement, the insistence on valuing your work and your capability, and what it means to own your intersectionality.

To Andrea and May, our mentors in this process. Few people get the opportunity to work through incredible and life-changing experiences in a process that affords them the opportunity to grow and reflect. The journey to creating this collection made that possible—and along the way, I was able to be in the presence of two masters (or mistresses). Thank you!

—Alyssa Teekah

A big thank you to everyone who has participated in the rich, intense and often overwhelming discussion about SlutWalk—regardless of the outcome, the conversation makes our feminist spaces richer. Many thanks to Alyssa, Erika, and Andrea for their amazing work and their shared passion for this project. And my thanks to Dan and the kids for ensuring that "slut" is a word that keeps us talking in the playground, around the dinner table and in our day-to-day lives.

—May Friedman

This is dedicated to my grandmother, the fiercest woman I have ever known. Thank you for showing me the importance of never giving up on others and most importantly, myself. Je t'aime. To my partner, Mike (and Sammy), who has supported me throughout all of the chaos and was the very person to push me into the advocate life. I love you.

My deepest thanks to the staff and the entire TRCC/MWAR family and community of survivors and allies. Your endless commitment, passion, and determination towards ending sexual violence and seeking justice for all survivors is unsurpassed and are power of examples of the importance of fighting the good fight.

Finally, much love and respect to my colleague and homegirl, Alyssa Teekah. I would not have survived the last five years without you by my side. I am your biggest fan. And my eternal gratitude to Andrea and May, it has been an honour to have had this opportunity to collaborate with two of wisest, committed and loving women I have ever met. Thank you for continuously pushing the limits and letting our voices be heard.

—Erika Jane Scholz

As always, a HUGE thank you to the fabulous women at Demeter Press who made possible the publication of this book; particular thanks to Katherine Barret, Nicole Doro, Tracey Carlyle, and Angie Deveau. And thank you to my co-editors who always kept the faith, and to our contributors who believed in the importance of this collection. I attended the first SlutWalk with several women from MIRCI's Mother Outlaws group: thank you to Linn, Renee, Christina and Kim for being the feisty feminists you are and for sharing that splendid day with me. Thank you to my two fabulous

feminist daughters Casey and Clementine who I marched with that day and who give me such hope for our feminist future. Finally, the international SlutWalk movement and this book would never have happened had it not been for the courageous women who organized the first SlutWalk march. Thank you Heather Jarvis, Colleen Westendorf, Raisa Bhuiyan, Jeanette Janzen, Laura Mc-Lean, Sonya J. F. Barnett, Alyssa Teekah, and Erika Jane Scholz.
—Andrea O'Reilly

Introduction

MAY FRIEDMAN, ANDREA O'REILLY, ALYSSA TEEKAH
AND ERIKA JANE SCHOLZ

WHEN WE BEGAN WORK on this book, we were inundated with responses: the submissions were overwhelming and we received query after query about the collection. In the midst of all the positive reinforcement, we received an isolated, hateful, misogynist email, an email that was disturbing enough we chose to file a police report in the event of any further escalation. Thus, the following surreal conversation between one of the book's editors and a member of the Toronto Police Services took place:

Editor: Thank you for coming so quickly. The situation is that I'm working on a book and all of the editors have received this nasty email. The book is about SlutWalk, which is a—

Toronto Police Officer (dryly): I'm familiar with SlutWalk, thanks.

He was familiar with SlutWalk. The awkwardness of the Toronto Police, catalyst for the international SlutWalk movement, being called upon to serve and protect the editors of this volume, was lost on neither party. Notably, the officer required no description, no prompting to jog his memory of this contemporary protest movement. SlutWalk, initially conceived as a gathering of a several hundred pissed-off feminists taking to the streets in Toronto, Canada, has instead spawned a global movement. We are all familiar with SlutWalk: whether we love it or hate it, joined in proudly or emphatically took a pass—we are all familiar with SlutWalk.

This book was created to consider the impact of an emergent global feminist movement. The book is not a ceaseless celebration of SlutWalk—though it's relevant to note that two of the editors were among the organizers of the inaugural Toronto event, the other two were proudly in attendance, and that we've had varying degrees of ambivalence about SlutWalk in the aftermath—nor is it a ceaseless critique. Rather, this collection aims to understand how a modest political action hit such a nerve that it morphed into an international feminist protest movement. We want to understand what went right—and what went wrong. We aim to explore the growing pains that come from such explosive progression, and to unpack some of the cogent critiques that SlutWalk engendered. By exploring SlutWalk as a case study for robust, albeit controversial, feminist engagement, we aim to take lessons away about maintaining and building a multifaceted feminist consciousness across space, place, age, and other critical diversities.

The chapters in this collection begin from many different places. Some focus on the movement's strengths; others on its failings. Several chapters hone in on specific SlutWalks to consider the particularities of the movement as it was adopted, in varying form, in a range of jurisdictions. What the chapters have in common, however, is that they honour the impact of the movement while maintaining a dialogue about how it was done well, how it might be done better, how it could be done again, and whether it should be abandoned.

BACKGROUND

The SlutWalk movement was catalyzed by the January 2011 comment by Toronto police constable Michael Sanguinetti that women should stop "dressing like sluts" in order to avoid sexual violence, although it is pertinent to note that founders' always saw Sanguinetti's comment as merely emblematic of a broader rape culture deserving of protest. In less than two months, a group of Toronto women organized a protest in response to the officer's comments, culminating in Toronto's first SlutWalk, held on April 3, 2011. Moving beyond this homegrown response to a local controversy, SlutWalk has since grown into a global phenomenon, with hundreds of marches planned or held throughout North America, Latin America, Europe, Africa and Asia. It is important to note, however, that the SlutWalk movement came on the heels of broader feminist genealogy.

Feminist organizing has often solidified around particular rallying points. The first wave[1] of the women's movement gained traction around organizing for women's right to vote and the push for Prohibition. Likewise, the women's movement of the 1960s and 1970s gained solidarity looking at abortion and women's rights within both familial and employment roles (Dow; Purvis). Despite both legal and substantive gains for women, however, women of every age, sexual orientation, race and class continue to experience sexual violence. While all women, gender non-binary folks, and trans folks are at risk of violence, this threat is greater for women from particular social locations, especially women of colour and women with disabilities. SlutWalk responded to the epidemic of violence, but it did not emerge exclusively in response to frustrations with the continuing assaults against women, gender non-binary folks, and trans folks. Rather, SlutWalk exemplified a response to the climate in which that violence occurs, a climate that continues to blame victims for their own victimization (Attwood; Ringose and Renold). In responding to the dismissive and misogynist comment of Officer Sanguinetti, women in attendance at SlutWalks responded less to their individual abusers and more to a climate that allows such violence to occur unchallenged, that valorizes women's fear as an appropriate method of attempting to maintain safety.

In response to the climate of victim blaming and woman shaming, some organizers took on what Jessica Ringrose and Emma Renold, borrowing from Judith Butler, call a "feminist politics of re-articulation" in which the word slut is reclaimed from its negative imagery and rehabilitated (Ringrose and Renold). Thus some folks who attended Slutwalks did so in deliberately provocative dress, and many placards at the rallies invoked the language of sex-positive feminism, resulting in what Glick has termed "a politics of transgression." Such a response also draws on feminist literature about agency and sex-positivity (Buszek; Payne; Martin). Other people dressed in everyday wear that would not be normatively identified as "slutty" in the effort to also mock assumptions around how rape and sexual assault works and to trouble the notion of protective forms of dress.

THEMES

As with any major feminist movement, SlutWalk hasn't been coherent. In different places SlutWalk has meant different things and has sometimes had different names, showing both the international, multilingual response to the movement (as in Latin American marches called Marchas de las Putas) but also differing responses to engagement with the word slut. Within the diversity of responses to SlutWalks, three major topics emerge. First, SlutWalks generated significant controversy, particularly in their potential to exist as privileged spaces that maintain oppressive social relations instead of combatting them. Perhaps in contradiction to this first idea, however, the second major point about the SlutWalk movement is the extent to which it has resulted in an exponentially greater uptake than ever considered by its Toronto founders. The explosive growth across such an extraordinary range of jurisdictions is definitely a hallmark of the movement. Finally, in the several years since their inception, SlutWalks require introspection in establishing the future of the movement and its evolution, or demise, in the many different spaces it has come to take up, as well as its role within the genealogy of feminist organizing. We aim to explicate these themes in greater detail before discussing the focused analyses of this collection in more depth.

CONTROVERSY

The "politics of re-signification" that attempted to rehabilitate the word slut were not uncontroversial. As many chapters in this collection articulate, the movement faced an overwhelming critique, not only from expected right wing corners, but also from across social justice movements. The controversy largely centred around the fact that the word slut (and the type of action undertaken at SlutWalks) remains within the purview of only particular bodies.

Many of these critiques referred to Slutwalk as emblematic of the problem of many mainstream, white, Western feminist efforts that affirm racism, colonialism, and a lack of transnational analysis in their efforts to be "feminist." The Black Women's Blueprint, for example, argued in an Open Letter that, "'slut' has different associations for Black women. We do not recognize ourselves nor do we see our lived experiences reflected within SlutWalk and especially not in its brand and its label." Jennifer Scott, blogging at *Ms. Magazine,* shared a similar sentiment around women with disabilities: "The word 'slut' has never felt like mine to reclaim. While women all over the world are waiting for people to stop seeing them as sex objects, women with disabilities are still waiting to be seen at all." Likewise, SlutWalks have been critiqued as harmful to folks across the spectrums of sexuality and gender (Dow and Wood). Apart from concerns about exclusivity, many women and feminists felt that the word slut was beyond rehabilitation, and the movement was critiqued for mounting a spectacle for the male gaze in the choice by (some) participants to dress provocatively. Other critiques, specifically relating to SlutWalks that involved police presence or reference to legal discourse, pointed out the issues around feminisms that invoke the nation state and military, police, and prison industrial complex.

The initial controversy, in an era of social media, spun off to a meta-controversy. Images of particular SlutWalks generated robust discussion and debate. Arguments weren't restricted to planning meetings or town halls, but occurred throughout cyberspace. This has presented a unique moment in the history of feminist organizing, in that much of the controversy and discussion has been archived and preserved for future analysis and engagement.

Responses to the controversy likewise varied. Organizers of the inaugural Toronto SlutWalk attempted to hear the many critiques of the event and immediately presented a response on their website aiming to articulate changes intended for future organizing, though many found this response lacking and hollow. Perhaps unsurprisingly in the realm of feminist debate, critiques weren't monolithic and generated a further level of discussion. For example, groups of women of colour expressed resentment at being represented by the Black Women's Blueprint. Hobson suggested that "black women, rather than oppose SlutWalk, should think of the ways it can be appropriated to serve our needs. I would like to see a SlutWalk with black women front and center" (Hobson qtd. in Carr, 34). The threads of discussion and debate which have emerged since April 2011 are overlapping strands of a vast engagement with the movement and defy easy analysis.

GLOBAL IMPACT

Initially a very Western movement, SlutWalk has had astonishing uptake across all corners of the globe. Unsurprisingly, both the strengths and challenges of the movement have varied from place to place. While an exhaustive analysis of each SlutWalk is obviously beyond the purview of this volume, it is nonetheless notable that the movement engendered dialogue far, far beyond its initial intentions. For example, Borah and Nandi suggest that the primary tension in India's Delhi SlutWalk was based on the presumption of an urban elitist movement that held no relevance for rural women experiencing poverty. They contest this point, arguing:

> We find that women who express their sexuality positively either in clothing or in choice of sexual relationships or by breaking any kind of sexual norm are called by exactly the same name everywhere.... For them, SlutWalk could be as relevant as it is to women and girls living in a big city. Is our discomfort with SlutWalk about urban elitism or about our unease with a positive (rather radical) articulation of sexuality?" (Borah and Nandi 418)

The nuances of the Indian experience of SlutWalk rearticulate the politics of exclusivity in uniquely postcolonial ways. While the controversy has been as successfully adopted as the movement itself, thus far there has been little analysis of what about SlutWalk, in particular, lent itself to such a passionate need for reproduction across so many diverse global locales. Perhaps the movement's focus, not merely on sexual violence, but on the specifics of slut-shaming at institutionalized levels, speaks both to the relative silence world wide on this topic, and also the transferability of this experience.

It is trite to point out the universality of sexual violence, but perhaps SlutWalks have shown that the experience of being blamed and silenced, and the outrage that rises in response, is similarly transnational?

While much of the controversy in virtually all jurisdictions was rooted in claims of exclusivity, it is the very portability of SlutWalks that have also led to their success. Each SlutWalk had its own flavor and flair; each drew on site-specific experiences. This does not mean that SlutWalks were not exclusive: movements can be both homegrown and tailored to specific locales and also ignore many of the constituents of a given space. Nonetheless, it would appear that while SlutWalks aimed to consolidate and homogenize diverse experiences, it was precisely their capacity to morph over time and space that allowed for the growth of the movement. This is an important observation, not because SlutWalks deserve ceaseless valorizing; rather, because in looking at what allowed SlutWalks to flourish and what caused them to flounder, we may widen our lens on how to successfully engage in global feminist action moving forward. It would be fascinating to see leaders of the movement across the world come together in a forum to discuss the unique strengths and challenges; such a dialogue might engender the type of open-mindedness that the feminist movement often lacks, and which SlutWalks are often accused of avoiding.

MOVING FORWARD:
SLUTWALK IN THE FOURTH, FIFTH OR SIXTH WAVE?

In many respects, SlutWalks appeared to be uniquely contemporary feminist actions. The passion of the movement and its specific manifestation in the gleeful spectacle which ensued drew on the camp sensibilities that are often ascribed to "third wave" feminism. Likewise, the portability and relative diversity of the movement, and, indeed, the calling to account about the limitations of that diversity, were similarly evidence of SlutWalks position as uniquely contemporary.

If, as Purvis asserts, "the third wave reflects an awareness that any attempts to bring feminisms to totalizing unity are prone to failure because they are annihilating and dishonest" (Purvis 97), how can the SlutWalk movement grow and contend with critiques of exclusivity and homogeneity? It may well be the critical self-awareness of SlutWalk founders and organizers that has led to the slowing of the movement in recent years. It is possible that this is an appropriate acknowledgement of contemporary feminism's fervent attempts to contend with difference, a growing awareness that SlutWalk can never truly meet the needs of all possible constituents. At the same time, we attend to Dow and Wood's compelling query: "Can any feminist action effectively represent the diverse experiences of all women?" (Dow and Wood 34) What are the expectations of feminist organizing going forward? Is it enough to have multiple parallel actions and an acknowledgement that each and every action will betray some participants? Is the action itself important, or is the dialogue in its aftermath where the true work is done?

It is tempting to engage in an analysis that runs toward binaries. Such an analysis cries "good riddance" to SlutWalk as the movement finally comes to grips with the exclusion of marginalized women and trans folk. Alternately, SlutWalks can be seen as evidence of feminist collective action brought down by concerns about inclusion. Neither response, however, truly contends with the depth of engagement with the movement, the diversity of its manifestations and the legacy of SlutWalk moving forward. Perhaps the lesson is the need to constantly invent new events, new ideas, working solutions that inch us toward social transformation, rather than aiming for any kind of annual battle cry.

It remains too soon to truly assess the long-lasting impact of SlutWalk on the face of feminism. It is our supposition, however, that SlutWalk has the capacity to live on as a pivotal event in feminist engagement, especially for young women. That engagement might have grown through passionate participation in SlutWalk, or, equally, through fiery opposition to SlutWalks for any number of reasons. Nonetheless, SlutWalks may have, in their capacity to shift complacency, moved a generation.

ABOUT THIS BOOK

Having explored some of the themes that the SlutWalk movement itself engendered, the chapters of this collection go further to interrogate the movement with the benefit of four years distance from its inception. They explore the specificities of reactions to the movement and the global spread of both SlutWalk and its detractors. The contributions explore the intergenerational nature of SlutWalk and the ways that it was founded on a much longer history of feminist organizing and awareness of sexual violence. Using many different methodologies: media analysis, photo content analysis, autoethnography, memoir, poetry and other representations, the chapters in this book aim to do justice to SlutWalk by reflecting the complexity of the movement in a nuanced and detailed analysis of its historical precedents, contemporary path, and future directions.

The collection opens with a poem by Clementine Morrigan and a photograph from Nish Israni, both of which engage with the visceral impact of slut-shaming and the individualizing of responsibility for safety. In the first chapter, "Slut Pride: A Tribute to SlutWalk Toronto," Andrea O'Reilly outlines the origins and development of the first Slutwalk march and shares with the reader her experiences attending this first SlutWalk event. O'Reilly argues that it is precisely the failure to locate the first SlutWalk in its specific historical and social context that has caused the event to be misunderstood and criticized by so many. She asks that we begin a new and different conversation on the SlutWalk movement, one fully grounded in the social, historical and linguistic context of the initial SlutWalk and the subsequent global movement. The following chapter, by one of the founders of the first SlutWalk, Alyssa Teekah, "Feminism Forged through Trauma: Call-out Culture and SlutWalk," considers one of the primary frameworks that currently disciplines modern feminism: "call-out culture." Using the aftermath of SlutWalk as example, Teekah riffs on the "stages of grief," instead suggesting the "stages of trauma" that one experiences as they are borne into and navigate mainstream feminism. Nancy Effinger Wilson's chapter, "Dirty Talk: A History of 'Slut,'" traces the word slut from the 1400s to present, observing how "slut" has been used specifically to signify a woman who violates the ideals of domesticity, obedience, purity, and piety. Using published instances of "slut," Wilson demonstrates how, for at least the past six hundred years, "slut" has supported an androcentric, misogynist double standard. The following chapter, "Practicing Intersectionality: Re-examining 'Third-Wave' Perspectives on Exclusion and White Supremacy in SlutWalk" by Jacqueline Schiappa, argues that feminist debates about SlutWalk serve as a useful microcosm for understanding the state of contemporary "third-wave" blogosphere discourse. She argues that while some feminists of colour generated necessary, productive critiques of SlutWalk's Whiteness and exclusivity, others constructed a hypercritical, narrow interpretation of the walk that erased the diverse experiences and testimonies of women of colour who participated. Nicole Pietsch in her chapter "'Doing Something' about 'Coming Together': The Necessary Surfacing of Intersections of Race, Sex and Sexual Violence in the SlutWalk Movement" interrogates the SlutWalk movement, its constructs of White femininity and the implicit racism in feminist activism—and considers strategies for intersectional sexual violence work, moving forward. Pietsch articulates that nowhere do the intersections of social location—race, class, sexual orientation, age and other factors—plainly disrupt notions of monolithic feminist collectivity than do women's diverse experiences of (1) sexuality and (2) gender-based violence. Diverging and socially-located constructs of "womanhood" have profound implications on women's experiences of femininity, sexuality, sexual violence and, therein, connotations of the term slut.

Dan Garret's chapter "Three Times a Lady: Images from SlutWalk Hong Kong" briefly discusses the importance of social movement visuality by considering SlutWalk in particular. It contends that visual methods and empirical-based strategies can aid scholars in grasping SlutWalk as it actually manifested— especially in indigenous settings. In the following chapter Angie Ng discusses some of the obstacles SlutWalk Hong Kong (SWHK) has encountered, along with its achievements. Within this non-Western context, the movement could not be minimized on the grounds of "white privilege"; instead, other rationalisations were employed by the mainstream media to undermine SWHK. Additional obstacles, including pre-existing local perceptions of sexual violence and feminism, are also explored. Andrea O'Reilly's chapter, "'It Happens Here Too': The SlutWalk Movement in Hong Kong and Singapore," explores how these two Slutwalk movements powerfully challenge and effectively correct many of the misconceptions of the SlutWalk movement particularly as it developed in so called non-Western contexts. The organizers and attendees of SlutWalk marches and events in Hong Kong and Singapore were anything but homogeneous or privileged; as well, though cognizant of the controversy surrounding the word slut particularly in non-Western contexts, the organizers strategically used the term to meet the needs of their particular community and fulfil the goals of their specific SlutWalk movement. Most impressive, O'Reilly argues, was how each SlutWalk developed, grew and flourished in response to the unique challenges and possibilities of their specific cultural locations. These SlutWalks were anything but derivative: they did not simply duplicate or replicate Western SlutWalks as is often assumed but rather created unique and vibrant movements of their own.

The following three chapters consider the impact of SlutWalk in the context of social media and popular culture. The chapter "Mapping the SlutWalk Paradox: Challenges and Possibilities of Using Raunch in Transnational Feminist Politics" by Amanda D. Watson and Corinne L. Mason explores what they call the "Slut-Walk paradox." They present the use of raunch as a contested strategy that forecloses some activist possibilities while giving access to others. They argue that SlutWalk has coincided with the mainstreaming of helpful terms like "slut-shaming" and "rape culture," but also that these terms are at the same time exclusionary, relying on racism and ableism, and thus, further complicate the im/possibilities of SlutWalk as an anti-violence platform. In their chapter "This Is What a Feminist Looks Like: An Understanding of the SlutWalk Movement Through Internet Commentary," Norah Jones and Margaret Nelson explore the Internet discourse focused on the first SlutWalk New York City which took place on October 1, 2011. They found that within that discourse there were significant disagreements about whether SlutWalk enhanced the sexual empowerment of women or resulted in the objectification of women, about whether it was possible to reclaim derogatory terms, and about whether one group of leaders could speak on behalf of others. They found as well that, in spite of these areas of discord, SlutWalk generated an "overarching unity" of commitment to a common cause. In "An Open Letter to Sinead O'Connor and Miley Cyrus," May Friedman considers the implications of sluttiness in popular culture and both the celebration of, and the backlash against, a type of packaged "sluthood" in the public sphere.

The following four chapters consider the movement from a more personal and experiential perspective. "Halt! Don't Do What You Want with My Body" by Raushan Bhuiyan briefly details the author's experiences as a former SlutWalk Toronto organizer. It is written with the spirit of encouraging efforts to continue to make organizing and activist spaces accessible, kind and gentle. In the next chapter "Single Mothering in Rape Culture: Confronting Myths and Creating Change," Shannon Salisbury pushes at the assumption that reclaiming the word slut has universal implications for all women. She explores how young people internalize messages about sexuality and sexual violence that they learn from the adults in their lives. She also provides an alternative, consent-based framework for addressing rape culture with children and youth. Similarly, in her essay titled "Sluthood & Survival: A Reflection on the Merits of Reclamation," feminist sociologist Tracy Citeroni employs autoethnographic reflection to highlight the intersectional nature of sexual violence and feminist action, pointing out that embracing a slut identity is more risky for members of some social groups, and considers the complications of reclaiming a slut label in the service of gender justice. As a primary tactic of feminist organizing, she argues, it falls short. She suggests we recognize SlutWalk as an inspired but limited activist strategy that undoubtedly contributes to our ongoing struggle to eliminate sexual violence and realize gender justice. "Loud, Proud, Fat Slut" by Morrisa Silvert takes a very intimate and personal look at the SlutWalk movement through the lenses of both internalized victim blame and fat shame.

CONCLUSION

In considering what SlutWalk has accomplished and what it was not able to do, the threads of this argument echo the conundrum of modern Western feminism: To be accurately intersectional requires a diversity of strands in order to formulate a cohesive, powerful feminist analysis.

Limitation, by way of energy, resources, barriers, and more, makes the task of a diverse, powerful feminist analysis more difficult than we'd like to imagine. In continuing to craft a collective, robust dialogue on the SlutWalk phenomenon, future research that centres and foregrounds intersectionality would do well to consider the following themes in relationship to SlutWalk and, of course, other areas of intersectionality. We would also pose questions as to why, in the midst of a robust debate that often reproduced overlapping analyses, these following areas were given less or no space by comparison.

To widen a critical engagement of SlutWalk, consideration of the LGBTQAAII spectrum, with special attention to the less considered queer women-identified community and trans, nonbinary, gender fluid community, the asexuality community, BDSM/kink culture, polyamory, casual sex, open relationship and multiple partner relationships should be included. In addition, exploration of different aspects of disability, including physical, mental, and behavioural would be invaluable. Looking at age (especially considering the intersection with gender) as well as sex work would be important. The politics of geography, including considering the urban space, the suburban and the rural would further expand the discussion, as would the study of spirituality, the sacred and the natural.

These sites of concern would help to expand analysis of the heteropatriarchal, monogamous, "vanilla" culture of normativity that manages gender, sexuality, and life at large. They would also help to explore what "sluthood" means, and what it can be and cannot be for varying marginalized folks, as well as how it interacts with other parts of identity. Delving into these areas could address how ableism and age are often left out of discussions on sexuality, how to think about consent, sluttiness, "safety" and harm by looking to our sex-worker positive movements, and finally, how to grapple with a non-religious Eurocentric culture that devalues the "feminine" in all interpretations.

This interaction of so many strands of feminism remains the potential and present power of SlutWalk. It was a movement that somehow, through fate, timing, and incredibly hard work, seemed to unify folks globally through shared debate and love of feminist politics. While SlutWalk has had its valid sites of critique that weave throughout the entire movement, it also became a poignant moment in remembering the sheer fire and passion that is lit by feminist consciousness. In reflecting on SlutWalk, our team has been, and remains excited by what SlutWalk can teach us about the future of feminism. We hope you enjoy this collection as a meditation on where we have come from, where we need to go, and what we are capable of when called to action.

ENDNOTES

[1]Regarding the use of the "wave" model, the editing team would like to simultaneously acknowledge the wave model and its uses within the Western feminist context while also questioning the model and its underlying philosophies. Issues around employment of the model include reifying the idea within feminism, and Western politics at large, that feminism began with the first wave. This type of positionality carries with it the connotations of white supremacy insofar as there is a belief that feminism began with the West and at this moment in time. However, an anti-racist and decolonial reading of history will point to feminisms present throughout space, place and time—critically, feminism present in non-Western empires (even if referred to by other names or without name). The wave model, if used without interrogation or contextualized as referring specifically to Western feminism (the conflation of "feminism" at large with Western feminism itself is revealing), re-centers whiteness as objective truth and reality. The wave model also may simplify the robust history of feminism into neat categories along a singular teleology that is prevalent in Western epistemes and philosophies. Liberal Western feminism has been called out for ironically reinforcing Western philosophies that marginalize and dispossess groups and seat humanity within the Western sphere. We are mindful of the erasure of histories and realities outside of the West, particular indigenous histories, and that notions used by Western feminists may not necessarily reflect or serve all. At the same time, given SlutWalk's original context

within a Western space, and its original intent as a Western activism, it can place itself within the Western feminist history and Western wave model. To do so can also serve purposefully in the pursuit of grappling with Western feminism, its history and future—as is done in this book. It is this reason we have chosen to refer to the wave model—but remain with ambivalence, as this term depends on its context.

[2]Throughout this book, the word "woman" is used. We would like to acknowledge the histories of heteropatriarchy, as well as cis-focused feminisms, that refuse to acknowledge and give equitable footing to trans, transitioning, gender fluid, gender queer, and non-binary folks. This often becomes a violent act of refusing to accept the falsity of the gender binary, which harms folks in various ways and often leaves trans* folks outside of accessing feminist spaces, resources and groups. In our use of the word, we firmly commit to allowing the word "woman" to be self-defined irrespective of biology. We do not use the word in reference to the binary, essentialized, cissexist formations of "womanhood." For the sake of grammar and word flow, we have opted to employ "woman" but use the word to refer to the spectrum of self-identifications.

WORKS CITED

Black Women's Blueprint. "An Open Letter from Black Women to the SlutWalk." *Black Women's Blueprint.* September 23, 2011. Web. October 2, 2014.

Attwood, Fiona. "Sluts and Riot Grrrls: Female Identity and Sexual Agency." *Journal of Gender Studies* 16.3 (2007): 233-247. Web. May 10, 2014.

Borah, Rituparna and Subhalakshmi Nandi. "Reclaiming the Feminist Politics of 'SlutWalk.'" *International Feminist Journal of Politics* 14.3 (2012): 415-421. Web. May 10, 2014.

Buszek, Maria Elena. *Pin-up Grrrls: Feminism, Sexuality, Popular Culture.* Durham: Duke, 2006. Print.

Butler, Judith. *Excitable Speech: A Politics of the Performative.* New York: Routledge, 1997. Print.

Carr, Joetta L. "The SlutWalk Movement: A Study in Transnational Feminist Activism." *Journal of Feminist Scholarship* 4 (2013):

24-38. Web. January 29, 2014.

Dow, Bonnie J. and Julia T. Wood. "Repeating History and Learning From It: What Can SlutWalks Teach Us About Feminism?" *Women's Studies in Communication* 37 (2014): 22-43. Web.

Glick, Elisa. "Sex Positive: Feminism, Queer Theory, and the Politics of Transgression." *Feminist Review* 64 (2000): 19-45. Web.

Martin, Nina K. "Porn Empowerment: Negotiating Sex Work and Third Wave Feminism." *Atlantis* 31.2 (2007): 31-41. Print.

Payne, Kathryn. "From Abject to Subject: Some Thoughts on Sex Work as a Missing Link in Feminist Understandings of Sexuality." *Atlantis: Critical Studies in Gender, Culture and Social Justice* 31.2 (2007): 53-63. Web. February 10, 2012.

Purvis, Jennifer. "Grrrls and Women Together in the Third Wave: Embracing the Challenges of Intergenerational Feminism(s)." *NWSA Journal* 16.3 (2004): 93-123. Web. March 6, 2014.

Ringrose, J. and E. Renold. "Slut-Shaming, Girl power and 'Sexualisation': Thinking through the Politics of the International SlutWalks with Teen Girls." *Gender and Education* 24.3 (2012): 333-343. Web. February 10, 2012.

Scott, Jennifer. "Thoughts on SlutWalk from a Wheelchair." *Ms. Magazine*. October 11, 2011. Web. May 21, 2014.

yes i am a slut

CLEMENTINE MORRIGAN

YES I AM A SLUT. because i have big tits that pour out of pretty much every shirt. because i like to show them off. because i used to charge 200 an hour and sometimes i would come and my client wouldn't cuz that's how much i was into fucking. because i've had trains run on me. because i liked it. because in grade eight a boy pulled down my shirt and bra in front of the whole class and my teacher and everyone saw my nipples. because he got a slap on the wrist and i was told by the principal that it was partially my fault because of the shirt i was wearing. because after that i started showing my tits to guys cuz i figured i was used goods. because when i was nineteen and being assaulted by a bunch of guys for not shaving my armpits they felt the need to pull my tits out of my shirt. because when i was twelve my grandfather forcibly made out with me. yes i am a slut. because i love sucking dick and i'll take his load all over my face and tits and in my mouth. because i used to get drunk and fuck random guys all the time even on weeknights. because i'm bisexual and everyone assumes bisexuals are slutty even when we're in monogamous relationships. because i'm a femme queer grrrl and everyone thinks femme queer grrrls are just 'doing it for attention' and are accessible to men. because the first time i was kissed in a way i actually liked my girlfriend and i were told we were disgusting and going to burn in hell. yes i am a slut. because i fucked my boyfriend in the ass with a strap on. because i used to work in a sex shop. because i love the night. because i wear miniskirts. because i flirt. because i've gone to bars by myself. because i've pissed in alleyways. because sometimes

17

i like sex. because sometimes i don't like sex. because i've been raped. because i'm a feminist. because i'm a survivor. because i'm a cum guzzling nympho. because i own sex toys. lots of them. because the only person who can make me come is myself and i'm fine with that. because i rub my clit when i'm being fucked. because i've done webcam work. because i've posed naked for pictures. because i like to masturbate. because i've always loved to masturbate. because i used to jerk off to naked pictures of women when i was like ten years old and i thought there was something seriously wrong with me. because there is nothing wrong with me. yes i am a slut. because my boyfriend called me one. because he got on top of me and screamed it in my face. because he called me it on my birthday. because random men have yelled slut at me more times than i could possibly count if i tried to sit down and write a list. because i have been called an ugly bitch, sweetheart, honey and other degrading names more times than i could count too. because i've been called a dyke and told to shave my armpits and my pussy and told to shut up and told to say yes to my pedophile grandfather. because i am sick of being told and this time i am telling you. yes i am a slut. because my pussy is beautiful and insatiable. because i love my body. because the clothes i'm most comfortable in apparently make me a target for rape. because when i was raped i was in my bed at home. because my body belongs to me no matter how many times i have been violated and none of it was my fault ever. yes i am a slut. because yes, i do fucking know what the word means and yes i am a feminist and yes i am intelligent and yes i do choose to say yes i am a slut. because the police officer who said women should stop dressing like sluts to avoid being victimized was talking about me and he was talking about you and he was talking about all of us. and because if we say it's okay to rape any of us then it's okay to rape all of us. because the slut card can be pulled out at any time and you never know when it will be used against you. because it can always be used against you, even if you've tried hard to make the 'right' choices. because all of us are sluts because in a rape culture women are considered inherently rapable. because none of us can be free of the word until those of us who choose to are free to embrace the word. because the word will never lose its power to hurt as long as we allow them to control it. because i respect a person's right to self identify and i expect the same respect in return. because i am taking a cue from my queer sisters who helped in the reclamation of words like queer and dyke, words that mean so much to our history and struggle. yes i am a slut. yes it is a complicated identity full of disempowerment, empowerment, struggle and resistance. yes it was forced on me and used against me and yes i and many of us were able to find different, new and empowering ways of relating to the word. yes we are sluts. so please hear us out. hear what we have to say. don't condescendingly tell us whether or not we are sluts or whether or not we can find empowerment this way. yes we can, yes we do, yes we are.

This piece was written in 2012. It was inspired by the SlutWalk movement. It has been translated into Spanish and Italian and has circulated widely on the Internet. I have received many messages from people who this piece spoke to. I no longer understand my sexuality in the way I did in 2012. Currently, I identify as demisexual and have a very different relationship to sex and desire. I share this piece because, while it is no longer representative of where I am, it speaks to a moment in time in my life and may resonate with others.

Caution

NISH ISRANI

ADORNING MY BODY with caution tape for SlutWalk was very symbolic for me. I wanted to challenge the notion that if what I wear is an invitation for sexual assault, what statement would I be making if my outfit screamed "Caution" loud and clear? And as someone who tends to spurn inappropriate sexual advances, I feel as if my outfit was also a warning, kind of an "approach at your own risk" expressing a side of me that is inherently angry about the misconceptions, stereotypes and objectification of women's bodies and sexualities. I feel like my outfit was drawing attention to rape culture while at the same time mocking it.

Slut Pride

A Tribute to Slutwalk Toronto

ANDREA O'REILLY

THE INTERNATIONAL SLUTWALK MOVEMENT began with twelve short words: "Women should avoid dressing like sluts in order not to be victimized." These words were spoken by Constable Michael Sanguinetti from Police Division 31 on January 24, 2011, at a safety forum that took place at Osgoode Hall Law School at York University in Toronto, Canada. He prefaced his remark with the following statement: "You know, I think we're beating around the bush here. I've been told I'm not supposed to say this, however...." And then he uttered the now infamous phrase. Significantly, there were only ten people in attendance at the forum that day, and it took a few weeks before the story spread by word of mouth across the York campus to be later picked up the Toronto media. On February 18, 2011, the *Toronto Star* ran a story on the event that included the police officer's apology, which had been sent earlier that week to the dean of Osgoode Law School: "I made a comment which was poorly thought out and did not reflect the commitment of the Toronto Police Services to the victims of sexual assaults." Sanguinetti commented further: "I am embarrassed by the comment I made and it shall not be repeated. I apologize for any ill feelings my comment may have caused" (Rush). Along with many others, I initially heard of the story in late February, as the media story ran during York's Reading Week when students and faculty were away from campus.

A few days after Reading Week I returned to my class to find the students actively engaged in a discussion on the Sanguinetti slut comment and its media coverage; the discussion continued well into the class lecture. I contacted my daughters later that day, both of whom were Women's Studies majors at York, and they, too, had been discussing the event with classmates and in courses. Within hours, it seemed, the story exploded and went viral across social media. A week later, a student in my third year Women's Studies course who was a member of the group who organized against Sanguinetti's comment reported that a rally and march had been planned in response to the comment. The event was intended to protest the victim-blaming and slut-shaming seen both in the police force, and in our larger patriarchal culture. SlutWalk, as the event obviously came to be called, took place April 3, 2011, at Queen's Park in Toronto, Ontario, and was attended by between 3,000 and 5,000 people.

I share the factual details of the origins of the first SlutWalk as I believe, if my many past discussions on the topic are any indication, that few fully appreciate how swiftly and spontaneously this protest unfolded. In my view, it is precisely this failure to locate the first SlutWalk in its specific historical and social context that has caused the event to be misunderstood and criticized by so many. Ten short weeks from the comment being heard by a group of ten people, and six weeks from the first media report of the comment, a feminist protest took place that was far greater, in both numbers and enthusiasm, than any feminist march or rally in the city of Toronto over the previous two decades. As a frequent attendee at feminist protests in Toronto over the past thirty years, I can attest that SlutWalk exhibited vibrancy and energy seldom experienced since the pro-choice marches of the early to mid 1980s. Indeed, the scope and range of this movement is unprecedented in contemporary feminist organizing and recalls the potent response to the reproductive rights movement of 1970s and 1980s.

In the four years since the first SlutWalk, there has been much reflection on and consideration of what about this contemporary moment has made this particular issue such a rallying point for feminists from diverse social locations; likewise, we have attempted to understand how the SlutWalk movement grew extremely quickly and reached around the globe. While future research will no doubt offer many and diverse reasons for the meteoric rise of this global feminist movement, what needs to be emphasized here is that the initial SlutWalk was initiated and organized by a handful of young women with no money, little time, and no formal support from any governmental, university, or social agency or department, and all in a matter of six weeks. Moreover, while the organizers oversaw the logistics of the event, securing permission from the city for the rally and march, inviting speakers, and setting up the SlutWalk Facebook page and website, the movement spread and grew outside any formal direction from the organizers. Importantly, the SlutWalk Facebook page explicitly invited all members of the feminist community to participate in planning and attending the event; it also asked organizations to list and register their organization on the site. I registered my organization *Mother Outlaws*, a feminist mothers' activist/community group; likewise, my two daughters listed their young women's feminist group.

Many groups met on their own, and in conjunction with the organizers, to strategize, make signs, and plan for the big day overall. One planned event open to all, the SlutWalk Prep Day on March 26, had 352 guests planning to attend. The SlutWalk Toronto website read: "Join us in our mission to spread the word that those who experience sexual assault are not the ones at fault, without exception … we are asking you to join us for SlutWalk, to make a unified statement about sexual assault and victims' rights and to demand respect for all":

WE ARE COMING TOGETHER. Not only as women, but as people from all gender expressions and orientations, all walks of life, levels of employment and education, all races, ages, abilities, and backgrounds, from all points of this city and elsewhere. Whether a fellow slut or simply an ally, *you don't have to wear your sexual proclivities on your sleeve*, we just ask that you come. *Any* gender-identification, any age. Singles, couples, parents, sisters, brothers, children, friends. Come walk or roll or strut or holler or stomp with us. This has become a global movement, with satellites happening all over the world. (SlutWalk, Why; emphasis in original)

I emphasize these details to correct the misconception, now unfortunately accepted as fact by many, that the organizers excluded certain groups such as trans people, sex workers, and women of colour from the movement. Such criticism betrays a lack of understanding of how this movement unfolded: there was no formal organization that could or could not exclude people; via the Facebook page, all were welcome to connect with those planning the event, list their organization, and attend the planning event as well as the march itself. Arguably, these young women could have done more to reach out to diverse women's groups and make them part of the organizing team; likewise, perhaps the initial impetus for the event betrayed some ignorance of the differential impact of the word slut on women from different social locations. Such critiques ignore, however, that SlutWalk was organized in less than six weeks and with no formal infrastructure. Moreover, and as importantly, these young women had no idea they were about to create a global movement that would later put their initial SlutWalk under worldwide scrutiny. These young women simply planned a one day protest in response to a sexist remark made by a police officer on their university campus, to demand accountability (not an apology) and a response to their proposed recommendations from the Toronto police force, and finally to take a stand against the victim-blaming and slut-shaming so rampant in our contemporary culture. As the organizers state on the SlutWalk Toronto website: "What began as a reaction to one comment, a reaction that we had originally imagined only to include a handful of our closest friends, exploded into a kind of movement that we never could have expected" (SlutWalk, How).

The Toronto organizers of SlutWalk have been highly criticized for choosing the term SlutWalk as the name for their event. As Gail Dines and Wendy J. Murphy wrote in the UK *Guardian,* "the focus on 'reclaiming' the word slut fails to address the real issue. The term slut is so deeply rooted in the patriarchal 'madonna/whore' view of women's sexuality that it is beyond redemption. The word is so saturated with the ideology that female sexual energy deserves punishment that trying to change its meaning is a waste of precious feminist resources." Similarly, as Keli Goff commented in the Huffington Post, "the images from SlutWalk send the message

Top, from left to right, Nish Israni, Clementine Morrigan, Andrea O'Reilly, Casey O'Reilly-Conlin.
Bottom, from left to right, Casey O'Reilly-Conlin, Clementine Morrigan, Andrea O'Reilly.

Top, from left to right, Andrea O'Reilly and May Friedman.
Bottom, Mother Outlaw banner.

that when push comes to shove, young women will always fall back on taking off their clothes to get attention, even when it comes to making a serious political statement." But such criticisms fail to locate the first Toronto SlutWalk in its specific social *and* linguistic context: the organizers chose the word slut in direct response to Police Constable Sanguinetti's use of the term. Furthermore, and as the organizers explain on their website: "Historically, the term 'slut' has carried a predominantly negative connotation ... so we're taking it back. Slut is being re-appropriated" (SlutWalk, Why). While it is beyond the scope of this article to revisit the debates on such a strategy as they have played out this past year, the organizers are hardly unique in reclaiming a derogative term: this tactic has a long tradition in feminist and social justice activism. Terms such as spinster, witch, bitch, queer, cunt, breeder, mama, crone, and hag, to name but a few, have been reclaimed and redeployed in both feminist activism and theory. Without minimizing the unique impact of this particular word on varying and diverse women, I would argue that it was precisely the use of the word slut that made the first walk the huge success that it was, for had a more benign term such as Stompin' been used, as was done with later walks, I doubt the event would have caught the media's attention, attracted the numbers that it did, or led to a global movement. In deliberately and strategically deploying the term slut, the first walk resonated with many women, particularly young women and sex-positive feminists, precisely because it challenged the anti-sex and slut-shaming views and values of our dominant culture, and those conveyed in much of second wave feminist writing.

Following the media coverage in the first year after the inaugural SlutWalk in Toronto, I became increasingly dismayed, troubled, and angered by the feminist response to, and representation of, the first SlutWalk and the subsequent global movement. Across feminist blogs, email list serves, Facebook, articles, and in personal conversations, the SlutWalk movement was judged, ridiculed, and demonized with mean-spiritedness and self-righteousness that often surpassed that conveyed in the mainstream media, and that has, in my view, been unparalleled in feminist activism over the last three decades. I was left asking: what about this particular event in this moment in history has made it so unsettling and unnerving to so many in the feminist movement? While such a discussion is beyond the scope of this paper, I raise the issue here in the hope that we can begin a new and different conversation on the Slut-Walk movement, one fully grounded in the social, historical, and linguistic context of the initial SlutWalk and the subsequent global movement. Such a conversation is necessary and long overdue.

I attended the first SlutWalk with friends from our *Mother Outlaws* group and as we marched we were joined by my two daughters. Twenty-plus of us marched together, us with our *Mother Outlaws* banner, and the young women with creatively handmade placards that read: "Slut Love," "Society teaches don't get raped, rather than don't rape," and "There is no such thing as an invitation to rape." That early April day held the promise of spring in the air, and as we marched the sun came out, warming our hearts and bodies. Contrary to what the media reported, the event was attended by a wonderful and diverse range of people: young and old; straight and queer; men and women of all sizes and from all nationalities, ethnicities, and abilities. Some of us dressed in fishnet nylons, others in jeans. One seventy-something-aged women wore a long heavy winter coat along with a placard that read "I am a proud old slut," and one participant, profiled in this book, wore a dress made, appropriately enough, of yellow crime scene tape. Mothers with babes in arms walked alongside high school students and children holding dogs on leashes chatted with grandmothers. What distinguished this march from so many I have attended over the years was the joy and camaraderie of that day. We were women, defined and lived in many diverse ways, and we were proud to be so. On that day our gender and sexuality were a place and position of power and strength, not of weakness and shame.

Finally, I could not share this story without acknowledging and thanking the young women that made that day possible and gave rise to the global SlutWalk movement. Most people do not know their names or appreciate all that these young women have endured, both to make the first SlutWalk happen, and to survive the subsequent media backlash. The student in my class had to take incompletes in all her courses and postpone graduation because of the time and energy SlutWalk demanded of her at the conclusion of the school year. I cannot say often or well enough how proud I am of these young women; in these so-called post-feminist times they give us much cause for hope and celebration. It is time they are recognized and honoured as the sheroes that they are. Thank you, Heather Jarvis, Colleen Westendorf, Raisa Bhuiyan, Jeanette Janzen, Laura McLean, Sonya J. F. Barnett, Alyssa Teekah, and Erika Jane Scholz.

This chapter is a revised and updated version of my article that appeared in Feminist Studies *38.1 (Spring 2012): 45-50.*

WORKS CITED

Rush, Curtis. "Cop Apologizes for 'Sluts' Remark at Law School." *The Toronto Star.* October 18, 2011. Web. 25 Feb. 2012.

SlutWalk. "Why." http://www.slutwalktoronto.com/about/why.

SlutWalk. "How." *SlutWalk Toronto.* N.d. Web. 25 Feb. 2012.

Dines, Gail and Wendy J. Murphy. "SlutWalk Is Not Sexual Liberation." *The Guardian.* May 8, 2011. Web. 25 Feb. 2012.

Goff, Keli. "Dear Feminists, Will You Also Be Marching In N***erwalk? Because I Won't." *The Huffington Post.* October 3, 2011. Web. 25 Feb. 2012.

Feminism Forged Through Trauma

Call-Out Culture and SlutWalk

ALYSSA TEEKAH

THREE YEARS AGO, a team of four other women and I organized what would come to be known as the first ever SlutWalk. In the years since, I related to SlutWalk like one with post-traumatic stress disorder may relate to events that reminded them of their trauma. It has taken a lot of listening and talking with others, distance, writer's block, fear, shame, acceptance, and working on myself and my politics, to be able to get to a place where I could write this piece. It seemed as though I went through "stages" to overcome a traumatic experience.

At the time of the aftermath of the first Slutwalk, the critiques pointed out how much work I had to do and how much my feminism was lacking. It was definitely hard to take so much criticism. Now, my politic is one where I could actually see myself being one of the people critiquing SlutWalk— as life works in such funny and strange ways. At the same time, I believe my critiques would be different from many that emerged from the Internet and in every day life, because I experienced the 'receiving' side of things. SlutWalk was a lesson in how we are all capable of both great and not so great things; sometimes within the same instance.

In this chapter, I hope to share with you my reflections on what some term "call-out culture," the way current, heavily-Internet based feminism can turn into a process of publicly shaming people for not enacting the most 'foolproof' politics. Using the aftermath of SlutWalk as an example, I'll aim to flesh out the 'stages' of experiencing this feminism, one that forges feminists through trauma. Riffing on the 'stages' of grief, I'll name the 'stages' of going through an experience of call-out culture: 'Experiencing the Trauma', 'Shame and Dismissal', 'Burying', 'Reflecting', 'Coming to Terms Publicly', and 'Contextualizing.'

Am I better for going through the traumatic aftermath that was the barrage of SlutWalk critiques? It's hard to say. My feminism and politics have grown exponentially since, and I am so thankful for that turning point. I see how it has shaped my journey. At the same time, I see the costs of how it has marked me, taught me lessons about the worst parts of people, and how it has left me fearful. That's the paradox of a feminism forged through trauma, I think.

CALL-OUT CULTURE

"Call-out culture" is a veritable shark tank, where online feminism becomes a never-ending, cyclical critique— an unwanted child of intersectionality theory. It's often paired with an impulse to name all of your social locations, and to have this naming suffice as your anti-privilege activism. The champions of intersectional theory would likely be shocked learning about this dastardly interpretation of their theory, meant to complexify and broaden historical white feminism. In this interpretation, intersectionality becomes ironic— so static that we can fail to see fluidity and diversity. By focusing inward and maintaining analysis at the level of the self, call-out culture obfuscates the larger structures which implicate all of us. It becomes more important about what "you" have done wrong to "me".

In academia, students are often taught through critiquing what is "problematic" about a given work, resulting in a speed and fury—a race to be the first to cry out against what's "wrong" with an act. This quick-to-judge attitude is found in organizing as well, creating a hyper-consciousness that can reduce the space and time for creating new acts. Regardless of how one has learned feminism, the omnipresence of online feminism reifies these call-out tendencies. The mechanics of blogging, where users can "share" and "follow" particular posts or authors, results in a loop where some content rises and becomes gospel, an exercise in "who can shout the loudest". The most bombastic critique is king— shared with the same juicy fervour as celebrity gossip.

While critique is necessary and important, a problem occurs when an entire argument is *only* made up of negative critique. There is no more room for both the positives and negatives, or complexity, as single-track thinking is preferred over nuance. Mired in toxicity, the process of critiquing conflates single moments with the entirety of a person, an "excommunication" that works similar to practices of public shaming. Redeeming value is no longer present, as phenomena is made two-dimensional, the critiquing author forgetting that humans and human productions can be many things at once. Nobody is good enough, and folks should not organize unless they will get it right. One is in the position of proving they are "good enough" for the "movement", and yet could never be by callout culture's standards.

These ideas pervade some arenas of feminism today. We can access a plethora of knowledge, interact, and create our own feminisms like never before. Yet through the same measure this may mean the cost of going through trauma, a twisted rite of passage involving being shamed for comments, arguments or questions short of "acceptable" levels of awareness and/or education, and torn down to the point of rebuilding. One can rebuild, keeping that sense of shame as memory— or may not rebuild, choosing to exit feminism and organizing for fear of re-traumatizing themselves.

This painful process strikes deeper and wounds stronger, as it often comes from the communities one hoped would be the place find solace, heal, and grow in the face of a wider oppressive culture.

Experiencing the trauma

The reactions to SlutWalk serve as a strong example of how call-out culture plays out. I won't go into detail about SlutWalk as other chapters in this collection already cover this terrain. Instead, this story begins after the march. To situate the following, I'll name my social locations so that you can understand where I'm coming from. I identify as a queer, brown (mixed South Asian roots), fat woman with middle class privilege, graduate level formal education, relative able-bodiedness, and "Canadian" citizenship status. These various social locations were factored into my experiences as a co-founder of SlutWalk Toronto.

In the aftermath of the first ever SlutWalk, the feminist and mainstream Internet start to take a bite. We were called out as being colonial when SlutWalk entered other geographic spaces, despite the fact that locals had brought the idea in and not us. We were called out as immature and petty, ignorant and redundant. Older white western feminists seemed to yell at us from their self-imposed pedestals, decrying the shame to *their* legacies. We were called insulting and sexist from anti-sex work feminists who scoffed at the idea of "empowered sexuality". We were called out as idealist and flighty by liberal feminists who insisted attention should be on economic and capitalist forms of "equality."

We were seen as symbolic of the supposed non-legitimacy of "social media" by traditional feminists. We were called "elitist" by mainstream feminists who erroneously believed we were all "sheltered university students." Some of the time, these critiques ended up demonizing the very things that had historically been considered part of a feminist worldscape (e.g access to education).

Mired in the paradox of these critiques, I now understand that they signal a sense of impossibility in doing feminism well. How mundane, that a movement primarily of women-identified people would make its own feel not good enough. How have we re-articulated some of the biggest violence that patriarchy produces?

It was the other critiques, however, particularly around race, that held more weight for me given my intersectionality (discussed in detail in other chapters). The lack of analysis on dis/ability, sex worker solidarity, and the police industrial complex was important too. A transnational analysis that tied SlutWalk into a global understanding of patriarchy and marginalization would have been critical. All these things exploded and challenged my analyses in ways that I am thankful for today.

The critiques came as a crashing wave that knocked us down. We were hearing it from all sides. Some were silly, but many of them were valid—and there were just so many. Every hour there were new articles. People posting, reposting, tweeting and retweeting critiques. Everywhere I turned people were shaming, reviling, shitting on SlutWalk. It didn't stop at the level of intellectual critique. It became so overwhelming, seeing hundreds of new posts, messages and articles. Each one, utilizing its shaming language of call-out culture, made me feel smaller and smaller.

On both sides—those critiquing, and those 'receiving'—no communication was truly happening. Ugliness reared its head. Instead of pausing and aiming to practice any sort of feminist ethic to discuss what needed to be worked on, white, straight, middle-class and otherwise privileged feminists (who could not see the point of marginalized naysayers) dismissed the critiques of Slutwalk as "oh! those are haters! Those people don't get it, they are just trying to divide us! They don't get the message!" In these cases, privilege and feminism colluded to create a shield of denial.

I consider this reaction as that of one who has been repeatedly harmed. One has to develop a thick skin in order to stay afloat. Or it could simply be privilege. Either way, one develops methods of coping with a culture that will actively harm you through constant critique. The sad part is, by these feminists ignoring the words of the most marginalized, they were reproducing the same kind of harm we'd expect from oppressive groups, in our "own" communities. Call-out culture has built within it its own undoing, in that we learn to develop scars from experiencing its wrath, ones that actively create barriers to creating positive change.

There was no saving of SlutWalk in this trauma-producing feminism. It was thrown out, the baby with the bath water. It felt like everyone started to singularize SlutWalk as a white supremacist, ableist, homophobic, cis act. While it reified those systems of violence, it was rendered as *only* indicative of those systems, and nothing else. It was worthless. It was terrible. It was horrible, it was embarrassing, and stupid.

And so, by proxy, we the Slutwalk organizers and participants were worthless, terrible, horrible, embarrassing, and stupid. Our inboxes started filling up. Hate mail. Death threats. People reviled us. It wasn't a process of critique any more. It was a full out damning. People wanted us dead. People wanted us to disappear. It was an unforgettable thing to see in writing. It was hard to remember that it was a critique of a specific action we had done, because so much of the critique focused on and questioned our internal selves.

On the SlutWalk Facebook group, people who held important, real, and necessary antiracist views went from active participation to a furious flooding, a barrage of posts, comments, and nonstop activity. It was a public shaming, laying waste to every part of us.

We were ascribed actions we never committed, as the fury grew stronger.

The lines started to blur between critique and assumptions, critique and falsities. Call-out culture is set up in a way where folks could not oppose the most vocal critiques. A commenter saying "this critique feels like we are being a little strong— we can do this with kindness or basic respect" would get the response of "you're just as bad as them!" The arguments moved so fast and became vile. I remember trying to engage in a conversation, with a few brief comments. I was obliterated. At the time, I had no rigorous anti-racist analysis. I did not understand the theoretical, practical, and historical nature of white supremacy nor its material and symbolic effects in the ways that related to the effects of SlutWalk.

SHAME AND DISMISSAL

I was hurt, and felt ashamed. These people who were queer, brown and radical—people who "should" be my community—were calling for my head. It hurt more, and compounded differently, for those organizers who were white. It was harder to place myself amongst it all, and made it more confusing to defend myself. This struck me raw. At first, I tried to defend. But then I stopped. And listened. And realized that some of what they were saying was right. While they were right, it did feel cruel. I do stand by the feeling that the way call-out culture lets people know they could have done better feels violent. This is what leaves trauma.

I began to engage in measures to distance myself and to dismiss what had happened—enacting the action that follows shame. I stepped down. I left SlutWalk. I watched, and read, and took in the stream of critiques that came, steeping myself in them. I came to understand completely where the critiques were coming from. But on a personal level, I wasn't sure how I could reconcile my participation in SlutWalk, and also understand the critiques. I was told I had failed, and I wasn't sure where to go from there. So I stayed entirely away. I didn't engage in community. I dropped out of any activist projects I had planned. I felt uncomfortable going to events for people of colour and queer folks. I felt that they knew who I was and would find me unredeemable. I was terrified they would find me out.

Sometimes I would get really down about it, feeling as though I had kicked myself out of the community before I really got to join. I did and continue to get anxiety, feeling that everyone who is queer and racialized is looking at me in a way where they've decided I'll never be worthy, because, in that one instance, years ago, I didn't have the right knowledge and experience— and thus I could never have it have it.

A key part of what I'm trying to share is the fact that although I speak here in past tense, these feelings remain. I am overly cautious about participation and still feel I am unwanted in community. I have a deepened political analysis and have learned so much, but this is paired with a sustained isolation. That is what a feminism forged through trauma feels like. It is living in a paradox of intellectually understanding what is fucked up in the world, yet struggling to find a way to address it because the 'fuckery' infiltrates your own method!

The lessons offered from this cruel feminism were rough and plain: never dare to try and make a change unless you know how to do it right. Never comment on fucked up things unless you know how to please all with your effort. This lesson not only came from feminists who were of comparable schools of thought as me, but from elders, from those who were staunchly anti-feminist, from mainstream observers and everyone in between. It's one thing when outsiders want to make sure you are harmed— it's an entirely differently thing when it's people with whom you thought you were "safe". All the critiques that attacked our person echoed the idea that we were worthy of revulsion, that we were just fools. This shame became part of my feminist upbringing.

BURYING

The next stage of trauma is the burial. When it gets to be too much, and when nothing has become resolved, the solution seems to be to just bury it, and hope it goes away. Trying to bury my participation in and memories of SlutWalk, however, became a funny thing— because it was completely unavoidable! It would come up in conversations, where I would look away and pretend to fade out. It would even come up in dating situations, me once comforting a male identified rape survivor who told me of healing through SlutWalk. The biggest moment was it coming up in grad school, as a case for discussion on white liberal feminism. Reading academic work on SlutWalk was like seeing those swirling thoughts in my head articulated. While hesitant and concerned about the day of discussion, upon arrival, I found myself actively participating, both critiquing and defending SlutWalk. My classmates were surprised as I confessed my participation, and intrigued that I could take this nuanced stance. I realized the freeing dimension of being able to perform an actual rigorous feminist engagement that could still save some grace and respect for the effort.

After occasions like these, I realized that I did, and could, have pride in SlutWalk after all. And that this was okay. I didn't have to feel ashamed, or bury it: rather, I could admit it as part of my wider story—when I was younger and newer to politics—my first experience that just happened to be a 3,000-plus person march. A thing that did some good, and some bad, but was still something I helped create, and was still a pivotal moment in modern feminist movements.

REFLECTING

I talked with a few people in the years that followed the first Slutwalk to try and grapple with the critiques and where to place myself, not to mention the mix of emotions. I felt that because I did not have a strong critique of white supremacy at the time, I was seen to be especially problematic as a person of colour.

The overwhelming message was that as a person of colour, "I should already have known know those things". But one's understanding of white supremacy, anti-racism, and the host of other system oppressions is largely shaped by one's own intersectionality. Black, Indigenous and People of Colour (BIPOC) have a variety of experiences and social locations— there is no one 'BIPOC' reality. While BIPOC come disproportionately from immigrant, lower income social experiences, this cannot account for all people. Thus, even if 'dominant' BIPOC narratives exist, they do not represent the full spectrum of narratives. In labelling me a "bad person of colour," there was no consideration or allowance for my own intersectionality and how those factors might have come into play. The idea that all BIPOC know "what whiteness is about" presumes that all of us go through institutions in the same way and are aware in the same way. Social location factors, like class, gender or so on, can actively set up barriers to awareness or shape awareness in particular ways. I was bothered by the incredulity that I should have "known better than to organize with white people" (a phrase I would come to learn was often repeated in BIPOC social justice circles in Toronto), from folks who presumed I had had particular, in depth contact with white folks. While whiteness and white people are indeed everywhere, in my own life growing up, whiteness manifested differently from many dominant BIPOC narratives of whiteness. The awareness of whiteness was contoured and shield from me by my particular privileges, and white people were a rare sight.

The folks who called me out had "learned better" through organizing with white people and experiencing whiteness, in cases that were probably very similar to SlutWalk. And yet for some reason, I was barred from being allowed to have that same twisted 'rite of passage.'

The use of "BIPOC" as a term is difficult in its crystallization— simultaneously offering the opportunity for solidarity, but also possibly presuming a monolith across a variety of groups (and within those groups). The critiques I received obscured any possibility of considering context, chalking me up to being a 'failed' person of colour. So many statements about what BIPOCS are and are not, have experienced and have not, were projected onto me, that the true effect of how systemic power, privilege and harm befalls each person differently was totally erased, barring me from full personhood in the process. The logic seemed to suggest that '*all*' BIPOC "knew" certain things about racism, homophobia, and systems of power, and by organizing Slutwalk - an even that was racist, homophobic, and otherwise oppressive - I had failed to perform that knowledge. By that logic, I could not be a 'real' BIPOC—or I would have "done better." In fact, my particular privilege and power meant I learned those knowledges in some ways, and not in others. The way we learn and do not learn is a critical part of the story, and it's part of the fight too.

I also see how this culture of toxicity grows stronger in the case of BIPOCs, particularly (and likely paralleled yet unique in other marginalized groups). A co-worker of mine pointed out that some of the most vocal people of colour will be much more vigorous with other BIPOC than with white folks. Somewhere along the way, colonization and white supremacy taught us not to trust each other or to give each other the same kindness we've been ingratiated to give to white folks. For our own "s/kinfolk," call-out culture is extra biting– whether it's because we "expect better," "see ourselves in them," or don't allow ourselves to fuck up as much because we're often never given second (or first) chances.

I realized that some of the trauma for BIPOC comes from trying to organize with white folks in a white supremacy where "their" (white) actions are automatically seen as the most valid; they are seen as doing the most work; and are least questionable. My co-organizers attempted to make me a token for SlutWalk, which in itself became traumatizing as I struggled to articulate why their actions were not okay. It's something else to be working within an organization as a minority, and then also being critiqued without care from the outside. The trauma starts to work on so many levels, as call-out tactics can't be contained and keep spreading.

The collusion of call-out toxicity, intra-community expectations, white supremacy and colonialism's legacies on the BIPOC mental and emotional spectrum also meant that I ended up believing that SlutWalk held no value and was a waste of time. It was only in hearing other people reinforce its positive aspects, and through time and perspective, that I could remember its value and goodness, too.

COMING TO TERMS PUBLICLY

While I seemed to have come to a better place internally, for many months, I still fretted over how folks would interpret my association with SlutWalk. I was concerned it might signal to people that the same politics which produced SlutWalk's problematics were the politics I still held (as that's the job of call out culture).

By entering the stage of burying and refusal, one loses touch with the variety of ways of being, lives, and types of social justice attitudes that exist. I felt that the attitudes I had come across were the only ones I would continue to see - enough to scare one out of any future hope.

A turning point came when I applied to work at a well-known feminist community organizing group. I hesitated whether to include SlutWalk on my CV. It could signal my strengths—or it could turn people off. I chose not to include it. A few months into the job, I became aware of how open minded and caring my co-workers were, and shared, as they discussed things in a way respected my basic humanity. I was grateful and became aware of the fact that these folks could understand nuance because they were used to an environment that was so highly charged it could get toxic—they knew the meaning of organizing in a healing way (and the high cost of not doing so). My suspicion is that many Internet commenters may have never experienced this kind of environment. It also helped me to become aware of the fact that as more people become brutalized by this toxic discourse, people become less willing to engage in such behaviour. I think the culture has become so cannibalistic that we are reaching a breaking point.

CONTEXTUALIZING

The last stage comes in the form of being able to contextualize the event within a wider web, and understand what influenced the myriad factors that came into being. I think that one of the critical things we have to work on in the "social justice" community is the idea that we expect each other to not grow. By throwing each other under the bus for making wrong moves or oppressive actions, we assume that we are not capable of growth.

If I were to critique an action like SlutWalk in the future, I wouldn't want to call for the beheading of organizers, nor would I flood their inboxes with vitriol, or damn them to a state where they could never transform or learn anything more. I would aim to critique the action itself and keep in mind the ever-fluid nature of our being (I know this is easier said than done). I've noticed the cooling of my own knee-jerk impulse to critique, and I see how I now attempt to engage differently. My critiques may not get as many 'reblogs' or be seen as feisty enough, but I am thankful. Neither knowledge nor politics nor people are crystallized or infallible and that is a lesson I hope is remembered within marginalized, feminist communities.

Since SlutWalk, I have participated in other spaces that have tried to do similar work. And more often than not, it crumbles into a state of dramatics, personal vendettas, and burnout. I think this is because of the difficulty of trying to organize while being situated within the heteropatriarchal ableist white supremacy, a system that has "built in" measures to ensure the shutting down of our organizing and resistance. Trying to exist in a system that blatantly does not want us is going to come with real difficulty. While as humans we may have a guttural feeling that things have got to be better, and the desire to realize that, call-out culture thrusts us into a state of reproducing the very mechanisms that ensure our continued oppression. This combines with the prevention of us working across boundaries—further upholding the myths of the system which requires our continued division.

Call-out culture teaches us that violence is a viable answer; that positivity will come out of causing pain; that there is only one true representation of reality; that the urge to complicate is unnecessary; that we are always to be our best and never slip up; that growth is not feasible nor important to remember in considering others; and that once something has been defined, it can never transform. This becomes more sad when we remember a key aspect of feminism's power is the ability to show that all phenomena exists along spectrums—and all reality forms complex matrices that are forever in motion.

We may forget that political progress is a process and how long it took ourselves to get to where we are. I had hoped and thought feminism would have unraveled all these egocentric ideas—instead, we sometimes make them stronger. If ego was, unfortunately, not so often found linked to politicking, we could have used Slut-Walk as a conversation. Some may articulate Slutwalk as 'five people ending up reproducing harmful, problematic paradigms in the attempt to do something feminist'. That is easy enough to identify. But to ask *why*, in conjunction with our critiques, would have done us a service in terms of thinking about SlutWalk more widely as an example of the emergence of a specifically Canadian, modern feminism.

Asking "why" would have us sit down in dialogue on the power of white supremacy, and how BIPOC and white "Canadians" often refuse to acknowledge the ongoing existence of systemic and material racism in our country, ranging from Indigenous genocide to the harm of model minority myths and everything in between. Asking "why" would also open up a conversation on how our how our conceptualization of freedom, rights and humanity have become disciplined and bound to the realm of western liberal notions, the very notions that work to strip folks globally of their rights and freedoms. To ask "why" would mean discussing how capitalism has co-opted feminist concepts like empowerment and led to western feminism reifying oppression while trying to break it down. "Why" would mean coming face to face with the teleology of western feminism that often invokes "it gets better",obscuring how things may not have changed much, may just have morphed, or have actually become worse (especially considering white women feminists' economic success to the direct disadvantage of global south women of colour). It would also acknowledge the competing and colliding feminisms that make a singular history, teleology or argument impossible.

But instead, when dealing with a feminism that works by way of trauma, we never reach the point of "why"—everyone is either dishing out the hurt, recovering from it, or escaping it. We don't work to facilitate an environment where we can get to the harder questions, because the level we're at gets too toxic. The "who" and "what" become the primary concern. This is what modern "social justice," in so many ways, has become, and the level at which it has gotten stuck.

We have forgotten how to be kind, and what "community" actually means—dealing with a lot of people who fuck up, but still trying to do better and still being there for one another. We have forgotten the critical meaning of having "ancestors" and being part of generations of feminists. Inter-generational knowledge sharing and action does not mean looking down at others from afar, but means that our mutual liberation is tied to each other. As bell hooks says, if we perceive "love" as actionable rather than just as a feeling, it means we invite accountability and responsibility into maintaining the existence of love. When we think about our actions, we understand the power of our influence on one another and the type of energy we get back. The message that I received from call-out culture— that holding care for one another is not an essential part of how we "do" feminism now in the mainstream— ignores the ways that we are all capable of action and responsible for what our actions create. Maya Angelou's invocation that "when we know better, we do better" is forgotten as we reproduce the harm we learned through living in oppressive structures in our own "chosen" communities.

SlutWalk was important as a political movement, including in its problematic aspects, for helping to rupture silence, rape cultures, and modern life. It facilitated rigorous debate in a huge range of spheres—and brought terms like "victim-blaming" and "slut-shaming" into greater mainstream use. Strangely, it also revealed the ruptures within our own feminist communities. It ruptured some folks' idea of a single cohesive feminism. We could not understand each other—we became lost in translation, in denial, and in distance. SlutWalk thus became a mirror held up to ourselves. It conjured up the undead ghosts of previous feminisms and made us face the unsettled terrain of feminism in a world marked by some as "post-feminist." It laid out on the table the nagging emotions that for all our work in the past odd century or so in the west, we still had so much further to go. It reflected to us that by believing in idealized forms of feminism, we undermined the pervasiveness of structural harm, and created impossible standards for us to live up to. It is no wonder we need to delve into practices of shaming just to cope with the structures we created.

CONCLUSION

After years of going through the stages of "traumatic" feminism (and slipping back and forth between them) I've come to a growing acceptance and a place where I can talk about SlutWalk. In reading my story, I hope folks see it as emblematic of many people's journeys into social justice in this current moment, for good and bad.

What can I say about this cruel teacher, the traumatic experience? For better or worse, it has influenced who I am today. I'm conflicted, because I feel nothing else taught me as much as that experience did. I'm flabbergasted by the leaps I've made as a result. By addressing the trauma of call out culture and where we've gotten stuck in mainstream feminism, perhaps we can move towards forms that let us keep basic humanity and remember complexity. I am thankful I have had an opportunity that many have not, in being able to reflect on, work through, and share my journey. I am grateful to SlutWalk for all the lessons about politics, people, and myself. I've learned to listen when critiques come up that you work so hard not to hear. It is scary— but refusing to hear is much more dangerous. I've learned about what it means, and the real work required, to be in real "solidarity." I've learned to think about how to practice politics that can be challenging but do not re-inflict harm, about limits, self-care, and finding what kinds of attitudes to align with.

Most of all, I've learned about the magic that is always potentially there—the magic that creates feminism and its never-dying flame, the type of magic that happens when people, even in agreement and disagreement, share dialogue and share honesty, and connect across boundaries of all kinds. It is that magic that I hope I and we can learn to honour through caring practice of critical feminism.

Dirty Talk

A History of "Slut"

NANCY EFFINGER WILSON

The word 'slut' (in patois) was repeated over and over, until suddenly I felt as if I were drowning in a well but instead of the well being filled with water it was filled with the word 'slut,' and it was pouring in through my eyes, my ears, my nostrils, my mouth.
—Jamaica Kincaid, *Annie John*

IN THE 1999 BOOK *Slut!*, Leora Tanenbaum cites twelve positive expressions for a sexually active man ("stud," "player," "stallion," and so on) and only two positive expressions for a sexually active woman ("hot" and "sexy"); on the other hand, she cites twenty-eight negative expressions for a sexually active woman ("slut," "whore," "tramp," "ho," and so on) and only three for a sexually active man ("womanizer," "wolf," "can't keep it in his pants") (7). Although we cannot ascertain precisely when "slut" was first coined, for at least six hundred years it has supported the sort of androcentric, misogynistic double standard shown above.

In this chapter, I trace the word "slut" from the 1400s to present, observing how "slut" has been used specifically to signify a woman who defies the "Cult of True Womanhood" because she 1) fails to maintain a clean home and clothing, thereby neglecting the ideals of *domesticity* and *obedience*; 2) behaves in a sexually lascivious way, thereby violating the ideals of *chastity*, *obedience*, and *domesticity*; and 3) is impudent and therefore neither *silent* nor, yet again, *obedient*. Moreover, because all of these behaviours conflict with the "chosen plan" for women as servants to their superior husbands, a slut is not *pious*. Although I attempt to tease each of these definitions out, in actuality they conflate, so a woman may be called "slut" because her home is unclean, but that fact likewise suggests that she is failing to obey her husband and societal roles. Similarly, in the 1700s, the physical dirtiness of a woman was taken as a sign of sexual availability. In short, as Feona Attwood observes, words such as "slut" expose "the connection often made in language between sex, women, service, class, dirt and pollution" (234).

Of course, we must add race to Attwood's list. In his 1885 journal, British Major-General C.G. Gordon used "black slut" to refer to Sudanese women and men. The term, always used to demean, thus became a racist pejorative used to justify colonization. Black Women's Blueprint notes a similar use of "slut" in the United States to refer to Black women in order to justify "Jim Crow kidnappings, rape and lynchings, gender misrepresentations." As a result, they argue, "'slut' has different associations for Black women" than White women.

"Slut" has thus functioned throughout time as a catch-all pejorative for prevailing human prejudices, both reflecting and perpetuating (hetero)sexism, classism, and racism. Fortunately, though, by the mid-twentieth century, meta-awareness of long-standing scripts that shame and restrict women had led to an interrogation of the "cult of true womanhood" and the word "slut." In her 1964 article "Slut," for example, Katharine Whitehorn embraces her lack of domesticity, and in the 2009 *The Ethical Slut*, Easton and Hardy re-appropriate "slut" to positively represent polyamorous people. In her fiction, Jamaica Kincaid explores how the word "slut" is used in the West Indies to colonize women's sexuality. These authors challenge not only the pejorative nature of the word "slut" but also the anti-female sentiments that lie beneath. Whether a word such as "slut" that has been used for centuries to signify misogynistic beliefs and justify misogynistic actions can be/should be reclaimed, I will leave to the reader to decide.

I. *Slut,* n. A dirty or slovenly person, usually a woman

In the Middle Ages, when "slut" first surfaced in print, it signified an "unclean woman," one who neglected to keep a clean home and appearance (*OED*). For example, "slut's corner" is a corner that has been left uncleaned; a "slut-hole" is a receptacle for trash; and "slut's wool" is dust left behind after sweeping (*OED*). In actuality, women *and* men would have been "dirty" in the Middle Ages because personal cleanliness would have been a costly endeavour. And, in fact, until the sixteenth century, males were referred to as "sluts."

However, "slut" came to designate not only a "dirty" but also a "contaminated" woman. The 1440 *Palladius de Rustica* (a translation of an agricultural treatise by Palladius) contains one of the earliest published uses of "slut" and captures both fifth-century Roman superstitions concerning the contaminating qualities of women and the medieval translation of those superstitions. Palladius tells farmers, "Do not dig up the weed, but pull it with your hand. Fully feared is the touching of unclean women—**sluts**,[1] I suppose it to mean (Liddle 137).[2] In other words, pull up your weeds and keep "unclean women" (probably a euphemism for menstruating women) out of your garden because women's menstrual blood was thought to contaminate agriculture, causing "fruits not to germinate, wine to sour, plants to parch, trees to lose their fruit" but also "iron to be corroded, bronze to turn black, and dogs to become rabid if they eat anything that has come into contact with the blood" (Salisbury 24). As Bullough and Brundage astutely note, "medieval science offered a biological explanation for almost any gender stereotype they wanted to promulgate" (92).

This link between women, pollution, and the word "slut," Bonnie Blackwell notes, may be linked to an increase in infection by syphilis (156), a connection evident in the 1717 medical book entitled *Syphilis: A Practical Dissertation on the Venereal Disease*, by Daniel Turner. In the book, Turner describes a variety of scenarios in which syphilis is contracted, always by a male and typically from a prostitute. In one example, "a Young Lad" was "carried to a scandalous House, by one of his Companions, who had been there before, and came off without Injury, engaging notwithstanding with the same **Slut**" (146). The next day the man visits Turner and reports "*Dysuria*, or scalding Urine" (146).

Although *syphilis* is allegedly a medical treatise, the difference in Turner's treatment of the two men and the woman is worth noting. For example, Turner only discusses how men "contract" (as opposed to "transmit") syphilis. In fact, the men (who are given the friendly nicknames "Young Lad" and "the young Spark") are presented as happy-go-lucky young men whose sex acts are discussed euphemistically: the man "engages with" the woman, as opposed to "pays for sex," and the friend "came off without Injury," as opposed to "avoided a sexually transmitted disease." By using passive voice (the man was "carried to a scandalous House"), moreover, Turner casts the man as a victim of circumstances as opposed to a man driven by his sexual desires.

In other words, these men are not animals, and they are not responsible for a disease, even though *they* paid *her* for sex. Actually, Turner suggests that they are not responsible perhaps precisely *because* they paid her. The "Slut" is a product these young men purchased, but the problem lies in her being a faulty product. Thus, although she could likewise benefit from treatment, Turner does not suggest informing her of the man's syphilis. Perhaps Turner only had interest in those who could pay his fee.

The association of "slut" with the lower classes is also obvious in its use as a term for a female domestic (seventeenth century) and eventually any poor woman (nineteenth century) (Blackwell 142). For example, in Henry Fielding's 1742 *Joseph Andrews*, Betty, the chambermaid, is called a "slut," and in Samuel Richardson's 1740 *Pamela, or Virtue Rewarded*, Mr. B. uses several variations of "slut"—"foolish slut" (16), "saucy slut" (269), and "artful slut" (264)—when referring to the maidservant Pamela, with whom he is infatuated.

Germaine Greer theorizes that this casting of female domestic servants as not only inherently unclean but also suspiciously immoral (i.e. the dirty maid) arose "when most lower-class girls were making a living as domestics, struggling to keep clear of the sexual exploitation of the males in the household" (260). Greer adds that "the language of reprobation became more and more concerned with lapses in neatness, which were taken to be the equivalent of moral lapses" (260). In other words, dirtiness shifted from being an effect of poverty to a sign of immorality, which was in turn a sign of sexual availability. How ironic that a woman hired as a domestic would have been perceived as "less noble" than an employer who sexually harassed/exploited her.

Unfortunately, the association of lower class women with dirtiness persisted well into the twentieth century (and continues still). In the 1912 *Pygmalion,* George Bernard Shaw opens with precisely this stereotype: Eliza Doolittle, the flower seller, is physically dirty ("her hair needs washing rather badly" and "she needs the dentist"), her clothing is dirty ("she wears a little sailor hat of black straw that has long been exposed to the dust and soot of London" [187]), and she is even warned that she appears to be a prostitute (to which she replies, "I'm a respectable girl: so help me, I never spoke to him except to ask him to buy a flower off me" [190]). In the final scene of the play, after Eliza announces that she will become a teacher of phonetics in competition with Higgins, he exclaims, "You damned impudent **slut,** you!" (292). The use of the adjective "impudent" reinforces societal displeasure at a woman who "exceeds her station." However, Higgins is not the hero. In fact, it is embarrassing to witness Higgins clinging to such an outdated and limiting view of women and social class, like so many others before and since.

The demeaning function of the slut label is also obvious in the use of "slut" to denote the colonized and the enslaved, groups stereotyped by the colonizer as lazy and dirty. Writing in 1885 from Khartoum, British Major-General C.G. Gordon describes escaped soldiers as they look at their "black pug faces" in a mirror for the first time, faces he asserts are "all alike" to him (25). He is particularly interested in "the black **sluts,** who think themselves 'Venuses,' and shove their hands into their mouths, which is a general sign among blacks of great modesty, like the casting down of the eyes with us" (42). Gordon's use of quotation marks around "Venuses" is intended as a wink to his British/White audience as clearly an African woman's belief in her own beauty would be laughable. Even a display of modesty is depicted as crude coming from an African woman, especially when contrasted with the British woman's "casting down" of one's eyes. Gordon thus supplies an apt example of what Black Feminist scholar Patricia Hill Collins refers to as the "intersecting oppressions of race, class, and gender" (8). Gordon does not question that women, unlike men, should demonstrate modesty, but even among subordinate women he further demeans African women as inferior to British women. Thus "slut" becomes not only a sexist and classist term, but a racist one, as well.

II. *Slut,* an impudent woman

By the seventeenth century, "slut" had shifted to signify a woman who lacks respect for men/society, an attitude made manifest in her immodesty, rudeness, boldness, and audacity. Thus, whereas in the Middle Ages a "slut" signified a dirty woman, the term shifted from physical dirtiness to moral dirtiness. A slut thus came to signify a woman who was *deliberately* unclean—who *neglected* to keep a clean appearance, a clean house, and a "clean" (i.e. monogamous) sexual life. This emphasis on women's agency also explains the special condemnation "slut" carried: these women were *choosing* "dirty" behaviours and thereby betraying and perverting the "natural" order of things, including women's subservience to men.

For example, in the 1621 *The Anatomy of Melancholy,* Robert Burton writes, "Women are all day a dressing to please other men abroad, and goe like **sluts** at home, not caring to please their owne Husbands whom they should" (37). Although these women's choice to dress well while travelling seems innocent, in doing so they are violating the ideals Barbara Welter cites as part of the "Cult of True Womanhood," namely "modesty" and "domesticity"; however, since they are "pleasing other men" and neglecting their husbands, they are violating the ideals of purity and piety as well. As the First Epistle of Peter commands, "you wives be submissive to your husbands.... Let not yours be the outward adorning with braiding of hair, decoration of gold, and wearing of robes, but let it be the hidden person of the heart with the imperishable jewel of a gentle and quiet spirit" (1 Peter 3:1-4).[3] Clearly a woman should not dress to please other men, or herself, nor even have a voice for that matter.

To help her honour her duty to family and church, women were relegated to the private sphere; the public sphere would have been reserved for men. In fact, Warner observes that "public" is derived from "the Latin *poplicus,* for people, but evolved to *publicus* in connection with *pubes*, in the sense of adult men, linking public membership to pubic maturity" (23). In Burton's example, women are transgressing their sphere by "all a day" travelling abroad even though they should be home.

Of course, because the woman has disobeyed, it is *her* fault if she is ogled. In fact, Burton emphasizes women's responsibility for any male attention by noting that they dress *in order* to please other men and thus elect *not* to please their own husbands. In short, by dressing a certain way, women are "asking for" the sexual attention of men. Sound familiar? Just as in Turner's treatise, the men who are actually engaging in the forbidden activity (having sex with prostitutes and leering at a married women) are not to be blamed.

However, where there is oppression, there will be rebels, and by the eighteenth century, "slut" had become a mainstream term to disparage "uppity" women who defied subservience. In Henry Fielding's 1742 *Joseph Andrews*, for example, we hear about "forward Sluts" (64), and in Trollope's *The American Senator*, Mrs. Masters calls her lovely but intransigent stepdaughter an "ungrateful, sly, wicked slut" (242). In *Pamela*, as well, Mr. B. consistently calls Pamela a slut. Even if the tone of these texts is playful, the subtext is clear: these female characters are *defying* the roles assigned them—to be good (i.e., submissive and quiet) (step)daughters, wives, and servants—and their punishment is the stigma of being called a slut.

III. *Slut*, a lascivious woman

In *Vagina*, Naomi Wolf asserts that "no historian has conclusively explained how women lost status in the transition from the earliest civilizations to those of classical antiquity"; however, by Plato's time (427-347 BCE), sexual perfection was seen as the union between a man and a boy; Greek wives were strictly for reproduction (129-30). Thus somewhere along the line women became second-class citizens.

Perceptions of women, and especially sexual women, do not improve in Christian texts. In the Old Testament we learn that "because the daughters of Zion are haughty and walk with outstretched necks, glancing wantonly with their eyes, mincing as they go, tinkling with their feet" (Isaiah 3:16), the Lord will punish them. Specifically, "instead of perfume there shall be rottenness; and instead of a girdle, a rope; and instead of well-set hair, baldness; and instead of a rich robe, a girding of sackcloth; instead of beauty, shame" (Isaiah 3:24). The Lord will also take away the women's jewelry and clothing (a list of twenty-one different items is included in the scripture). Put simply, as penance, the women will lose their feminine markers and their sexuality.

In the First Epistle of Paul to the Corinthians, Saint Paul simplifies matters even further, stating simply, "It is well for a man not to touch a woman" (1 Corinthians 7:1). Such disgust for women led to their casting in the Middle Ages as possessing "insatiable sexual appetites" (Bullough and Brundage 92), and it was a short step to the actual demonization of women. As Dyan Elliott reports, in the fifteenth century there was a rise in accusation of women/witches copulating with the devil (283). This belief in women as less than human informs the nineteenth-century use of "slut" to refer to a female dog.

However, according to Peter Heinegg, Jesus "seems to have gotten along well with women" (50). In John 8:3-7, for example, the scribes and the Pharisees bring before Jesus a woman accused of adultery, attempting to test Jesus' obedience to Jewish law by asking him to weigh in on the woman's punishment. Jesus replies, "Let him who is without sin among you be the first to throw a stone at her" (John 8:7).

The fact that the 1468 mystery play *The Woman Taken in Adultery*, performed by the Grey Friars, is based on this scripture suggests a bright spot of charity toward women in an otherwise misogynistic climate. Although it is true that the play conveys Jesus' compassion for the adulterer, this occurs only after a vicious verbal assault by the scribes and Pharisees. In the play, the female adulterer is summoned thusly,

> Scriba: "Come forthe, thou stotte! Come forthe, thou scowte! Come forthe, thou bysmare and brothel bolde! Come fforthe, thou hore, and stynkynge byche clowte! How longe hast thou suche harlotry holde? ...Come forth, thou quene! Come forthe, thou scolde! Com forth, thou sloveyn! Com forthe, thou **slutte**!" (Halliwell 217-18)

As Richard Grant White notes, the language used is "far more pharisaic than decent" (341). Of course, one could argue that the misogynistic language the Grey Friars employ in the play is intended to cast the Scribes and Pharisees as unchristian; however, such a goal could surely be accomplished with less vehemence and vulgarity. Of special note is the fact that the language is so sexual: "stotte" (slut), "hore" (whore), "bitch clout/ /byche clowt" (a profane term for a woman), and "slutte" (slut). She is also called a "quene," a term of abuse to signify a "lowborn woman," an interesting pejorative given Christ's championing of the poor.

Ironically, Douglas Kelly cites the "virtuosity" taught "through the education of the monks" as a major source of medieval misogyny (86). That is, during the Middle Ages, the more closely one held to misogynistic religious teachings, the more misogynistic one became. It was precisely to challenge misogyny, including misogyny in the church, that Christine de Pizan (1364-1430) wrote her letters. For example, in *L'Epistre au Dieu d'Amours*, she questions the traditional interpretation of Eve's responsibility for original sin "by proposing another occasionally heard, but less damning reading; both the man and the woman cooperated in the sin" (Kelly 83). Christine de Pizan also argues that, "if women had written the books that were written by clerks, those books would have contained very different things (a claim made by Chaucer's Wife of Bath)" (Bornstein 13).

A "translation" of Christine de Pizan's *L'Epistre au Dieu d'Amours* by medieval writer Hoccleve should likewise challenge misogyny. However, whereas Christine seeks to challenge men's refusal to take responsibility for their own behaviour, in "The Letter of Cupid," Hoccleve writes, "it shall not be their choice to refuse the foulest **slut** in the town, despite what they might imagine."[4] That is, because the man *cannot* resist the sexual temptation of a woman, even one who is ugly and/or diseased, it is not the man's fault if he makes sexual advances. Instead, "Cupid is the culprit who makes clerks fall in love with worthless women" (qtd. in Bornstein 13).

Hoccleve also neglects to include examples of women's good deeds (14) and men's bad ones (12). Ironically, then, Hoccleve co-opts a work that challenges misogyny and instead creates a text in which he perpetuates misogyny, including using pejoratives such as "slut" in his translation that were not in the original. As Bornstein notes, Christine de Pizan's accusation that men make bad translators seems to have been borne out (13).

Unfortunately, as Mills reports, in the twentieth century, slut became "a widespread term of abuse, synonymous with scrubber and slag, applied to any woman who does not accept the sexual double standards of society" (224). For example, in *Promiscuities*, Naomi Wolf writes of her personal experience coming of age in the 1950s: "If we were out of line sexually, we could become sluts; if we became sluts, we could die several deaths. This equation was so much a part of the air we breathed that we could scarcely examine it. The impulse to equate women's being sexual with their suffering a swift, sure punishment is reflexive" (64).

Jonathon Green in *Green's Dictionary of Slang* also reveals that in the twentieth century, "slut" became pejoratively linked to lesbians and gays: a "slut hut" is a gay brothel, and "slut-puppy" is a derogatory term for a gay man (1060). Even in this context, "slut" is meant to criticize men who are "acting like women," but not demonstrating the shame that women are told to exhibit when it comes to sexuality. Likewise, contemporary synonyms for "slut" such as "jezebel," which is meant to impugn African American women's sexuality, and *puta*, which according to Sandra Cisneros is the Latina's unfortunate destiny if she does not embrace her "destiny—marriage and motherhood" (176), are predicated on a virgin/whore, Mary/Jezebel, virgen/puta dichotomy that privileges the submissive, pure, and pious.

Thus, given that "slut" retains its association with dirtiness, immorality, and impudence, the word has not been completely reclaimed, although the following examples offer evidence of a trend in the right direction. In particular, we can witness in popular culture three important shifts in how the word is viewed.

First of all, although people continue to this day to call women "slut," those people are challenged, publicly. In other words, whereas throughout most of its history "slut" was uttered by men (and women) to denigrate women, in the twentieth century, "sluts" began fighting back. For example, in the 1970s a recurring *Saturday Night Live* skit entitled "Point/Counterpoint" featured

actors Dan Aykroyd and Jane Curtin debating one another. Aykroyd
routinely uttered the line, "Jane, you ignorant slut." The sexism
and anger inherent in the word "slut" was deliberate, reflecting
the chauvinism of the pompous character Aykroyd played and the
exasperation this character felt with having to debate a woman.
During this period in the U.S., Equal Rights Amendment (ERA)
opponents were claiming that the ERA was anti-family and denied
women the right to be supported by their husbands. Jane Curtin
represented the pro-ERA feminist who both angered and challenged
Aykroyd's conservative character. Importantly, Curtin was able to
reply, even if her response, "Dan, you pompous ass," was likewise
juvenile. Nonetheless, the skit provided a much-needed opportunity
for women in the 1970s to interrogate misogynistic words such
as "slut." For instance, if women were truly sexually liberated,
why did a suggestion that they were sexually "dirty" still pack a
punch? Perhaps it was the knowledge that men continued to view
women as inferior, dirty, and deserving of the slap that a word
like "slut" provides.

A second shift in the use of the word slut in U.S. popular culture
is represented by Blanche Devereaux, a character on the mid-1980s
television program *The Golden Girls*, who was proud to refer to
herself as a slut:

> Dorothy: So [Rose] had fifty-six boyfriends in one year. That
> doesn't mean she's a slut. She is THE slut! She is the grand
> Poobah of sluts! She is the easiest woman in this room!
> Blanche: Dorothy Zbornak, you take that back!... *I'm* the
> biggest slut. ("Old Boyfriends")

Had another character, especially a male character, labelled
Blanche "the biggest slut," one would characterize this as misogynistic language. However, as Judith Butler explains, "the
interval between instances of utterances not only makes the
repetition and resignification of the utterance possible, but
shows how words might, through time, become disjoined from
their power to injure and recontextualized in more affirmative
modes" (15). For Blanche, being referred to as a "slut" signified
the fact that she continued to engage in an active sexual life and

to be sexually attractive. Given that definition, and since she was single, what could be wrong with being a slut? Unfortunately, the fact that Blanche's female housemates regularly use the word slut "lightheartedly" against Blanche with resignation but also disapproval reveals that the term, as well as the behaviour, remained socially stigmatized.

In the 1997 book *Ethical Sluts*, Easton and Hardy's use of the adjective "ethical" more directly defuses accusations that sexually promiscuous women are inherently unethical or immoral. Rather than focusing on the number and identity of one's sexual partners, Easton and Hardy emphasize "finding a place of sanity with sex and relationships" and "freeing ourselves to enjoy sex and sexual love in as many ways as may fit for each of us" (5). Because the activities associated with "slut" (e.g., public displays of sexual lascivity, multiple sexual partners) are neutralized, the word "slut" is neutralized, as well.

The third shift is an interrogation of the *intentions* behind using "slut" to shame and blame women. The SlutWalk movement, for example, challenges assumptions about women's sexuality, including several that I have excavated in this article, such as the belief that a woman by her choice of dress is asking for male attention (Burton), that a man is powerless to resist women (Hoccleve), and that a sexual woman is dirty and deserves punishment (the Grey Friars). Amelia Abraham, a Slut Night organizer in London, explains that "the goal isn't to reclaim the word 'slut'; it's to completely undermine it" (qtd. in Heawood, n.p.).

Critics of the SlutWalk movement, however, argue that despite their efforts to reclaim it, "slut" still functions as a signifier for a dirty, poor, sexually available, and bad woman, so it should not be used in feminist protests. In 2011, for example, the Board of Directors and Board of Advisors of Black Women's Blueprint stressed their support of "a woman's right to wear whatever she wants anytime, anywhere." However, they argued that SlutWalk would not make women safer and may actually harm women by "normalizing the term on T-shirts, buttons, flyers and pamphlets."[5] Unfortunately, as Black Women's Blueprint note, misogynistic beliefs have material consequences, especially so for women with racialized bodies.

Jamaica Kincaid's short story "Girl" is worth noting, however, as it provides an example of challenging sexist language by employing it. The text of "Girl" is a list of life lessons told by a West Indian mother to her daughter. The mother seems most concerned with teaching her daughter to be a "true" woman: domestic, obedient, silent, and chaste. For example, the mother instructs, "this is how to sweep a corner," "this is how you smile to someone you don't like at all," and "on Sundays try to walk like a lady and not like the **slut** you are so bent on becoming." And yet, as Bonnie Blackwell observes, "to belittle a woman with the gravest term of pollution represents a refusal of empathy" (158). In fact, in this short piece, the mother mentions the probability of her daughter becoming a "slut" three times. And yet, by witnessing this painful exchange, the reader can acquire empathy, not only for the daughter whose mother has such a harsh opinion of her, but also the mother whose exposure to the systemic sexism of West Indian society has led her to feel such fear for her daughter. The use of the actual word "slut" is imperative in this mission.

Unfortunately the scenario that Kincaid captures remains a reality for many, and it is naïve to hope that this will end any time soon. However, the transgressive uses of "slut" included in this history represent an important paradigm shift and hopefully a sign of advances in gender equity to come.

CONCLUSION

As this article reveals, "slut" functions as a palimpsest, revealing how men (primarily) have cast women as the Other: Adam was created first, so he must lead Eve, his inferior, who must obey him and confine herself to the private sphere. Even today, a woman who is "public" about her "privates" and thereby defies societal (patriarchal) norms is seen as a pariah, as a slut.

However, as this article also reveals, when we excavate the word, the sources tend to be male. Except for Christine de Pizan, few women prior to the twentieth century were in a position to challenge the "slut" (or the "virgin") label or to question the man-made ideals of female behaviour, namely chastity, obedience, piety, silence, and domesticity, that limit women's agency and power.

It is precisely because the woman/slut's perspective is largely absent from history that Jane Mills questions the *OED*'s classification of the use of "slut" as a term "used playfully, or without any serious imputation, or bad qualities" (224). In particular, in reference to the example cited in the *OED*—Samuel Pepys' 1664 *Diary* "our little girl Susan is a most admirable *slut*, and pleases us mightly"—Mills shrewdly observes, "there is no record as to whether Susan actually enjoyed the playfulness of her employer, a self-avowed lecher" (224). In other words, perhaps our judgment of whether or not a term has "bad qualities" should not be based on how the user of the term feels about it. It's time to hear from the sluts themselves.

An awareness of how "slut" has functioned for the past six hundred years to support a patriarchal and oftentimes racist and elitist agenda is crucial if we hope to dismantle the misogynist ideology on which the word's pejorative meaning is predicated.

ENDNOTES

[1]All bolded text is my emphasis.
[2]Original Middle English text: "Ne delve' awey the weed, but pull with honde. / fful ferd is hit for touching of vnclene / Wymmen — and slottes y suppose hit mene."
[3]All biblical quotations from *The Oxford Annotated Holy Bible* (May and Metzger).
[4]Original Middle English text: "It shal nat been in hir elleccioun / The foulest slutte in al a town refuse / If that us list, for al that they can muse."
[5]Please refer to the introductory chapter for a detailed discussion of Black Women's Blueprint and their critique.

WORKS CITED

Attwood, Feona. "Sluts and Riot Grrrls: Female Identity and Sexual Agency." *Journal of Gender Studies* 16.3 (2007): 233-47. Print.
"bicche clout." Def. 2. *Middle English Dictionary*. University of Michigan. 2001. Web. 10 November 2013.
Blackwell, Bonnie. "How the Jilt Triumphed Over the Slut: The

Evolution of an Epithet, 1660-1780." *Women's Writing* 11.2 (2004): 141-61. Print.

Black Women's Blueprint. "An Open Letter from Black Women to the SlutWalk." *NewBlackMan*. 23 September 2011. Web. 10 November 2013.

Bornstein, Diane. "Anti-feminism in Thomas Hoccleve's Translation of Christine de Pizan's *Epistre au Dieu D'Amours*." *English Language Notes* 19.1 (1981): 7-15. Print.

Bullough, Vern L., and James Brundage, eds. *Handbook of Medieval Sexuality*. New York: Garland, 2000. Print.

Burton, Robert. "Democritus Junior to the Reader." *The Anatomy of Melancholy*. Vol. 1 Ed. Thomas C. Faulkner, Niocolas K. Kiessling, and Rhonda L. Blair. New York: Oxford University Press, 1989. 1-114. Print.

Butler, Judith. *Excitable Speech: A Politics of the Performative*. New York: Routledge, 1997. Print.

Cisneros, Sandra. "Guadalupe the Sex Goddess." *Women's Lives: A Multicultural Perspective*. 4th ed. Ed. Gwyn Kirk and Margo Okazawa-Rey. New York: McGraw Hill, 2007. 175-77. Print.

Collins, Patricia Hill. *Black Feminist Thought: Knowledge, Consciousness, and the Politics of Empowerment*. 2nd ed. New York: Routledge, 2000. Print.

Easton, Dossie and Janet W. Hardy. *The Ethical Slut: A Practical Guide to Polyamory, Open Relationships, and Other Adventures*. 2nd edition. Berkeley: Celestial Arts, 2009. Print.

Elliott, Dyan. *The Bride of Christ Goes to Hell: Metaphor and Embodiment in the Lives of Pious Women, 200-1500*. Philadelphia: University of Pennsylvania Press, 2011. E-book.

Fielding, Henry. *Joseph Andrews*. Ed. John Berseth. Mineola, NY: Dover, 2001. Print.

Gordon, C. G. *The Journals of Major-Gen. C.G. Gordon, C.B., at Kartoum*. London: Kegan, Paul, Trench, and Company, 1885. Print.

Green, Jonathon. *Green's Dictionary of Slang*, Vol. 3. London: Chambers, 2010. Print.

Greer, Germaine. *The Female Eunuch*. St. Louis, MO: McGraw-Hill, 1971. Print.

Halliwell, James Orchard, ed. *Ludus Coventriæ: A Collection of*

Mysteries, Formerly Represented at Coventry on the Feast of Corpus Christi. London: Shoberl, 1841. Print.

Heawood, Sophie. "I'd Much Rather Be a Slag Than a Slut." *The Guardian.* 6 October 2013. Web. 15 November 2013.

Heinegg, Peter. *Bitter Scrolls: Sexist Poison in the Canon.* Lanham, MD: University Press of America, 2011. Print.

Hoccleve, Thomas. "The Letter of Cupid." *Chaucerian and Other Pieces.* Vol. 1. Oxford: Clarendon, 1897. 217-32. Print.

"hore." Def. 1a. *Middle English Dictionary.* University of Michigan, 2001. Web. 10 November 2013.

Kelly, Douglas. *Christine de Pizan's Changing Opinion: A Quest for Certainty in the Midst of Chaos.* Rochester, NY: D. S. Brewer, 2007. Print.

Kincaid, Jamaica. "Girl." *At the Bottom of the River.* New York: Farrar, Straus and Giroux, 2000. Kindle file.

Liddle, Mark, ed. *The Middle English Translation of Palladius de re Rustica.* Berlin: Ebering, 1896. Print.

May, Herbert G., and Bruce M. Metzger. *The Oxford Annotated Holy Bible.* New York: Oxford University Press, 1962. Print.

Mills, Jane. *Womanwords: A Dictionary of Words about Women.* New York: Free, 1992. Print.

"Old Boyfriends." *The Golden Girls.* NBC. KXAN, Austin. 4 Jan. 1992. Television.

Pepys, Samuel. "Samuel Pepys Diary February 1664." 24 March 2011. Kindle file.

"quene." *Middle English Dictionary.* University of Michigan. 2001. Web. 10 November 2013.

Richardson, Samuel. *The Works of Samuel Richardson.* Vol. 1. London: Henry Sotheran, 1883. Print.

Salisbury, Joyce E. *Church Fathers, Independent Virgins.* New York: Verso, 1992. Print.

Shaw, George Bernard. *Pygmalion and Major Barbara.* New York: Bantam, 2008. Print.

"slut." *OED Online.* September 2013. Web. 10 November 2013.

"slutte." Def a. *Middle English Dictionary.* University of Michigan, 2001. Web. 10 November 2013.

"stot(t)e." Def 2. *Middle English Dictionary.* University of Michigan, 2001. Web. 10 November 2013.

Tanenbaum, Leora. *Slut! Growing Up Female with a Bad Reputation*. New York: Seven Stories, 1999. Print.

Trollope, Anthony. *The American Senator*. Detroit: Craig and Taylor, 1877. Print.

Turner, Daniel. *Syphlis: A Practical Dissertation on the Venereal Disease*. London: Bonwicke, 1717. Print.

Warner, Michael. *Publics and Counterpublics*. New York: Zone, 2002. Print.

Welter, Barbara. "The Cult of True Womanhood: 1820-1860." *American Quarterly* 18.2 (1966): 151-74. Print.

White, Richard Grant. *Memoirs of the Life of William Shakespeare with an Essay toward the Expression of His Genius and an Account of the Rise and Progress of the English Drama*. Boston: Little, Brown, 1865. Print.

Whitehorn, Katharine. "Sisters Under the Coat." *Observer*. December 1963. Web. 15 May 2012.

Wolf, Naomi. *Promiscuities: The Secret Struggle for Womanhood*. New York: Random House, 1997. Print.

Wolf, Naomi. *Vagina: A New Biography*. New York: HarperCollins, 2012. Print.

Practicing Intersectional Critiques

Re-examining "Third-Wave" Perspectives on Exclusion and White Supremacy in SlutWalk

JACQUELINE SCHIAPPA

AVING BEEN DESCRIBED in many ways, ranging from "an incredibly badass protest" (Adelman) to "a product placement ad for capitalist patriarchy itself" (Miriam 266), SlutWalk has proven to be a subject of powerful, divisive feminist debates. Activist Yasmin Nair authored an essay titled "Is Slutwalk the End of Feminism?" only a year after *Feministing.com* founder and best-selling author Jessica Valenti declared: "Slutwalks have become the most successful feminist action of the past 20 years." Indeed, the publication of this book is a testament to the volume and range of responses to SlutWalk as feminist controversy. Here, I review a selection of feminist essays on SlutWalk to show how although *some* perspectives productively mobilize "third wave" feminist critiques, others take a hypercritical position that minimizes counter-testimonies and misunderstands how the original SlutWalk Toronto was organized. The first section of this chapter outlines my understanding of what constitutes "third-wave" feminism; I briefly review and question the tradition of the "wave" metaphor for historicizing feminism, thereby mitigating the commonly held notion that women of colour and other marginalized social groups were not actively contributing to feminism or resisting its exclusivity prior to the "third wave." The following section examines the arguments of three popular critiques of SlutWalk, including Black Women's Blueprint's "Open Letter to Slutwalk," Chai Shenoy's "Why I don't care to Slutwalk," and Aura Bogado's "Slutwalk: A Stroll through White Supremacy." Each of these essays is commonly cited in what has been described as the "feminist blogosphere," a robust communicative space in which feminists have debated SlutWalk and continue to dialogue. Importantly, I incorporate divergent perspectives from less-cited sources, such as Global Women's Strike, to increase their counter-testimonies' visibility and to describe SlutWalk more fully. I also include comments from the only active, original SlutWalk Toronto organizer, Heather Jarvis, whom I interviewed in person during a research trip to Canada for this project. The firsthand insights I gained during that travel and research process transformed my perspective of SlutWalk Toronto and revealed unexpected tensions within many popular criticisms of the walk and its organizers, which ultimately inspired this chapter. I share these essays and insights to consider their implications for how we might reinterpret SlutWalk and related feminist debates. Finally, I argue that while many of these types of critiques intelligently interrogate "third wave" issues, other critiques paradoxically reproduce the inappropriate practices they decry, such as essentializing and limiting the testimonies of women of colour in SlutWalk, and failing to recognize the material realities of how the movement was organized. I illustrate how two of SlutWalk's principle points of controversy, intersectionality and white privilege, serve as a useful microcosm for assessing and understanding the state of third-wave feminist discourse. I refer to the practice of intersectionality and problematization of white privilege as "third wave" throughout this chapter to situate my work within an intellectual and organizational tradition, however it should be remembered that scores of marginalized feminists have engaged in such work long before mainstream (that is, dominant) feminism realized its necessity.

ON INTERSECTIONALITY:
SITUATING "THIRD WAVE" ISSUES IN FEMINIST HISTORY

Many feminists recognize the metaphor of "waves" and its chronology as useful insofar as it provides a common understanding by which significant shifts in feminist history may be viewed and reviewed. Often, that history tells us that first wave feminists were primarily focused on attaining suffrage in the mid-nineteenth century through the early twentieth century, while second-wave feminists prioritized issues of equal pay, employment opportunities, and reproductive health rights, such as abortion. The most popular rendering of feminist history does not typically recognize the contributions and criticisms of women of colour until the "third wave." However, women of colour have always been present in feminism and critical of the ways in which the feminist majority marginalized their voices to prioritize white middle-class heterosexual women.

By compartmentalizing feminist histories as distinct waves, feminist paradigms expedite a teleological organization to the detriment of a more accurate, complete history that resists chronologizing (Sandoval). Leandra Zarnow suggests that the feminist wave metaphor is therefore not only artificial, but detrimentally "compresses the highly nuanced reworking of feminist thought and practice" (274). In her work recovering marginalized feminist histories, Becky Thompson asserts that "the most significant problem with this litany [of waves] is that it does not recognize the centrality of the feminism of women of color in second wave history"; she adds, "missing too from normative accounts is the story of white antiracist feminism, which, from its emergence, has been intertwined with, and fueled by the development of, feminism among women of color" (39). For example, during the timeframe designated "second wave," many Black, Latino, and Asian women created and sustained important collectives, such as the Chicana *femenista* group Hijas de Cuauhtemoc, the Asian-American women's group Asian Sisters, the Native American organization Women of All Red Nations, and the Third World Women's Alliance, later also known as the National Black Feminist Organization. To exclude feminists of colour in second wave history is, therefore, not only hegemonic but factually inaccurate. Thus when "third wave" feminism is described as unique in its attention to race and class, the interrogations of those factors by women of colour, which traverse the boundaries of each "wave," are diminished within the wave metaphor (Fernandes; Thompson). Recognizing that women of colour, queer communities, and class activists have been, and continue to be, consistently erased in the history of feminism should not obscure the related fact that such groups were always, and remain, excluded by mainstream (popular, dominant) feminism.

The "third wave" of feminist progress marks enormous issue expansion, introducing many ideas and questions that both make and strain connections between disciplinary perspectives. For example, Judith Butler's notions of gender and performativity have wildly complicated assumptions about how bodies function as sites of sociopolitical constructions and expressions of gender. And where second wavers largely objected to the ways in which sex/uality is tethered to the female body, some third wave feminists have found an opportunity to question the inherent moralization of sexuality, ushering in pro-sex, or sex-positive, positions that reject many second-wave assumptions about the injury of sex culture. At the same time, Black feminist thinkers have resisted strands of sex-positivity which minimize the historical hyper-sexualization, fetishization, and exoticization of bodies of colour, while queer authors interrogate the implications of centering conversations about gender oppression around sex at all. Diversifying narratives, challenging interpretive frameworks that emerge from particular standpoints and geopolitical locations (white, hetero) is therefore a signature of third wave thought. Difference itself has become one of the most valuable truth-tools feminism has skilled. Rather than divide feminist agendas along lines of difference, third wave theorists suggest that difference be recognized, articulated, re-spected, and empowered as a mechanism of solidarity. Pursuing freedom from oppression involves recognizing the ways in which systematized exclusions are distinctive *and yet also* emerge and are sustained by intertwined dominant cultural logics. Thus, many feminists agree that "third wave" feminism must be particularly alert to issues of intersectionality, multiculturalism, and identity politics (Fernandes), thereby emphasizing how various forms of institutionalized inequity, such as racism and classism, are not only necessarily relevant to feminism but are inherently interconnected processes and must be discussed together. Despite intersectional criticism being a trademark of third wave feminism, mainstream feminists relentlessly prioritize white, hetero, middle-class expe-riences.

It is not surprising, then, that many women of colour and their allies continue to condemn mainstream third-wave feminism's commitment to racist, classist, heterosexist logics for perpetuating the exclusive practices that the first and second waves made so normative. Consider the prolific conversations provoked on Twitter by the #SolidarityIsForWhiteWomen hashtag created by Mikki Kendall, where hundreds of users networked an ongoing conversation explicating feminism's predominantly white supremacist culture. Twitter user @sanaa_cue authored one such tweet, directly linking feminism's exclusivity with SlutWalk: "#solidarityisforwhitewomen when i'm expected to support slutwalk but y'all carry on celebrating the french ban on hijabs and niqabs." Consequently, having emerged when it did, and whether or not anyone intended it as such, SlutWalk Toronto became an immediate emblematic figure of third-wave debates regarding intersectionality and enduring white supremacy in feminism. In what follows, I review popular critiques of SlutWalk that problematize its name and related exclusivity; within these critiques I find an opportunity to recognize third-wave feminism as both advancing and limiting its reflexivity on issues of intersectionality in feminist practices.

"THIRD WAVE" OR HYPERCRITICAL?
PATTERNS OF CRITIQUE ON SLUTWALK

To begin, I examine a pattern of third wave feminist critique I describe as hypercritical, represented in an essay by Chai Shenoy which seeks to deny any legitimacy to SlutWalk as a feminist activity. By "hypercritical" I mean excessively critical, unreasonable argument positions that are impractical to engage with or satisfy. Such a hypercritical pattern is indicative of an increasingly popular habit of rejecting the feminist practices of a person or group when they do not meet a specific set of "third wave" expectations. Moreover, I argue that this habit frequently fails to attend to divergent experiences of SlutWalk and flatly ignores how SlutWalk Toronto, among other SlutWalk events, were *actually* organized.

I take Shenoy's online essay, "Why I don't care to Slutwalk" as a representative example because it is comparable to other popular critiques of SlutWalk. An overwhelming majority of the essays, blog posts, tweets, and conversations that I have analyzed for a larger project take similar liberties in presuming how SlutWalk Toronto came to be and how subsequent organizers pursued building their own versions of the walk in their communities. For example, the author's argument depends on a definite notion of how SlutWalk Toronto emerged, one that is factually inaccurate and directly misinforms interpretations of SlutWalk as a movement. Shenoy's essay also represents a propensity of feminist writers, especially online, to use third-wave values to indict SlutWalk as an inadequately intersectional feminist practice, while contradictorily demanding a singular, specific reading of its meaning, especially for women of colour. Finally, I find that feminist critics denouncing SlutWalk for claiming to speak "for" Others tend to do that very same speaking "for" Others to carry their claims, erasing divergent narratives from women of colour on the meaning(s) of SlutWalk and limiting the intersectional feminist thinking they support.

Shenoy begins her critique of SlutWalk by suggesting that organizers failed to properly involve themselves in their communities. She calls on them to "take time off from work or school and sit in court rooms and hold judges and juries accountable," and to donate their earnings to existing organizations in their neighbourhoods rather than organize a new, separate initiative such as SlutWalk. Immediately, the author presumes quite a bit about SlutWalk's organizers, including that they refused to actively participate in established community projects/resources and that they do not sacrifice enough of their time to their activism. After likening SlutWalk to Take Back the Night, arguing that both merely "preach to the same choir" and that she is "tired of that," Shenoy calls for increased community involvement or "marches in our own backyard." Shenoy's refusal to grant SlutWalk validity as a "backyard" march opportunely obscures the fact that *all* SlutWalks are *locally* organized by volunteers and that SlutWalk Toronto organizers specifically sought to support and include existing local community resources such as the Toronto Rape Crisis Center, Multicultural Women Against Rape, The White Ribbon Campaign, and a well-respected two-spirited leader working on related local issues. Furthermore, SlutWalks (indeed many local activism events) are typically organized solely by volunteers who do not have the privilege or financial security to enact their activism with personal funds. Indeed part of SlutWalk's unique character is its strategic use of social media to disseminate information and network with other initiatives free of cost because of the lack of available resources (Jarvis). Insisting that a handful of volunteer organizers, many of whom struggle economically, should take time off work or school in addition to forking over their wages, is an expression of the "third-wave" fixation with finding no feminist practice good enough. Such hypercritique indulges in presumptuous thinking in regard to the intentions and material participation of both organizers and participants, making little to no effort to consider divergent reasoning, experiences, or meanings. The common assumption expressed in Shenoy's appraisal, that SlutWalk Toronto's founders were not already actively participating in their community and that SlutWalk was organized in a detached, privileged manner, constructs an unfair, inaccurate rendering of the original walk.

A different, more widely recognized feminist critique of SlutWalk was published by Black Women's Blueprint (BWB) in "An Open Letter from Black Women to the Slutwalk."[1] In their letter, BWB makes it clear that it is not just the name SlutWalk that requires critical attention, but the comfort with which organizers chose it, exemplifying "ways in which mainstream women's movements have repeatedly excluded Black women even in spaces where our participation is most critical"; the process of naming SlutWalk was inadequately intersectional. When I asked principal organizer Heather Jarvis to elaborate on how SlutWalk's name was chosen, she attributed it to fellow organizer Sonya Barnett's exchange with a coworker:

> I think she [Sonya] was talking to a colleague where she worked and telling the colleague about this [Sanguinetti's comment], and the colleague went, 'What do you mean, what are you gonna call it, like a slutwalk?' and she texts me and said 'What do you think of the name SlutWalk?' And I said, perfect, fine, done. He [Sanguinetti] threw this at us, we're going to throw it right back. (Jarvis)

That the name choice *unintentionally* excluded many women of colour is irrelevant, because, as BWB suggests, if organizers had involved more women of colour in their process, the exclusivity and privilege of that name-choice would likely have been addressed. The problem for BWB, then, is that neither organizer reached out or recognized the *necessity* of reaching out to women of colour from the beginning. Although not all of the original SlutWalk Toronto organizers were white, the thinking that enables the choice of "slut" without hesitation is made possible by the ignorance afforded by white privilege in a white supremacist culture that renders the different history of women of colour, and the sexualization of their bodies, invisible. On BWB's objection to SlutWalk's name, Jarvis replied, "I fucked up, and I try to be accountable for that, I can't take it away." She adds, "If I could go back and change anything it would be to have a deeper analysis of the language we used." Throughout my interviews with SlutWalk Toronto organizers I witnessed a consistent, reflexive consciousness of the privilege that named SlutWalk and a desire to redress that choice in ongoing conversations. By specifically highlighting the ways that SlutWalk's naming expressed white privilege, BWB's letter clarified how and why women of colour need to be included in and leading the feminist community. The selection of SlutWalk's name is not the only issue of concern regarding its relationship to third wave perspectives.

As the feminist blogosphere quickly disseminated BWB's letter, in many conversations it was presented as a definitive perspective of women of colour. However, positions on SlutWalk are articulated by women of colour in divergent and myriad ways; this has received far less attention. Here, I include some of those perspectives to diversify our understanding of how women of colour describe SlutWalk and to suggest that their interpretations rebut the prevailing notion that Slutwalk can only be meaningful to women with white privilege.

Global Women's Strike, a collectivity of immigrant women, responded to BWB's letter, arguing that their critique affirms class distances between women: "They say they 'do not recognise' themselves in it, while ignoring many thousands of us who do" ("Women of Colour"). Their response continues, "Many mainstream feminists and journalists (of colour and white) are livid about SlutWalk, and refuse to support it because they don't want to identify with those of us who are often or always identified as 'sluts.'" Authors of the Global Women's Strike statement describe a desire and ability to reform the meaning of slut because doing so mobilizes a sense of agency that classism often deprives.

In a recent interview, esteemed Black womanist author Alice Walker responded to the word slut and its feminist reclamation:

> I've always understood the word 'slut' to mean a woman who freely enjoys her own sexuality in any way she wants to; undisturbed by other people's wishes for her behavior. Sexual desire originates in her and is directed by her. In that sense it is a word well worth retaining. As a poet, I find it has a rich, raunchy, elemental, down to earth sound, that connects us to something primal, moist, and free.

Further, Walker asserted, "The spontaneous movement that has grown around reclaiming this word speaks to women's resistance to having names turned into weapons used against them" (qtd. in Archer). Similarly, feminist blogger Crunktastic argues in a post circulated on the *Crunk Feminist Collective* and *Racialicious* websites that it is *because* Black women's sexual identity has been historically "deviant, hyper, and excessive" that "the word slut has not been used to discipline (shame) us into chaste moral categories, as we have largely been understood to be unable to practice 'normal' and 'chaste' sexuality anyway." Crunktastic goes on to describe herself as "somewhat ambivalent about accusing my white sistren of being racist" in SlutWalk because "we have come to a point in feminist movement-building where we need to acknowledge that differing histories necessitate differing strategies." Far from ignoring the implications of the name, Crunktastic's stance at once makes visible the racialized history of the word slut by asking white women to recognize the problematic language *and* makes space for differing interpretations of how that history may be experienced to "force an acknowledgement that the experience of womanhood being defended here—that of white women—is not universal, but is under attack and worthy of being defended, all the same." By recognizing the reality of divergent experiences without hierarchically organizing them or denying the ways white privilege was exercised, Crunktastic's argument successfully mobilizes "third wave" ideas that resist essentialism and prioritize intersectionality. To contrast, I next examine Aura Bogado's piece that champions "third wave" values such as intersectionality, but is so devoted to a definite vision of what that intersectional feminism should look like that it becomes hypercritical, overlooking the divergent interpretations and experiences of women of colour who chose to organize and/or participate in their own SlutWalk.

In the widely circulated essay "SlutWalk: A Stroll Through White Supremacy," Aura Bogado gave an assessment of SlutWalk, lambasting the organizers for not reaching out to black, poor, and transgender women. Her appraisal mobilizes many "third wave" concerns, noting that the systemic processes victimizing women are supported by white supremacist culture and thusly emphasizing the need for intersectional approaches to change-making. She also points to the privilege inherent in SlutWalk's attempts to communicate with the Toronto police, because for many communities of colour that communication is accompanied by risk and fear. On that point Bogado is cogently reminding feminists that privilege exists in all public spaces.

Responding to the news that her country of origin, Argentina, may host its own SlutWalk, Bogado made another critique drawing on "third wave" concerns. She identifies the problematic assumption that women experience the word slut universally and frames SlutWalk's movement into the Global South as an unwelcomed encroachment by white women. She is rightfully skeptical of a white-privileged movement "bearing down" on South American women, but deprives their agency in choosing to organize their own SlutWalk. She asserts: "I do not want white English-speaking Global North women telling Spanish-speaking Global South women to "reclaim" a word that is foreign to our own vocabulary. To do so would be hegemonic, and would illustrate the ways in which Global North "feminists" have become a tool of cultural imperialism." Bogado is correct to remind us that the word slut is not familiar to many non-English-speaking persons, not exactly. But terms akin to slut which demonize, criminalize, shame, and ostracize (often female) sexuality are most certainly familiar to the oppressed. In India, SlutWalk's name was transformed into "Besharmi Morcha," or "shameless protest" (Lahiri). In countries like Argentina, Columbia, and Honduras most marches were named la Marcha de las Putas; in Brazil, Marcha das Vadias. These alternate namings suggest that the common experience of sexual violence can be important enough to women of colour to come together in international solidarity with a North American movement.

Characterizing SlutWalk as a parade of privilege that silences women of colour oversimplifies the complexity of its development, the diversity of its enactments, the experiences of participants, and the critical reflexivity practiced by many within the movement. Ironically, it is in Bogado's own post that self-identified South Asian migrant "Creatrix Tiara" describes feeling erased by the essay and begs in one of her fourteen comments:

> Please PLEASE listen to WoC like myself and a couple of others who are actively involved in SlutWalk in our areas and have explained many times why we feel passionate about the cause. In this malarkey we're being overlooked here by EVERYONE, no matter what side they take, and personally I feel that it's not helping in the 'making sure the marginalised get heard' department—if you really want the marginalised to be heard, stop engaging with the trolls and engage with us instead!

Although a few other discussants respond sparsely to Tiara's pleas, most do not, including Bogado herself. SlutWalk Toronto authored a response to the essay on their Facebook page in a post titled "SlutWalk is NOT all white and not white supremacy at its finest." Among other points, the post refutes Bogado's assertion that the SlutWalk Toronto organizers were all white, that they did not involve local communities of colour, and that they are unwilling to educate themselves further on issues of privilege. The post concludes by openly inviting any who want to "share ideas, strategies, constructive criticisms and pragmatic actions" to allow SlutWalk to "continue to do better." There is a difference between critically examining the ways in which SlutWalk emerged from a privileged moment and indicting the movement as a whole as "typical of liberal white women who have never truly listened to begin with" [Bogado] and that difference represents the distance between a productive "third wave" critique and a hypercritical one. Janell Hobson notes that there are plenty of "third wave" feminists who seek to regulate women's practices of feminism, especially women of colour. I share Janell Hobson's concern expressed in her piece on MS *Magazine's* website, where she asserts, "If feminism becomes yet another space for the regulation of our differences, rather than an embrace of our differences, then we have impeded our progressive move forward in our collective political consciousness."

BETWEEN A ROCK AND A HYPERCRITICAL PLACE

I hope to have shown how some of the feminist perspectives on SlutWalk productively demonstrate "third wave" criticism, such as BWB's letter, while other critiques like those of Shenoy and Bogado participate in hypercritical arguments in which no SlutWalk event or participant is acknowledged to be a legitimate feminist practice. All of the positions I've reviewed are valuable, but I find that those which accept divergent perspectives represent more effective "third wave" discourse. I hope to have also shown that SlutWalks are experienced in diverse ways by women of colour, a diversity that has been obscured by hypercritical arguments that do not recognize it. Perhaps the enduring intensity of SlutWalks as feminist controversy attests to its resonating power and usefulness as a microcosm for feminist issues. Exploring feminists' concerns about SlutWalk's name and as a popular feminist organizing initiative, one that has both succeeded and failed in including women of colour, reveals that "third wave" feminist dialogues are contentious, diverse and, at times, hypercritical. Moving forward, I hope that feminists interested in SlutWalk take the time to listen to the divergent testimonies of women of colour, to examine the actual ways SlutWalks are organized, and to generally make efforts to not collapse its potential meanings. If we cannot do so, I fear that our conversations will fall between a rock and a hypercritical place, where the feminist movement is stagnated by narrow and overly regulated feminist expectations of what constitutes legitimate feminist practice.

ENDNOTES

[1]Please refer to the introductory chapter of this book for a detailed discussion of Black Women's Blueprint and their critique.

WORKS CITED

Adelman, Lori. "The Feministing Five: Sonya Barnett and Heather Jarvis." *Feministing.* Apr. 2011. Web. 1 Oct. 2013.

Archer, Michael. "Michael Archer: Q&A with Alice Walker." *Guernica.* 15 June. 2011. Web. 1 Oct. 2013.

Black Women's Blueprint. "An Open Letter from Black Women to the SlutWalk." *Black Women's Blueprint.* 23 Sept. 2011. Web. 1 Oct. 2013.

Bogado, Aura. "SlutWalk: A Stroll through White Supremacy." *To the Curb.* 13 May. 2011. Web. 1 Oct. 2013.

Butler, Judith. Performative Acts and Gender Constitution: An Essay in Phenomenology and Feminist Theory." *Theatre Journal* 40.4 (1988): 519-531. Print.

Crunktastic. "Slutwalk vs. Ho Strolls." *Crunk Feminist Collective.* 23 May. 2011. Web. 1 Oct. 2013.

Fernandes, Leela. "Unsettling 'Third Wave Feminism': Feminist Waves, Intersectionality, and Identity Politics in Retrospect." *No Permanent Waves: Recasting Histories of US Feminism.* Ed. Nancy Hewitt. New Jersey: Rutgers, 2010. 98-118. Print.

Hobson, Janell. "Policing Feminism: Regulating the Bodies of Women of Color." *MS Magazine.* 10 June 2013. Web. 1 Oct. 2013.

Jarvis, Heather. Personal interview. 14 Jan. 2013.

Lahiri, Tripti. "Converting Indian Slacktivists Takes (Offline) Time" *The Wall Street Journal* (India). Web. 2 Aug. 2011.

Miriam, Kathy. "Feminism, Neoliberalism, and SlutWalk." *Feminist Studies* 38.1 (2012): 262-266. Print.

Sanaa (@sanaa_cue). "#solidarityisforwhitewomen when i'm expected to support slutwalk but y'all carry on celebrating the french ban on hijabs and niqabs." *Twitter.* 12 Aug. 2013, 2:58 p.m. Tweet.

Sandoval, Chela. *Methodology of the Oppressed.* Minneapolis, University of Minnesota Press, 2000. Print.

Shenoy, Chai. "Why I don't care to Slutwalk." *Collective Action DC*. 8 Aug. 2011. Web. 1 Oct. 2013.

SlutWalk Toronto. "SlutWalk is NOT all white and not white supremacy at its finest." *SlutWalk Toronto Facebook Page*. 14 May 2011. Web. 1 Oct. 2013.

Thompson, Becky. "Multiracial Feminism: Recasting the Chronology of Second Wave Feminism." *No Permanent Waves: Recasting Histories of U.S. Feminism*. Ed. Nancy Hewitt. New Jersey: Rutgers, 2010. 39-60. Print.

Valenti, Jessica. "SlutWalks and the future of feminism." *The Washington Post*. Web. 3 June 2011.

"Women of Colour respond to Black Women's Blueprint attack on Slutwalk." Global Women's Strike | Huelga Mundial de Mujeres. n.d. Web. Oct. 2013.

Zarnow, Leandra. "From Sisterhood to Girlie Culture: Closing the Great Divide between Second and Third Wave Popular Feminism." *No Permanent Waves: Recasting Histories of U.S. Feminism*. Ed. Nancy Hewitt. New Jersey: Rutgers, 2010. 273-304. Print.

"Doing Something" About "Coming Together"

The Surfacing of Intersections of Race, Sex, and Sexual Violence in Victim-Blaming and in the SlutWalk Movement

NICOLE PIETSCH

IN 2011, A POLICE OFFICER'S REMARK that "women should avoid dressing like sluts" in order to avoid being victimized by sexual violence generated strong reactions from women in Toronto, Ontario. "Historically, the term 'slut' has carried a predominantly negative connotation," founders of SlutWalk Toronto stated in response. "Aimed at those who are sexually promiscuous ... it has primarily been women who have suffered under the burden of this label ... the intent behind the word is always to wound, so we're taking it back" (SlutWalk Toronto). SlutWalk aimed to identify and challenge sexual stereotypes related to womanhood. It also aimed to point out how these stereotypes put women at risk for targeted acts of victim-blaming and sexualized violence. SlutWalk Toronto thrived, attracting over 3,000 participants at its 2011 event and inspiring subsequent events challenging "slut-shaming" all around the world (Pilkington). Yet in the midst of this successful action, resistance from different communities of women also surfaced: Was SlutWalk's definition and history of the term slut complete? Which women—"sluts"— did SlutWalk's definition include? By extension, who did it *exclude*? Last, what were the implications of these inclusions and omissions upon sexual violence and victim-blaming?

This chapter will look at how different women experience sexual violence and sexual denigration—including the label slut—differently. In particular, I will argue that the experiences of women of colour are not reflected in the mandate and activity of the SlutWalk movement. I will identify historical contexts concerning (different) women's sexual accessibility, and how this constructed-accessibility informed which women were targeted for state-sanctioned sexual violence. These constructs continue today and remained unchallenged by SlutWalk. This chapter aims to bring to the surface aspects of systemic violence that SlutWalk could not, namely, how white femininity is implicated in contemporary notions of chastity (and, by extension, notions of "sluttiness"). Last, I will argue how this history is implicated in contemporary "rape culture."

"COMING TOGETHER": THE COHESIVE AND DIVISIVE MECHANISMS OF *SOLIDARITY* IN THE VIOLENCE AGAINST WOMEN MOVEMENT

Notions of consciousness-raising, solidarity, and collectivity are conveyed throughout most feminist struggles. Feminist equity-seeking organizations, for example, have "historically favoured a lateral, coalition building model," as well as incorporated the experiences and expertise of a community of women toward the end of collective action (Bonisteel and Green 20). Feminist concepts of shared experiential knowledge are particularly useful in articulating the "collective nature of traumatic experience" and the politicization of violence against women (Bonisteel and Green 29). This is an innovative and foundational strength of the feminist anti-violence movement. By definition, however, collectivity can also present inherent limitations.

While the notion of collectivity gives strength, unity, and clarity to a movement, it can also give rise to the marginalization of some voices and experiences. The intersections of social location—race, class, sexual orientation, age, and other factors—are obviously seen to plainly *disrupt* notions of monolithic feminist collectivity in women's diverse experiences of (1) sexuality and (2) gender-based violence. Constructs of intersecting womanhood and race, for example, have had distinct and divergent effects on North America's social conceptualizations, policies, and services addressing sexual and reproductive health. Intersections of womanhood and race also influence the efficacy of systems meant to address violence against women (see Donovan; Cossins; Pfeifer and Oglaff). These phenomena, in turn, have a significant impact on not only *state resolutions*, but also *feminist framing and problem-solving* of the question of sexual violence.

Social location has concrete impacts on one's experience of sexual violence. Canadian studies note that young women from marginalized racial, sexual, and socioeconomic groups are more vulnerable to being targeted for sexual harassment and sexual assault (Wolfe and Chioda qtd in Safe Schools Action Team). Community-based programs meant to support survivors are often less accessible to women from diverse racial and socioeconomic populations. And while feminists agree that the justice system's ability to address sexual violence is tepid overall, its response to racialized women as sexual assault complainants is decidedly poor. An American study on rape blame attribution, for example, found that "White male participants [in the study] viewed the Black victim as more promiscuous than the White victim when the perpetrator was White" (Donovan 733). In Canada, the Sisters in Spirit campaign reveals, likewise, that women of Aboriginal descent are overwhelmingly overrepresented as murdered, violated, and missing cases that are not adequately investigated by police (Native Women's Association of Canada). Women's experiences as survivors of sexual violence are divided along racial, ethnic, religious, age, and class lines because social cultures including "legal cultures create different categories of *Woman* according to these factors" (Cossins 78). It follows that women's experiences of the label "slut" are also divided along racial, ethnic, religious, age, and class lines.

Diverging and socially-located constructs of "womanhood" have implications for women's experiences of femininity, sexuality, and sexual violence. These overarching questions are ever-present—though historically, too often unspoken—within the feminist anti-violence movement. These questions were ever-present and unspoken within the inaugural activities and mandate of the Slut-Walk movement too. Certainly, different women experience sexual violence and sexual denigration—including the label slut—differently. If race-based constructs are significant and intertwined with women's experiences of sexual violence and victim-blame overall, how did SlutWalk omit them?

SlutWalk showed considerable depth in its capacity to discuss the root causes of sexual violence against women, surpassing superficial interpretations of sexual violence as a problem related to crime or mental illness. Like other aspects of the women's movement, early SlutWalk action indeed revealed that the "search for feminism and sisterhood" (Ringrose 413) does not necessarily interrogate the most complex and intersectional indications of patriarchal oppression.

SEXUAL VIOLENCE, WOMEN OF COLOUR, AND MARGINAL WOMANHOOD

For all women, sexuality, violence, and sexual violence hinge necessarily upon notions of hegemonic and intersectional womanhood. SlutWalk succeeded in its capacity to link stereotypical *expectations of femininity* with the *punitive threat of sexual violence* for women who failed to achieve these notions.

All women confront expectations of femininity in their lives. In Elizabeth R. Cole and Alyssa N. Zucker's *Black and White Women's Perspectives on Femininity*, the authors describe a socially-constructed "prescriptive set of normative feminine behaviors" and attributes. These include, amongst others, "beauty, demeanour ... sexuality, and (White) race" (Cole and Zucker 1). Dominant femininity, the authors argue—as well as "the typically White upper-middle class women who can achieve it" —are "conspicuously valued within mainstream [North] American culture" (Cole and Zucker 1).

In late eighteenth-century North America, however, a concept that separated marginalized women from privileged women was the notion of chastity. Women who could—or were perceived to— evade sexual impulses were awarded higher social and political status (Solinger *Pregnancy and Power* 52). This privilege was not afforded to Black women who faced the daily realities of slavery, including state-mandated tolerance of sexual violence perpetrated against them. In this, chastity became an ideological and political mechanism that functioned to differentiate subordinated women from privileged women. Being a *true woman* meant being sexually inaccessible.

Colonial history in North America and the accompanying "grotesque abuses of slavery" linked the lives of women of colour with sexual access from white men (Hillman 13). This history, in addition, drew a "dominant view, constructed on emotionology toward black females that, even today, scripts her as open, lewd and available" (Hillman 13). White supremacist social and economic policy that followed in the post-war years—such as income support programs, sterilization practices, and access to social housing— served to reproduce sexual stereotypes and "carnal images of and expectations for all black women" (Hillman 15). In *Pregnancy and Power: A Short History of Reproductive Politics in America,* author Rickie Solinger notes an example:

> For the purposes of excluding families of color, 40 percent or more of the states wrote "suitable homes" laws that barred aid to illegitimate children. Legislators accepted welfare rules that threw mothers and their children off the welfare roll if some official believed the woman had had sex with a man—whether the father of her children or someone else.... These rules targeted African American mothers,[1] who were instructed to stay away from men and punished them if they disobeyed. (146)

Social policies functioned to condemn and associate black women with the "racist image ... of the promiscuous breeder, populating the world irresponsibly, like an unspayed animal" (Bordo 79).

This sexual script worked to support patriarchal and white supremacist initiatives in more than one way. First, within this script, black women were reaffirmed as habitually sexually accessible to men, whether by consent or by force. Second, it assumed white women to be comparably "inaccessible, sexually prohibited and chaste" (Hillman 21). This script functioned to differentiate black women and white women as *qualitatively different and deserving* on this basis; the notion of *sexualized women* (any sexualized woman) was categorized, concurrently and automatically, alongside the (deficient) black women. It is here that contemporary hegemonic constructs of the "slut" are foregrounded. The term slut is not only a "negative connotation aimed at those who are sexually promiscuous," but a racialized label of subordinate femininity (SlutWalk Toronto).

Today, our sexual selves as women rely upon a history in which women of colour "fulfilled white men's sexual gratification while simultaneously protecting the virtue of white women" (Hillman 14). For black women, this means that the charge of "slut" is ever-present and endemic to their experience of daily racism. Black writer Aura Bogado notes it is "our skin color, not our style of dress, [that] often signifies slut-hood to the white gaze" (Bogado 5). The interconnections of racism, sexism, and sexual violence cannot be disentangled. Indeed, "one cannot write adequately about the lives of white women ... *in any context* without acknowledging the way in which race shaped their lives" as well (Brown 276).

Expectations of femininity are defined by constructs of what a racialized woman *isn't*; and negative interpretations of femininity (i.e. promiscuity) are informed by constructs of what a racialized woman *is*. These differences challenge "the idea of a unitary or universal 'women's experience,'" including women's experiences of sexual violence and victim-blaming (Cossins 78).

THE SLUTWALK CHALLENGE TO TORONTO POLICE: CHALLENGING *WHOSE* CONSTRUCTED "SLUT-HOOD"?

Toronto Police Constable Michael Sanguinetti's remarks in 2011 noted his opinion as a man and a member of frontline law enforcement (that is, a system) that women ought to avoid "dressing like a 'slut'" (SlutWalk Toronto) in order to avoid being targeted for acts of sexual violence. In Sanguinetti's words, the notion of chastity stands out: it is a marker of woman-based/originated integrity within his hegemony. Through Sanguinetti's eyes, chastity is largely achievable through (women's) action, behaviour, and dress. Further, chastity is constructed as an "actionable" virtue that, when practiced correctly, can exact a woman's safety. On the other hand, sexual availability and accessibility signifies an unskilled or unscrupulous woman. *That* woman, we read in Sanguinetti's words, can expect the threat of sexual violation to remain imminent.

Following Sanguinetti's comments, a group organized in protest and issued a response:

Historically, the term "slut" has carried a predominantly

82

negative connotation *aimed at those who are sexually promiscuous*,[2] be it for work or pleasure, it has primarily been women who have suffered under the burden of this label. And whether dished out as a serious indictment of one's character or merely as a flippant insult, the intent behind the word is always to wound, so we're taking it back. "Slut" is being re-appropriated. We are tired of being oppressed by slut-shaming; of being judged by our sexuality and feeling unsafe as a result. (SlutWalk Toronto)

Certainly, women in Canada live in a culture that continues to normatively differentiate between "good women who can be raped and bad women who cannot" (Cossins 95). In the mandate above, slut-shaming and the related threat of sexual violence is understood as a "negative connotation aimed at those who are sexually promiscuous" (SlutWalk Toronto). To women of colour, however, constructed "slut-hood" is not problematized as a question of action, behaviour, and dress. Instead, it is first a *clearly racialized differentiation,* and one that is both strategically and externally imposed upon black women by white supremacist values. The Black Women's Blueprint, an organization that aims to amplify the voices of women of African descent, notes that "where slavery constructed Black female sexualities, Jim Crow kidnappings, rape and lynchings, gender misrepresentations, and more recently, where the Black female immigrant struggle combine, 'slut' has different associations for Black women" than do features like "mode of dress" or behaviour (Black Women's Blueprint).

For racialized bodies, Sanguinetti's comments are particularly sobering. They reflect a lived reality where intersections of womanhood and race *explicitly predict* black women's vulnerability to being targeted for acts of sexual assault and harassment. His words, as a member of a police force, reaffirm what black women know and fear, and in addition, that the efficacy of systems meant to support survivors of sexual violence will not readily endorse black women as sexual assault complainants. This includes black women's experiences of navigating criminal justice systems; systems' framing of victim and offender responsibility; and systems' capacity to ally with the stories of violated racialized women (see

Donovan; Cossins; Pfeifer and Oglaff).

In a hegemony where black women continue to face racist stereotypes that depict them as socially and sexually *unqualified* to realize values associated with white womanhood, SlutWalk presented "itself to be a maddening distraction from the systematic and interpersonal violence that women of color face" (Bogado 3). Its starting point (an academic classroom, a female student who honestly queried a police officer for sexual violence prevention tips, and the resultant outrage at his response) identifies "a privileged position of relative power, replete with an entitlement of assumed safety that women of color would never even dream of" (Bogado 4). SlutWalk's inability to identify racialized understandings of "sluts"/slut-shaming within its activities, outreach, rhetoric or protest march revealed "an innocence that amounted to the transgressive refusal to know" experiences and reality outside white experience—including the impact of racism (and in that, sexual violence) on the lives of racialized women (Sullivan 127).

Like sexual violence itself, positioning the root causes of violence and enacting resistance to that violence must be contextual. Feminist thought and action does well to remember that being a woman is "not extractable from the context in which one *is* a woman—that is, race, class, time and place" (Brown 276). Black Women's Blueprint outlines this context by correcting SlutWalk on race, time, and place:

> As Black women, we do not have the privilege or the space to call ourselves "slut" without validating the already historically entrenched ideology and recurring messages about what and who the Black woman is. We don't have the privilege to play on destructive representations burned in our collective minds, on our bodies and souls for generations. … Even if only in name, we cannot afford to label ourselves, to claim identity, to chant dehumanizing rhetoric against ourselves in any movement. (Black Women's Blueprint)

The "slut" label remains the tool of the oppressor, and therein carries with it the pain of colonialism and bodily subjugation, including the imminent threat of racist sexual violence. The term "'reclaiming' is defined as taking something back," Aura Bogado agrees, "and the word 'slut' was never ours to begin with" (Bogado 4).

THE SLUTWALK CHALLENGE NOW

One of the strengths of feminist anti-violence work is the recognition that gender-based violence is a *social problem*. Patterns of violence against women are common to women, and different from those against men. Prevailing attitudes in most societies "serve to justify, tolerate or condone violence against women, often blaming women for the violence they experience" (World Health Organization). Without a systemic analysis—largely based on notions of commonality and patterns in women's experiences of violence globally—how do we frame gender-based violence, including sexual violence? We can't. The challenge facing SlutWalk now is to articulate a systemic analysis of collective rape culture, while at the same time recognizing experiences of difference within it.

In her essay *What Has Happened Here*, black writer Elsa Barkley Brown observes feminist anxiety toward recognizing women's various and diverging experiences of oppression. The prospect of recognizing intersectional—as opposed to common or linear—realities, she writes:

> makes us wary, fearing that layering multiple and asymmetrical stories will only result in chaos with no women's history or women's story to tell, that political community is a product of homogeneity, and that exploring too fully our differences will leave us void of any common ground on which to build a collective struggle. (Brown 281)

Furthermore, intersectional feminism is a demanding, ongoing process that challenges us to consider social issues from a variety of perspectives. This practice includes recognizing where we each have privilege and implementing ways to think alternatively about, or challenge, this privilege. All the more tricky is the fact that privilege—particularly racial privilege, or whiteness—itself passes as an element so hegemonic as to appear invisible, irrelevant, thereby "operating as a shield that protects a person from realizing her complicity in an oppressive situation" (Sullivan 158).

If we are to accept the criticism of SlutWalk—largely, that different women experience sexual violence differently; that different women experience different sexual assault myths; and that, consequently, different women will experience systems meant to support survivors differently—where does this leave SlutWalk as a movement? Its mandate identifies its key action and strength in its collectivity: "We want meaningful dialogue and we are doing something about it: WE ARE COMING TOGETHER ... to make a unified statement about sexual assault and victims' rights and to demand respect for all" (SlutWalk Toronto). How do we reconcile this mandate alongside the directives of intersectional feminist practice?

Brown's work speaks foremost to the strength and innovation of intersectional analysis in feminist action, as opposed to its challenges. Particularly, I note that Brown identifies the significance that intersectional feminist thought can have on complex policy, such as law. Citing present and complicated women's issues—for example, the workplace sexual harassment of women of colour and the pressure on white women to meet narrow "Victorian assumptions of sexuality and respectability," both of which have important legal implications for female sexual violence complainants—Brown notes that intersectionality is *a necessary tool* to elucidating the real issues at play (Brown 280). Only racial (including white) and gender contexts *combined* will effectively surface the realities of sexual violence. On the contrary, Brown states, the "liability here and the threat to creating a community of struggle [comes] from *not* focusing on differences among women and *not* seriously addressing the race and class dimensions of power" (Brown 281). That is, without intersectional framing of sexual violence, we will not have the foundational analysis to *effectively articulate* sexual violence as a social problem.

For SlutWalk, this means that the movement could just be starting to realize its potential. An intersectional analysis, for example, will better support SlutWalk in identifying sexual assault myths. This analysis, with its multiple intersectional herstories, will be useful in outlining how rape culture myths and misconceptions originated, and how they grew to be heavily entrenched in our social scripts. In my opinion, practiced intersectional thought also supports frontline workers in effectively advocating for survivors within justice systems, be they women of colour or not.[3]

This intersectional narrative, Brown acknowledges, may "not [make] good sound bites or simple slogans, for it would [be] far more complicated"; but this complication will allow for "a fuller confrontation" of the issue of sexual violence (Brown 280-281). Consider how useful it would have been, for example, to insert the black history of the label "slut" into SlutWalk's mandate.[4]

Black feminists caution, however, that a larger dialogue and greater inclusion must occur within the movement overall. While the 2012 Toronto-based SlutWalk indeed aimed to include speakers and stories from diverse populations of women (i.e., Kim Crosby and Crystal Mein, both women of colour), the fact that SlutWalk "organizers never reached out to women of color as equals to begin with" has fundamentally shaped the mandate of the movement (Bogado 3). This remains evident in SlutWalk's definition of slut, for example, and its manifestation as predominantly a protest march.[5] Increased and more meaningful relationships with diverse women, as well as a commitment to work collaboratively to build consensus on direction and actions, will improve SlutWalk's authenticity. As Black Women's Blueprint shares in its online letter to SlutWalk, collaboration with women of colour is not simply a measure of courtesy, but one of concrete strategy in the anti-rape movement.

This author agrees. Collaborative and coalition work between marginalized populations and privileged allies can build relationships. But only a genuine attempt to hear and understand racialized women's day-to-day experiences will challenge "the idea of a unitary or universal 'women's experience'" (Cossins 78).

CONCLUSION

Much successful feminist work—protest, lobbying, and consciousness-raising, for example—is comprised of acts and theories of gender solidarity. Yet a crucial consideration in feminist practice is also to resist the temptation to "land" on common bottom-lines or "linear order and symmetry" in our collaborative work and herstories (Brown 281). The quest for symmetry and order sets us up to compare women's narratives for evidence of similarity; to marginalize or invisibilize some at the expense of others; or worse, to prioritize them against one another.

Feminist practice finds strength in processes that support those working together to understand one another, to identify inequities, and to problem-solve inequities together. Elsa Barkley Brown's *What Has Happened Here* affirms that a *process*—that is, the ways in which we conduct our business and work together—while messy and elongated, is often more valuable than a concrete outcome.

Brown shares the story of author Luisah Teish, who travelled home to visit her Creole family in New Orleans, and found meaning in a social process built on difference and disarray:

> They [Teish's family] begin to talk gumbo ya ya, and it goes on for 12 days.... Gumbo ya ya is a creole term that means "Everybody talks at once."...It is through gumbo ya ya that Teish learns everything that has happened in her family and community, and she conveys the essential information about herself to the group.... They do this simultaneously because, in fact, their histories are joined—occurring simultaneously, in connection in dialogue with each other. To relate their tales separately would be to obliterate the connection. (Brown 274)

Similarly, within the SlutWalk movement, a useful process will engage different women to relay diverging experiences of sexual violence and victim-blaming. It recognizes that the narratives of black women occurred as the narratives of white women were also occurring. That is, our herstories are joined—occurring simultaneously—and they continue to inform one another.

Last, women of privilege do well to remember that we do not lose anything by telling our stories simultaneously with other women. Instead of "doing something about [sexual violence]" by "COMING TOGETHER" (SlutWalk Toronto), SlutWalk will gain strength by "doing something" about "COMING TOGETHER" first.

The author recognizes S. Batacharya, J. Benn-John and R.R. for their considerable influence in this work.

ENDNOTES

[1]Ricki Solinger's *Wake Up Little Susie: Single Pregnancy and Race before Roe v. Wade* outlines how young black single women in the post-war years were more likely to keep babies born outside of marriage than were young white women, who were pressured to relinquish their children for adoption in order to maintain the image of their constructed "whiteness." In this, black single mothers were also more likely to be forced to rely on social welfare programs than other populations.

[2]Italics are this author's addition.

[3]Sexual assault myths continue to be ever-present and used against victims within the Canadian criminal justice system. Offenders and defense attorneys commonly take up the alibi that a sexual encounter was consensual; or depict the "victim as delusional, vengeful, exploitive, or an attention-seeker," often relying on sexist constructs of good/bad femininity (hinged on white/racialized femininity) to do so (The Learning Network).

[4]Similar approaches have been effectively used by other activist movements to illuminate the pain and history behind offensive terms used to label marginalized populations. See: GLAAD Media Reference Guide, the Special Olympics' R-Word: Spread the Word to End the Word, and Western North Carolina Citizens For An End To Institutional Bigotry's informational page SQUAW – Facts on the Eradication of the "S" Word.

[5]Activism through marches and physical protest are less accessible to socially marginalized groups such as the working poor (who cannot afford to jeopardize their employment by attending a protest, either through missed attendance or discipline), racialized persons, and members of the LGBT/queer community (who are more vulnerable to public acts of violence or arrest). With this in mind, protest and/or resistance can take many forms, such as lobbying, community-based gatherings, boycotts, etc. Coates and Wade's work on survivor resistance to sexual violence notes that all forms of resistance, individual and systemic, ought to be recognized as relevant: "resistance [to violence] is ubiquitous: whenever individuals are badly treated, they resist" (Coates and Wade 502).

WORKS CITED

Black Women's Blueprint. "An Open Letter from Black Women to the SlutWalk." *Black Women's Blueprint*. September 23, 2011. Web. October 2, 2014.

Bonisteel, M. and Linda Green. "Implications of the Shrinking Space for Feminist Anti-violence Advocacy." Presentation to *Forging Social Futures*. Canadian Social Welfare Policy Conference. Fredericton, Canada. 2005. Web. March 9, 2015.

Bordo, S. *Unbearable Weight: Feminism, Western Culture and the Body*. Berkeley: University of California Press, 1993. Print.

Brown, Elsa Barkley. "What Has Happened Here: The Politics of Difference in Women's History and Feminist Politics." *The Second Wave*. Ed. Linda Nicholson. New York: Routledge, 1997. 271-287. Print.

Coates, L. and Allan Wade. "Telling it Like it Isn't: Obscuring Perpetrator Responsibility for Violent Crime." *Discourse & Society* 15.5 (2004): 499-526. Print.

Cole, Elizabeth R. and Alyssa N. Zucker. "Black and White Women's Perspectives on Femininity." *Cultural Diversity and Ethnic Minority Psychology* 13 (2007): 1-9. Print.

Cossins, Anne. "Saints, Sluts and Sexual Assault: Rethinking the Relationship Between Sex, Race and Gender." *Social and Legal Studies* 12.1 (2003): 77-103. Print.

Donovan, Roxanne A. "To Blame or Not to Blame: Influences of Target Race and Observer Sex on Rape Blame Attribution." *Journal of Interpersonal Violence* 22.6 (2007): 722-736. Print.

GLAAD Media Reference Guide. Terms To Avoid. n.d. Web. March 9, 2015.

Hillman, Philipia Lauren L. *Negotiating the Dominant Script: Middle-Class Black Girls Tell Their Story*. Diss. Faculty of Arts & Sciences, American University. 1999. Print.

The Learning Network. *Overcoming Barriers and Enhancing Supportive Responses: The Research on Sexual Violence Against Women A Resource Document*. May 2012: 17. Web. March 9, 2015.

Native Women's Association of Canada (NWAC). "Sisters in Spirit." *Native Women's Association of Canada*. n.d. Web. Oct. 2, 2014.

Pfeifer, Jeffrey E J. E. and James R. P. Ogloff. "Mock Juror Ratings of Guilt in Canada: Modern Racism and Ethnic Heritage." *Social Behavior and Personality* 31.3 (2003): 301-312. Print.

Pilkington, Ed. "SlutWalking Gets Rolling After Cop's Loose Talk about Provocative Clothing." *The Guardian* May 6, 2011. Web. January 17, 2014.

Ringrose, Jessica. "A New Universal Mean Girl: Examining the Discursive Construction and Social Regulation of a New Feminine Pathology." *Feminism and Psychology* 16.4 (November 2006): 405-424. Print.

Safe Schools Action Team. *Shaping a Culture of Respect in Our Schools: Promoting Safe and Healthy Relationships.* Safe Schools Action Team Report on Gender-based Violence, Homophobia, Sexual Harassment & Inappropriate Sexual Behavior in Schools. 2008. Web. March 9, 2015.

SlutWalk Toronto. "SlutWalk Toronto: FAQs." *SlutWalk Toronto.* n.d. Web. October 2, 2014.

Solinger, R. *Wake Up Little Susie: Single Pregnancy and Race before Roe v. Wade.* New York: Routledge, 2000. Print.

Solinger, R. *Pregnancy and Power: A Short History of Reproductive Politics in America.* New York: New York University Press, 2005. Print.

Special Olympics. "R-Word: Spread the Word to End the Word." n.d. Web. March 9, 2015.

Sullivan, Shannon. *Revealing Whiteness: The Unconscious Habits of Racial Privilege.* Bloomington: Indiana University Press. 2006. Print.

Western North Carolina Citizens For An End To Institutional Bigotry. SQUAW – Facts on the Eradication of the "S" Word. n.d. Web. March 9, 2015.

World Health Organization (WHO). "Understanding and Addressing Violence against Women." *World Health Organization.* N.d. Web. October 2, 2014.

Three Times a Lady

Images from SlutWalk Hong Kong (2011-2013)

DANIEL GARRETT

Activists articulate visual messages, their activities are represented in photos and video sequences, and they are ultimately rendered visible, or invisible, in the public sphere. (Doerr, Mattoni and Teune xi)

Visual representations play a crucial role in struggles over discursive power, the power to set agendas, and the power to define credibility. (Luhtakallio 28)

The image is at the heart of political struggle, which has become an endless process of images battling, reversing, erasing and replacing other images. (Khatib 1)

THIS SHORT ESSAY PROPOSES that studies of SlutWalk stand to benefit significantly from incorporation of visual methods and analyses as empirical-based strategies to better understand the movement *as actually manifested* in its multitudes of indigenous settings around the world. One such site, the Hong Kong Special Administrative Region (HKSAR) of the People's Republic of China, is discussed briefly in this chapter in the context of a visual essay covering three years of SlutWalk Hong Kong (SWHK). I begin with a general introduction to the intensely contested visual domain surrounding SlutWalk's image. I follow with a pithy discussion of how powerful images and visual frames challenging hegemonic norms such as rape cultures can potentially provoke social change. Next, I provide an account of the criticality of visual representations for social movements in their struggle for visibility. I then offer remarks on recent scholarly work that recognizes the importance of visual analysis of social movements before I delve into the background of SWHK. Lastly, I present visual arguments, expression, and visuality of SWHK in a series of representative photographs of processions and rallies from 2011 to 2013, all taken by the author, a SWHK supporter.

BACKGROUND

If the *image* of SlutWalk, the global anti-sexual violence movement confronting misogynistic attitudes, rape cultures, and patriarchal structures legitimizing the blaming and shaming of rape survivors on the basis of victims' appearance, behavior, or dress, had a Facebook relationship status it undoubtedly would be: "It's complicated." After thousands of SlutWalks situated across six continents and in over a hundred cities since 2011, there is little surprise that the nascent transnational movement has manifested in a diversity of incarnations, local adaptations, and images (Garrett and Ng; Carr). Yet, despite a multiplicity of embodiments SlutWalk Toronto's global progeny have remained generally faithful to its core social justice demands of no sexual violence, no victim-blaming, and no victim-shaming. This has held true even as local SlutWalks sometimes adapted the movement's more contentious identity, performances, and repertoires (Tilly and Tarrow; Tilly) to better negotiate local norms and to subvert oppressive power. And though frequently swaddled in Western criticisms regarding its transgressive identity, movement composition, and tactical repertoires, SlutWalk's essential image of spectacular defiance towards rape cultures and performative challenging of rape myths has, nonetheless, resonated with many people and in many places across the world.

That the visual narrative and stories surrounding Slutwalk have evoked a tidal wave of images, claims, representations, and imaginations about the movement, its actors, and repertoires is indisputable—and an understatement. Many of these verbal and visual images, good and bad, accurate and exaggerated, measured and distorted have sensationally and alternatively been used to variously construct SlutWalk as a Heroine or Villainess—when it is neither. This is partly because of the polysemic nature of images, but also because, as Edelman informs us, images are the "currency in which we think about and mutually negotiate changes in the world we inhabit" (12). In other instances, images may activate various preexisting assumptions that people hold and that have been socialized in to them through complexes of patriarchy and rape cultures or other systems of dominance. And though images may be variously construed, contested, and read, they still remain a "major influence on social change" because they fill in the details on significant events and processes that we rarely experience firsthand: "What happens instead is that one's ideas about occurrences are shaped by memorable pictures, placed there by journalistic accounts, everyday conversations, political oratory, or other sources of alleged information who devise striking images to win and hold audiences" (Edelman 11).

POWERFUL IMAGES AND VISUAL FRAMES

In this context, novel images, especially deployed as "image events" containing "mind bombs"[1] (Delicath and DeLuca)—arguably like those initially created with the launch of SlutWalk—have the potential agency to "upset the established order and can be revolutionary" because they can "disturb long-held beliefs and expectations" of the viewer (Edelman 13). Indeed, SlutWalk essentially confronts images of "ideal victims" (Christie) and sexual predators and reframes them in reality *as lived*—not as imagined in ivory towers, newsrooms, police stations, prosecutors' offices, or judges' chambers. In the case of global SlutWalk, as part of the "struggle to be seen" (Guidry), its core verbal and visual rhetoric has sought to smash everyday taken-for-granted media, societal, and individual frames (Entman). These are mental structures and images that enable secondary victimization of survivors and *redirects* society's *focus* and outrage *from* the rapist *to* the raped.[2] This image stands in marked contrast to the often sensationalist critique that SlutWalk simply "… struts around in their underwear as means of embracing of their femininity" (jbeyer) or that Slutwalks have "hundreds of women dressed in their underwear" marching through the city ("Slutwalkers").

Indeed, as most participants or first-hand observers of many SlutWalks around the world would likely attest, one typically sees more skin or provocative behaviour or outfits at the beach, a public swimming pool, a nightclub, or on television than they normally would at a SlutWalk. And while *some* SlutWalkers do dress sexually or suggestively (in various gendered capacities), wear costumes (ironic, humourous, satirical, or sexy), or embody or brandish provocative placards, this is not the preponderance of the movement. Exploratory media analysis of global SlutWalks between January 2011 and May 2012 conducted by Garrett and Ng, as well as three years of direct observations of SWHK by the author, suggests that various forms of everyday casual attire are far more the norm than lingerie, partial-nudity, or spangles and G-strings. And though not the focus of this essay, it may likely be the case that local (and popular) culture plays more of a role in generating such contentious expressions than any alleged ideology or project ascribed to SlutWalk.

THE STRUGGLE TO BE SEEN

Rather, as suggested above and in the epigraphs, visual representations of social movement organizations are powerful modes of visual discourse, politics, and struggle, intimately intertwined in on-going wars to be seen, recognized, and understood in today's image-saturated hegemonic mediascapes (Khatib; Luhtakallio). This struggle over visuality significantly affects how the public and other actors perceive movements, as explained by Luhtakallio: "Visual representations play a crucial role in struggles over discursive power, the power to set agendas, and the power to define credibility. What we think of as a collective struggle far away, or in the neighboring city district, is increasingly dependent on the images we have seen on TV, in newspaper reports, and the internet" (28).

Khatib also elucidates how images permeate a movement as contentious political discourse: "The visual manifests itself in several forms in processes of political struggle: as a mass media image; a digital image; a cartoon; a piece of art; a physical space or object; an emphemeral image on paper, a wall or another physical medium; and as a human embodiment. It can also be a conceptual image, a visual idea" (1). In turn, these "visual expressions" aid observers in making sense of the movement, its actors, and aims. In other words, visual utterances provide "important points of reference" in external observers' construction of "a picture of a social movement" as percived through their own lenses (Doerr, Mattoni and Teune xiii). Put another way, images and visual representations of social movements and their actors are competitors in the arena of symbolic contests where "competing sponsors of meaning" construct political significance for the broader public about the movement and their claims (Gamson and Stuart 55).

THE VISUALITY OF SOCIAL MOVEMENTS

As such, social and political science scholars are now increasingly attending to images associated with, about, and created by movements and the counter-visuality (Mirzoeff) potentials they posit in the public and visual spheres (Doerr, Mattoni and Teune; Nathansohn and Zuev). However, Doerr, Mattoni and Teune rightly lament that to date only scant attention to the visual has been made by most. More specifically, they detail that "systematic analyses of the visual or an integration of visual analyses within broader frameworks is still rare" and imply that "textual" tyranny reigns still (xi-xii). To better address these lacunae, Doerr, Mattoni and Teune convincingly lobby for increased focus in three areas related to social movements: visual expressions; differential representations across media; and their visibility or lack of visibility in the societies they inhabit (xii-xvi). The following visual essay briefly touches on elements of these recommendations but especially on the visual expression of SlutWalk through the case of SWHK.[3]

SLUTWALK HONG KONG

As suggested above, the HKSAR was one of many global outposts that picked up the SlutWalk fight. After hosting a maiden SWHK procession in 2011, three subsequent SlutWaks (2012, 2013, and 2014) were held with the fourth taking place in the midst of the Umbrella Revolution in the Hong Kong SAR following the completion of this essay. In addition, SWHK's visibility was not limited to only annual hallmark marches. Instead, as with many other SlutWalk organizations sprinkled throughout the world, more quotidian efforts aiding victims and fighting against local manifestations of "rape culture" were pursued. Typically, this consisted of public speaking engagements and participation in educational workshops with Hong Kong's larger, established, and more traditional sexual violence support groups and networks. Solidarity actions with other social justice organizations and aid societies concerned with preventing sexual violence, discrimination, and violence against women, Hong Kong's foreign domestic workers (mostly female) and transgendered people were also engaged.

Subsidiary SWHK activism occurred in street actions like Hong Kong Pride, local International Women's Day rallies, and more recently, One Billion Rising, where SWHK members encouraged the public to combat rape myths and stereotypes and confront victim-blaming and shaming. Well-known Hong Kong radical legislator "Long Hair" Leung Kwok-hung, from the League of Social Democrats, has also spoken a number of times the SWHK rallies and other local political pressure groups, such as Social-ist Action, and aided in promoting SlutWalk's core messages in their outreach to Hong Kong's migrant, refugee, and workers' communities. Complementing all of these actions were the usual assortment of traditional social movement organization protest paraphernalia such as banners, effigies, flyers, pins, and placards as well as embodied performance art that performatively and visually declared SlutWalk's demands and stance against rape cultures and myths (e.g., body painting, T-shirts, etc.).

VISUAL ESSAY

The data presented in this visual essay represents a small, purposeful sample from a larger corpus of photographic images of SWHK's annual processions and rallies between 2011 and 2013. They were taken by the author, a SWHK supporter, for personal photography and documentary interests. Image selection, by the author, was based on perceived representativeness of each march. Contextually, SWHK marches were held during the weekend afternoons on Hong Kong Island when maximum visibility of the procession could be assured. Three staging points in Causeway Bay, a major shopping and entertainment district on Hong Kong island with high-levels of pedestrian traffic, were utilized, namely the Patterson Street (2011), East Point Road (2012), and Times Square (2013) pedestrian areas. The protest route followed a main east-west thoroughfare to either Southorn Playground (2011 and 2013) or Charter Gardens (2012). Restaurants, shops, and major shopping complexes line the entire route thereby providing exceptional supplemental visibility of the marchers and their vocal (chants and slogans) and visual (banners, embodied visual messages, placards, etc.) displays. The staging and destination areas and protest route are traditional protest arteries in Hong Kong (Garrett).

IMAGES OF SLUTWALK HONG KONG (2011 TO 2013)

Figure 1 (p. 98). A SWHK supporter in the audience holds a mobilization placard emphasizing SlutWalk core messages, 2011.
Figures 2. & 3. Supporters marching though the city during the maiden SWHK in 2011.

Figures 4. & 5. SWHK 2012 was strongly supported by local rape prevention/crisis center groups and other justice organizations. Supporters decked out in Power Ranger costumes (to illustrate that anyone can be raped regardless of their apparel) pose with SWHK 2012 speaker League of Social Democrats legislator, Leung Kwok-hung, aka "Long Hair."

Figures 6. to 9. Various supporters of SWHK 2012. Despite a steady downpour shadowing most of the 3.5-kilometer march, turn-out by supporters and the public was good.
Translation, bottom left: "Don't teach me how to dress, teach people not to rape."

Figures 10. & 11. SWHK 2013 performance demonstrating the rape myths used to bind, silence, and subjugate victims of sexual violence. SlutWalkers and by-standers inscribed the various myths on the sheets that were used to tie-up the performers. Top, SlutWalkers bound by rape myths begin the nearly two-kilometer-long march. Bottom, they arrive at the rally point where, in front of the crowd, they dramatically and defiantly rip off their rape culture and myth chains. Translation of four front placards, Fig.10 (left to right): "Sex workers are regular people, if we are not willing then it is rape. Taking off condoms = rape"; "Don't teach me how to dress, teach rapist not to rape"; "Drinking: my drinking does not mean that you can violate me"; "Head-to-toe: being covered head-to-toe, does that guarantee no one will rape you?"

Figures 12. & 13. Top: SWHK 2013 supporters and placards. Bottom: SWHK 2012 placard. While many placards and flyers used in the various SWHKs were in English, many more were in Chinese and English or simply in Chinese. Other languages, such as Tagalog or Indonesian, which are used by hundreds of thousands of female Filipino and Indonesian foreign domestic workers in living Hong Kong were also represented. Translation of placard in Fig. 12: "My going to your place does not mean I consent to being violated by you."

ENDNOTES

[1] According to Delicath and DeLuca, image events are "staged protests designed for media dissemination" which are deployed as "a form of postmodern argumentative practice, a kind of oppositional argument that creates social controversy, and animates and widens possibilities for debate" (315). DeLuca also cites Hunter (22) in explicating that a "mind bomb" is "an image event that explodes 'in the public's consciousness to transform the way people view their world.'" (1)

[2] Following Entman, framing is the selection of "some aspects of a perceived reality [to] make them more salient in a communicating text, in such a way to promote a particular problem definition, causal interpretation, moral evaluation, and/or treatment recommendation" (52). Frames used by the media to construct a story are media frames; individual frames are those held by people used to make sense of the world.

[3] While not discussed more extensively due to space limitations, Nathansohn and Zuev lobby handedly for attention to "the visual sphere—where images are produced, circulated, interpreted, reproduced, and re-imagined" arguing that the visual is essential to better understandign the social world we inhabit (2). Saliently, they go on to note that this symbolic space also has the power to subvert social order and warn that the role of the visual at the nexus of "human agency and institutional constraints" is that juncture of paramount analytic importance (2). The implications for SlutWalk research are apparent for reasons stated elsewhere in this essay.

WORKS CITED

Carr, Joetta L. "The Slutwalk Movement: A Study in Transnational Feminist Activism." *Journal of Feminist Scholarship* 4 (2013): 24-38. Print.

Christie, Nils. "The Ideal Victim." *From Crime Policy to Victim Policy.* Ed. Fattah, E. Basingstoke: Macmillan, 1986. Print.

Delicath, John W. and Kevin Michael DeLuca. "Image Events,

the Public Sphere, and Argumentative Practice: The Case of Radical Environmental Groups." *Argumentation* 17 (2003): 315-33. Print.

DeLuca, Kevin Michael. *Image Politics: The New Rhetoric of Environmental Activism. Revisioning Rhetoric.* New York: Guilford Press, 1999. Print.

Doerr, Nicole, Alice Mattoni and Simon Teune. "Toward a Visual Analysis of Social Movements, Conflict, and Political Mobilization: Introduction." *Advances in the Visual Analysis of Social Movements.* Ed. Nicole Doerr, Alice Mattoni and Simon Teune. 1st ed. Vol. 35. Research in Social Movements, Conflicts and Change. Bingly, UK: Emerald Group, 2013. xi-xxvi. Print.

Edelman, Murray J. *The Politics of Misinformation. Communication, Society, and Politics.* New York: Cambridge University Press, 2001. Print.

Entman, Robert M. "Framing: Towards Clarification of a Fractured Paradigm." *Journal of Communication* 43.4 (1993): 51-58. Print.

Gamson, W. A. and D. Stuart. "Media Discourse as a Symbolic Contest: The Bomb in Political Cartoons." *Sociological Forum* 7.1 (1992): 55-86. Print.

Garrett, Daniel. *Counter-Hegemonic Resistance in China's Hong Kong: Visualizing Protest in the City.* Singapore: Springer, 2015. Print.

Garrett, Daniel, and Angie Ng. "Visualizing Slutwalk: Participants, the Public, and the Media." *ISA Forum of Sociology.* 2012. Print.

Guidry, John A. "The Struggle to Be Seen: Social Movements and the Public Sphere in Brazil." *International Journal of Politics, Culture and Society* 16.4 (2003): 493-524. Print.

Hunter, Robert. *The Storming of the Mind.* Garden City, NY: Doubleday, 1971. Print.

jbeyer. "Smoke and Mirrors." Looking at Slutwalk. 2012. Web. February 1 2014.

Khatib, Lina. *Image Politics in the Middle East: The Role of the Visual in Political Struggle.* London: I.B. Tauris & Co, 2013. Print.

Luhtakallio, Eeva. "Bodies Keying Politics: A Visual Frame Analysis of Gendered Local Activism in France and Finland." *Advances in the Visual Analysis of Social Movements.* Ed. Nicole Doerr, Alice Mattoni and Simon Teune. 1st ed. Vol. 35. Research in

Social Movements, Conflicts and Change. Bingly, UK: Emerald Group, 2013. Print.

Mirzoeff, Nicholas. *The Right to Look : A Counterhistory of Visuality*. Durham, NC: Duke University Press, 2011. Print.

Nathansohn, Regev and Dennis Zuev. "Sociology of the Visual Sphere: Introduction." *Sociology of the Visual Sphere*. Ed. Regev Nathansohn and Simon Teune. New York: Routledge, 2013. 1-9. Print.

"'Slutwalkers' Step up Demand for Justice of Rape Victims in London." *Sky News*. September 23 2012. Web. March 15 2015.

Tilly, Charles. *Contentious Performances*. Cambridge Studies in Contentious Politics. Cambridge: Cambridge University Press, 2008. Print.

Tilly, Charles and Sidney G. Tarrow. *Contentious Politics*. Boulder, CO: Paradigm Publishers, 2007. Print.

SlutWalk Hong Kong

"Western" Instead of "White Privilege"

ANGIE NG

S LUTWALK HONG KONG (SWHK) first took place on December 4, 2011, as the local manifestation of the international SlutWalk spirit within this Special Administrative Region of China. Being a former British colony, Hong Kong is definitely post-colonial; at the same time, it is considered by the United Nations Development Programme as a territory with very high human development (UNDP). Amid accusations of "white privilege" against the international movement, this piece explores the existence and experiences of a SlutWalk held in an Asian context and, to my knowledge, the only SlutWalk officially held within China. This chapter explores SlutWalk Hong Kong and my involvement as an organizer and participant.

Around the world, the fight against rape culture has met with resistance and criticisms about trying to change things that are "part of our culture." Cries of "Western culture" in the face of SlutWalk Hong Kong are far from a peripheral issue. These concerns serve as one of the main weapons used to discredit the movement in the territory and have given rise to other obstacles. Without denying that there are indeed cultural differences among peoples around the world, we must acknowledge that culture is not a static phenomenon; China, similar to other parts of the world, has seen times of stronger patriarchy and times of greater women's empowerment. We must also recognize that sexual assault and victim-blaming exist in different global contexts, and even "Western countries" continue to have varying levels of patriarchy and rape culture. There is a unified need to raise awareness concerning this problem, and generate or perpetuate discussion on the issue.

SWHK was initiated in the summer of 2011, with the first march taking place on December 4, 2011. As an organizer of SlutWalk Hong Kong, I felt that it was necessary to raise awareness around the issues of sexual violence and rape myths due to the high level of victim-blaming. I have gone on record as having experienced sexual violence myself in the territory and have been blamed for the assault.

SWHK has held various activities other than the main marches in 2011, 2012, and 2013, and plans to continue doing so. These include organising or participating in workshops with other feminist organisations, and holding discussion meetings and social events. Its members have also attended various other events concerning equality, including the Hong Kong Pride Parade and Occupy Hong Kong/Central.

In order to understand feminist organizing in Hong Kong, we must understand Hong Kong's historical background.

COLONIAL CONTEXT

In 1841, after China lost the Opium War, Hong Kong became a British colony, allowing opium trafficking activities to be transferred there from the mainland (*The Guardian* qtd in Naylor). After the Second Opium War, along with being forced to grant free trade to foreign powers, China also had to hand over control of foreign residential areas in major cities and lease what is now known as the New Territories of Hong Kong to Great Britain (Jaschok and Miers). Under colonialism, Hong Kong was allowed to preserve not only the customs but also the laws of China (Sinn). There was a symbiotic relationship between the British colonials and the local elite, in which the Chinese elite were officially protected by the colonials, while the colonialists were able to make use of Chinese trading networks throughout Asia and also receive the cooperation of these elites in managing the local community (Hui). The local bourgeoisie were able to maintain the status quo, as evidenced by the colonial government's resistance to the British government's protest against the domestic slavery of poorer girls in wealthier households; this system did not end until the 1970s (Carroll). In

1997, Hong Kong returned to China as a Special Administrative Region and was promised the ability to keep its own laws for the next five decades.

CULTURE

Despite Hong Kong's glossy exterior as a major international financial centre, it maintains highly traditional, Confucian ideas. As Confucianism places more importance on families, clan, and other groups over individuals themselves, there is a high priority placed on maintaining "social harmony," leading to an intolerance of any behaviour considered against the mainstream (Vagg). Rather than being an anomaly, this is just an example of a "tight" or homogeneous culture (Watters) in which individuals are interconnected rather than independent, although it may seem strange to those from Western, Educated, Industrialised, Rich, and Democratic (WEIRD) backgrounds (Henrich, Heine and Norenzayan).

In accordance, Confucianism also places a large emphasis on the opinions of others (Wong and Tsai); a person is said to lose face when they have been successfully shamed, and that results in a lowering or loss of social prestige (Vagg). Family members will also experience this loss of face when one of their members is considered a deviant (Wong and Tsai), and secrecy is expected to protect the entire family, including its ancestors (Tsun). There is an old saying, *jiachou buchuwaichuan* (family shame should not be transmitted outside).

Along with the colonialists came both Protestant and Catholic missionaries. Although Christianity is not widespread among the general population, its influence should not be underestimated as Christians both started and continue to be influential within the school system (Chan) and run many schools (Liu). Prior to this, Hong Kong only had about a dozen village schools, as wealthier families sent their children to China to receive a traditional Chinese education (Boyle). The importance of Christianity can be seen by the fact that, after the centralization of the school system in 1862, Scripture was one of the three main subjects, with the others being Chinese Classics and English (Boyle). Both Confucian and Christian systems of belief provide their own "reasons" to suggest why people who are perceived as sexual "deviants" are at fault (Chan 77).

GENDER

The combination of traditional Confucianism—in which the three submissions demand that women obey their fathers before getting marriage, their husbands after marriage, and their oldest sons after widowhood (Gao et al.; La)—and colonial Christianity resulted in a very high level of patriarchy, including sexual conservatism, in Hong Kong (Chang). In brief, Confucianism demands that one serve one's patriline by having male children, and this is the purpose of marriage and sexuality (Brownell and Wasserstrom). To be considered a morally virtuous woman, one is required to remain a virgin and have an intact hymen at the time of marriage (La). Confucianism also demands that women be faithful to husbands, even in widowhood (Gao et al.).

In Hong Kong and other Chinese societies, the topic of violence against women itself is considered taboo (Tiwari). Various institutions are seen to be sources of retraumatisation of victims, including but not limited to the police, the school system, the courts, and the Equal Opportunities Commission (Hung). In May 2013, Hong Kong's Secretary for Security, Lai Tung-Kwok, commented that he would ask "young ladies" not to "drink too much" to avoid being raped (Ip). Similar to other places around the world, women in Hong Kong typically internalise this blame (Tiwari). This context of colonialism, culture, and strict gender roles provided the backdrop to SlutWalk Hong Kong.

DISCUSSION

This study is based mainly on ethnographic observations carried out during the initiation and organisation of, and participation in, Hong Kong's local manifestation of the SlutWalk spirit in both 2011 and 2012. It is also supplemented by a qualitative, thematic analysis of the media coverage received in 2011.[1]

This paper discusses the reception by both local people and the media who used local constructions of "sluts" and "Westerners," some of which resulted from the former colonial environment. It then explores both particular obstacles faced, such as the inability of some to link the fight for sexual autonomy with the fight against sexual violence and societal pressure, and ends with some positive achievements. I begin with a discussion of how participants of SWHK, or feminists "sluts," were perceived by the local media and regular people. Participants were framed as Western-educated or inauthentic, or were seen as white outsiders. The point was that participants and the issues were "othered."

THE MEDIA

In 2011, the local media focused mainly on sensationalising SlutWalk and disparaging the movement. In terms of sensationalising, just as in other locations, stories focused on what protestors were or were not wearing. However, the spotlight seemed to be on me, as an organizer, and my previous experience of being sexual assaulted in Hong Kong, which was perhaps interesting to readers looking for tabloid gossip rather than real news.

Beyond sensationalizing, the "othering" of the protestors was also prominent. Media seemed to suggest that protestors were more privileged, as suggested in the headline "Sex Message for the Urbane" ("Sex Message"). While "white privilege" could not be used convincingly in this Asian context, the title suggests that protestors were limited to upscale urban-dwellers. Beyond this perception, the movement was largely stereotyped and constructed by the media as inherently "Western" in nature, with little local relevance (Garrett and Ng). This is regularly the case with certain ideas, people, or movements that go against the status quo, such as Occupy Hong Kong/Central, but not others, such as brand names from Europe. Organizers and participants were further distanced from the general public by being portrayed by the local media as what locals would imagine as "sluts." These two factors combined in the construction of my experience as an ethnic Chinese educated overseas who liked to go drinking in one of the territory's main bar areas, Lan Kwai Fong, and ended up being raped there. In the local context, being educated overseas to the university level is already seen as a sign of privilege. Also supporting the media's framing of Slutwalk as "Western" and for "sluts" was the focus on Max, the white foreign exchange student who showed up as his drag queen alter ego, Maxine, in a Santa's Helper outfit.

Given that Max was a volunteer with SlutWalk Hong Kong as well as a participant, the coverage was not completely unexpected. More surprising were the photographs and coverage focused one particular protester from Mainland China, a woman who was working in Hong Kong. Drawing on Hong Kong stereotypes of women from Mainland China as sexual "vixens" or "sluts" who seduce the men in Hong Kong and are out-competing the local women in the dating/marriage market, the focus on this participant was used to further alienate the public from the movement. Through media use of local constructions of "sluts," including Mainland Chinese women, participants were also "othered," making it difficult for the general public to relate to them.

While SWHK's volunteers, supporters, and allies understood the movement as uniquely home grown, from the outside the movement has mainly been viewed with suspicion as a "Western" phenomenon. As one Internet comment illustrated, the movement is accused of copying the West or *chaoxifang*. Understandably, there continues to be a post-colonial rejection of anything labelled Western. However, as mentioned above, this dismissal is thoroughly piecemeal and seems to be used selectively as a weapon against particular people or movements who threaten the current state of social inequality in the territory, echoing similar cries of lack of "patriotism."

This suspicion was also manifested in the "othering" of non-Asian and/or Westernized people, reflecting the Confucian disdain for anything different from the mainstream and also negative feelings left over from colonialism. More than one person with whom I spoke suggested that the march take place in Lan Kwai Fong, which is where many tourists and expatriates like to go for drinks. One reason was that we would find more participants there, since the girls who frequented the bars and clubs in the area were more Westernized and (therefore) would be more willing to identify with the term "slut." Another person suggested that the protest be aimed at Western men, since they, not Chinese men, are perpetrators of rape.

The suspicious construction of Westerners has roots in colonial times, during which the selling of sex was considered part of the maintenance of soldiers and other colonialists (Truong). Despite the end of colonial rule, in post-colonial Hong Kong there continues to be a large expatriate, male labour force working for global corporations and banks, for example, and making large incomes amidst a backdrop of extremely high income inequality. The minimum wage has only recently been increased from 28 to 30 Hong Kong dollars per hour, which is roughly four Canadian dollars per hour. This creates a large power imbalance between locals and expatriates, which plays a part in sexual politics and also creates room for tension and alienation between groups.

OBSTACLES AND ACHIEVEMENTS

SWHK encountered various obstacles, some of which were connected to certain perceptions of Westerners. However, it also experienced certain achievements, which partially dispelled any preconceived notions of what a feminist "slut" should look like.

One of the obstacles faced, and that SWHK continues to face, is the inability (for people in Hong Kong and beyond) to link battles against sexual assault with the battle for sexual autonomy. SlutWalk's name and one of its messages communicate that there is nothing wrong with a person choosing their own expression of sexuality or asexuality. SlutWalks assert that sexual autonomy does not cause victimization and should not be used as an excuse to blame victims. However, due to the high level of sexual conservatism in Hong Kong as a result of both traditional Confucianism and conservative Christian schooling, even many of the volunteers fighting against sexual violence are too embarrassed to talk about sexuality in general and do not see the broader link between sexual violence and sexual control of women and heteronormativity. Undoubtedly, in such a context, the fear of being seen as a "whore" rather than a "virgin" limits the number of those who are willing to attend an event with a title which includes the word "slut"; however, without accepting that it is okay for people to be sexual or asexual in their own way, it continues to be easy to blame people who experience sexual violence for their victimization.

Another difficulty is that the focus on family and community over individuality, as well as deep concerns for what others think over what one thinks, makes the idea of victims' having the right to speak publicly about their victimization quite difficult to grasp. Even if a victim does not care what people think about her, it is problematic for her to speak out due to fear of family pressure against "airing out dirty laundry in public" and family embarrassment. To illustrate this point: As an organizer, I publicly shared part of my story of being sexually assaulted, and this was run in the media; to this day, all the relatives who have mentioned SWHK, save for one, have felt too embarrassed to mention my sexual assault, and none have attended any SWHK activities. These factors, along with the smearing of social activists in the territory and ingrained disdain for anything which disrupts "social harmony," severely limited the number of supporters. In a city of over seven million people, the Facebook page for SWHK has less than 600 "likes," and less than half that number turned out for the marches (though according to other people involved in social movements, these numbers are considered high for Hong Kong).

THE GLOBAL PRESENCE OF SLUT-SHAMING

The aim here is neither to increase the number of protestors nor to resist the centrality of family and community in Hong Kong; it is to raise awareness and start conversations to slowly change local culture so that it is no longer politically correct to blame victims of sexual assault. Such a shift would provide a nurturing environment in which victims could expect to receive support from their families and communities instead of blame and embarrassment. Such an assertion leads to questions about how we can change the situation when it is, as some supporters put it, "part of our culture." Due to mainstream media constructions of Westerners, few local people in Hong Kong understand how different areas in Western countries also have varying levels of patriarchy and sexual conservatism. They are also not aware that culture is a dynamic phenomenon and, similar to other cultures around the world, Chinese culture has changed many times in history. "Chinese culture" can be liberalised and does not necessarily have to accept patriarchal ideas of Confucian orthodoxy.

The question of the "otherness" of Westerners is evidenced by the fact that even a SWHK supporter questioned whether "Western feminism" could provide solutions. Although this chapter is not about the debate between "Western" feminism and other types of feminism, I believe that the feminist goal of SlutWalk transcends differences between types of feminism and geographical locations, as sexual assault and victim-blaming are not limited to specific cultures or areas. SlutWalk does not ask that all participants become sexually liberal and self identify as "sluts"; rather, it requests that people not judge each other and reinforce rape myths and rape culture by blaming victims and considering them "sexual deviants." The movement also does not suggest there is anything wrong with attachment to family and community; instead, it is perpetrators, not victims, who should feel pressure from these institutions for disrupting social harmony.

Aside from causing increased discussion concerning sexual assault and victim-blaming, one of the greatest achievements of SWHK has been linking together NGOs and groups with diverse interests. Women's groups, migrant workers' groups, LGBT groups, academics, progressive politicians, and others all showed concern for the issue. Not only did it increase the social capital of all involved, it also prompted discussions among members of these groups, increasing the number of persons touched by the movement.

Another major achievement of SWHK has been its ability to bridge the gap between feminist activist and non-activist or non-feminist activist participants in the march and/or workshops. This allowed those new to feminism and/or activism to relate to other members of SWHK. It also helped to demystify and destroy existing stereotypes of feminists and/or activists. To give an example, I am the mother of a young child for whose care I am responsible full time. This is something that contradicts the perception of what a feminist "slut" should be, and this helped some to see that feminist and/or activists were just regular people. This illustrates the importance of involving the public in activities.

As mentioned previously, to have roughly 300 people show up at an event named "SlutWalk" is considered an especially large achievement in the context of Hong Kong. People from different genders, sexualities, races, socio-economic backgrounds, and ages all showed up to demonstrate that there is support for this issue from various communities and to help educate the public. Helping activists and supporters realise that they are not alone in the fight against sexual violence raised the morale of all those involved, energising them as they continue in the long process of social change. It also showed participants who were not sure of what to expect that there is no stereotypical mold into which a SlutWalk supporter fits.

CONCLUSION

Given Hong Kong's post-colonial context, labelling people, ideas, and movements that would like to change the current system of social inequality as "Western" has become a popular tool. The media in general used many typical tactics to discount the SlutWalk movement; however, as the organizer and most participants were not white, the cry of "white privilege" could not be used. Instead, privilege was merely suggested, while the suspicion of "Western" values was emphasized to "other" both the message of SWHK and the protestors involved. The local population also viewed not only SWHK but "sluts" and "sexual assault" in general as "Western" or "Westernized" phenomena, which are ideas perhaps rooted in colonial times.

Local obstacles faced include the high level of sexual conservatism and disdain for "deviants." Although the purpose is not to tell everyone in Hong Kong to behave sexually in any way or another, to avoid victim-blaming it is necessary that everyone accept others regardless of how they choose to express their sexuality or asexuality. Another challenge was the focus on family and community and concern for what others think. It is necessary for families and communities to provide support for victims, to recognise that it is no longer politically correct to blame victims, and at the same time, to start focusing responsibility on perpetrators.

Around the world, conservative resistance and even backlash is taking place in various forms. "Western," "white," "privileged," and "sluts" are just some of the terms used to: (1) "other" participants, making it more difficult for the public to relate to the

SlutWalk movement and fight against rape culture in general, (2) make it appear as though victim-blaming and sexual assault belongs only to some groups or cultures and not others; and (3) cause it to appear as though the solution is beyond the reach of the public due to the permanence of "our culture." In fact, patriarchy and sexual violence are issues faced by many cultures around the world, not just "Chinese" culture or "Western" culture. All cultures are dynamic in nature, and none have to accept patriarchal ideals, which include sexual control and heteronormativity.

In reality, cries of preserving "our culture" arise from conservative groups whenever the status quo is threatened or questioned in any way. Slavery, female genital mutilation, child marriages, child abuse, and wife battering are just some of the social injustices that have existed throughout the world in one form or another and at one time or another. The fact that some places no longer accept these forms of injustice is proof that cultures are not immutable. When we hear that something is threatening "our culture," we should always ask whose interests are actually being threatened.

ENDNOTES

[1]Since there was a near media-blackout in 2012, the media situation in 2012 is beyond the scope of this paper.

WORKS CITED

Boyle, Joseph. "Imperialism and the English Language in Hong Kong." *Journal of Multilingual and Multicultural Development* 18.3(1997): 169-181. Print.

Brownell, Susan and Jeffrey N. Wasserstrom eds. *Chinese Feminities/Chinese Masculinities.* Los Angeles: University of California Press, 2002. Print.

Carroll, John M. *A Concise History of Hong Kong.* Hong Kong: Hong Kong University Press, 2007. Print.

Chan, Phil C.W. "Stonewalling through Schizophrenia: An Anti-Gay Rights Culture in Hong Kong?" *Sexuality and Culture* 12 (2008): 71-87. Print.

Chang, Jui-shan. "Do We Need "Kinsey Reports" in Chinese Societies? An Alternative Paradigm for the Study of Chinese Sexuality." *Bulletin of Concerned Asian Scholars* 31.1 (1999): 40-42. Print.

Gao, Ersheng, Zuo, Xiayun, Wang, Li, Lou, Chaohua., Cheng, Yan, and Zabin, Laurie S. "How Does Traditional Confucian Culture Influence Adolescents' Sexual Behaviour in Three Asian Cities?" *Journal of Adolescent Health* 50 (2012): S12-S17. Print.

Garrett, Daniel, and Angie Ng. "Visualizing SlutWalk: Participants, the Public and the Media." Universidad Buenos Aires. Second International Sociological Association's Forum of Sociology: Social Justice and Democratization. Buenos Aires. 3 Aug 2012. Conference Presentation.

Henrich, Joseph, Steven J. Heine and Ara Norenzayan. "The Weirdest People in the World?" *Behavioural and Brain Sciences* 33.2-3 (2010): 61-83. Print.

Hui, Po-Keung K. "Comprador Politics and Middleman Capitalism." *Hong Kong's History: State and Society under Colonial Rule.* Ed. Tak-Wing Ngo London: Routledge, 1999. 130-145. Print.

Hung, Suet-lin. "A Study on Help Seeking Experiences of Sexual Violence in Hong Kong: Community Responses and Second Victimization." University of Hong Kong, Hong Kong. The Hong Kong Women's NGO Forum: Working with CEDAW. 7 May 2011. Conference Presentation.

Ip, Kelly. "Rapes Soar 60pc in First Quarter." *The Standard.* 15 May. 2013. Web. 7 Oct. 2013.

Jaschok, M. and S. Miers. "Women in the Chinese Patriarchal System: Submission, Servitude, Escape and Collusion." *Women and Chinese Patriarchy: Submission, Servitude and Escape.* Eds. Jaschok, M. and S. Miers. London: Zed Books, 1994. 1-24. Print.

La, C.-M. "How Virginity Enhances Masculinity: An Exploratory Study in Hanoi, Vietnam." Master's Thesis. San Francisco State University, 2005. Print.

Liu, Tik-sang. "A Nameless but Active Religion: An Anthropologist's View of Local Religion in Hong Kong and Macau." *The China Quarterly* 174 (2003): 373-394. Print.

Naylor, R. Thomas. *Hot Money and the Politics of Debt.* 3rd ed. Montreal: McGill-Queen's University Press, 2004. Print.

"Sex Message for the Urbane." *The Standard.* 05 Dec. 2011. Web. 29 May 2013.

Sinn, E. "Chinese Patriarchy and the Protection of Women in the 19th-Century Hong Kong." *Women and Chinese Patriarchy: Submission, Servitude and Escape.* Eds. Jaschok, M. and S. Miers. London: Zed Books, 1994. 141-167. Print.

Tiwari, Agnes. "Sexual Coercion in Intimate Relationships in Hong Kong." University of Hong Kong, Hong Kong. Symposium on Gender-Based Violence in Hong Kong: Sexual and Domestic Violence. 20 Nov. 2012. Conference Presentation.

Truong, T. D. *Sex, Money and Morality: The Political Economy of Prostitution and Tourism in South East Asia.* Dissertation, University of Amsterdam, 1998. Print.

Tsun, Angela O. K. "Sibling Incest: A Hong Kong Experience." *Child Abuse and Neglect* 23.1 (1999): 71-79. Print.

United Nations Development Program (UNDP). *Human Development Report 2013: The Rise of the South: Human Progress in a Diverse World.* UNDP. 2013. Web. 12 Dec. 2013.

Vagg, Jon. "Deliquency and Shame: Data from Hong Kong." *British Journal of Criminology* 38.2 (1998): 247-264. Print.

Watters, Ethan. "Universal Human Nature?" *Adbusters.* 05 Oct. 2013. Web. 06 Oct. 2013.

Wong, Ying, and Jeanne Tsai. "Cultural Models of Shame and Guilt." *The Self-Conscious Emotions: Theory and Research.* Ed. Tracy, Jessica L., Richard W. Robins and June P. Tagney. New York: Guilford Press, 2007. 210-223. Print.

"It Happens Here Too"

The SlutWalk Movement
in Hong Kong and Singapore

ANDREA O'REILLY

IN THE FALL OF 2013, I had the good fortune of being on sabbatical with plans to visit my son in Asia for three weeks at the end of his teaching contract in South Korea. I saw this trip as an ideal opportunity to interview founders and attendees of SlutWalk marches in Asia. A Google search revealed that both Singapore and Hong Kong had active SlutWalk Facebook pages, and had hosted various SlutWalk events since the start of the international SlutWalk movement in the spring of 2011. As a proud attendee of the first SlutWalk march in Toronto, and a passionate defender of the international SlutWalk movement, I was keen to examine how SlutWalk happened and developed in a cultural context radically different than my own. In exploring the "how, why, when, where, who and what" of SlutWalk in both countries, I was particularly interested in addressing the central criticisms of the SlutWalk movement, namely the assumed homogeneity of SlutWalk marches globally; the presumption that SlutWalk was largely a feminist movement for and about privileged, Western, white, educated, young women; the alleged lack of diversity in SlutWalk participants; and finally its uncritical use of the term slut. The interviews were conducted in December 2013. In Hong Kong, due to the holiday season, I was only able to interview one person, Dan Garrett (who has also contributed a chapter to this collection). In Singapore, I had the good fortune of conducting a group interview with seven women and one man, attending one of their monthly business meetings, and giving a talk on SlutWalk Toronto at a women's community centre.

Due to seemingly endless demands on my time, I was only able to begin writing this chapter in the fall of 2014. While certainly not planned, the delay proved to be fortuitous as the thinking and writing for this chapter took place when violence against women became *the* topic of Canadian public and media discourse as a result of the Jian Ghomeshi "scandal" and the marking of the 25th anniversary of the Montreal Massacre on December 6th. It seemed as though everyone had something to say about sexual and physical violence against women as 2014 drew to a close. As yet another woman came forward to disclose the sexual assault she experienced by Canada's former media darling Ghomeshi, as one more story of sexual violence was shared via the hashtag #Iwasraped on Twitter, and as our country remembered and mourned the murder of fourteen female engineering students who were killed for simply being women, the outrage and outcry of the SlutWalk movement again became timely and relevant. As people asked why the many women assaulted by Ghomeshi never reported the crime to the police, feminists found themselves needing to explain once again the concepts of slut-shaming and rape culture; women—even privileged women like those assaulted by Ghomeshi—are seldom believed and readily blamed when the crime is sexual assault.

As the themes in my transcribed interviews from Asia coalesced with those in Canadian social media I found myself returning to and re-reading some of the earlier media coverage of the SlutWalk movement in the hopes of becoming better prepared to deal with and respond to the current cohort of slut-shaming/rape culture nonbelievers and naysayers. In so doing, I came across Margaret Wente's *Globe and Mail* column of May 12, 2011, titled, "Embrace your inner slut: Um, maybe not," written one month after the inaugural SlutWalk in Toronto. In the column, Wente writes: "SlutWalks are what you get when graduate students in feminist studies run out of things to do. In fact they're flogging a dead mare. The attitude that rape victims bring it on themselves has largely (though not entirely) disappeared from mainstream society." She goes on to write: "...the highly educated women who join SlutWalk are among the safest and most secure in the world. But you would never know it from the fevered rhetoric. I guess they mean well. But really, they're so privileged." The stories of the many women who were sexually assaulted by Ghomeshi but never reported it to the police remind us that, contrary to Wente's claim, victim-blaming has anything but "disappeared from mainstream society" and that "privileged" women are not immune to sexual violence. And for the journalism students who were sexually harassed by Ghomeshi, not to mention the fourteen female students murdered at École Polytechnique in 1989, educated women in Canada are anything but the safest and most secure in the world. Wente ends her column by asserting: "There's no shortage of other causes for feminists to take up…. Anything would be a big improvement over the narcissistic self-indulgence of the SlutWalkers." Reading Wente's column alongside the seemingly endless Facebook debates on violence against women over the last several months, I was reminded again of the importance of the SlutWalk "cause" so disparaged by Wente and, indeed, most thankful for the opportunity to meet with, and hear the stories of Slutwalkers from the other side of the world. To that discussion I now turn.

"IT'S IMPOSSIBLE TO BE INVISIBLE"/"NO MARCHES EVER": LOCATING AND UNDERSTANDING SLUTWALKS IN THEIR SPECIFIC CULTURAL CONTEXTS

I opened my interview with a set of questions on the background of the SlutWalk movement in each country, as I was particularly interested in how the so-called "western" feminist movement of SlutWalk occurred and developed in so-called "non-western" countries like Hong Kong and Singapore. Questions asked included: "How/when did you first hear about the SlutWalk movement?"; "Why did you plan a SlutWalk march/event in your community?"; "In doing so, were you aware of the criticisms of SlutWalk as a western feminist movement?"; "In planning your events were you mindful of these criticisms and did you seek to develop events specifically in and for a 'non-western' context?" What surprised me most as these questions were answered was how inapplicable this binary was for an understanding of the SlutWalk movement in these two countries and, I suspect, for the movement more globally.

In designing my research questions, I naively, and I now see very problematically, positioned Canada as "western" and both these countries, being in Asia, as "non-western." But what became most startling as the interviews unfolded was how radically different Singapore and Hong Kong are as countries and subsequently how radically differently the SlutWalk movement occurred and developed in each country. At the time of my interview with Dan in December 2013, Hong Kong had held three SlutWalk Marches: December 2011, November 2012, and November 2013. Between 100 and 300 people attended each march, and the marches lasted approximately 45 minutes on what Dan described as a "popular parade route ... these marches have visibility and lots of people. It's all about public transportation and people on buses, trains and people on the sidewalks." Dan went on to explain that "since 1997 we have had 50,000 demonstrations so we've had rallies as big as half a million or a small as a couple of people. At SlutWalk marches people watching were mainly on the sidewalk. So it's impossible to be invisible. People may not understand it, but they see it, which I think is important." Speaking later about the lower numbers at the third SlutWalk, Dan suggested that this may have been the result of what he described as "protester fatigue":

> 2012 and 2013 have been the most politically contentious years since 1967. Lots of authorities described 2012 as Hong Kong's most anti-communist since the '67 riots so it is a big political situation right now. In 2012 there were several protest and rallies with over 100,000 people; one in July reached 180,000. This may explain why there was not quite as much energy and support for the last SlutWalk march: SlutWalk was competing with other protests going on at the same time. It's hard for the same speakers to be at different locations.

Dan went on to explain that the tradition of large protests in Hong Kong and what he termed the "rich civil society movement" has created "a diverse and large activist community with a core set of activists that all know each other." Awareness of and support for the Hong Kong SlutWalk movement was disseminated and developed through these networks via Facebook and email.

In contrast to the public visibility of Hong Kong SlutWalk marches and the overall vibrant protest culture of Hong Kong, public demonstrations are illegal in Singapore and hence SlutWalk was not enacted as a march but rather through a series of events. As one of the organizers of SlutWalk Singapore explained: "We are not allowed to march in Singapore. No one marches ever, unless it is state sanctioned." The organizer went on to explain that since marches are not legal in Singapore, SlutWalk occurred and developed through events: the first event was a gathering where women came together to do life drawings and talk about SlutWalk; the second was a screening of a film and a discussion on how rape culture affects sex workers; another was a martial arts class; and another a Speakers' Corner in a park attended by about 600 people. They also secretly screened porn videos in someone's house as well as held consent workshops. SlutWalk Singapore was also initiated and established in secrecy: "We started with a small group of 10-12 people. We had a secret Facebook page. We invited people who would be interested so we wouldn't be open to criticism too early. So that's when the discussion started, and then we took it offline." Most of the organizers also did not tell friends or family of their involvement with SlutWalk Singapore. Significantly, though both of these SlutWalks took place in Asia, the development and design of each movement could not have been more different: each was influenced and shaped by the specific historical, cultural, and political context of their respective countries.

"IT WAS MAINLY ACTIVISTS"/"IT HAPPENED THAT THE PUNKS CAME IN": CHALLENGING THE ASSUMPTIONS AND PRESUMPTIONS OF PRIVILEGE AND HOMOGENEITY IN THE SLUTWALK MOVEMENT

As these two SlutWalks call into question the presumed uniformity of SlutWalk events globally and the view that non-western SlutWalks unproblematically replicate and duplicate western Slut-Walks, they likewise reveal that SlutWalks are more diverse than assumed and presented in media discussions and representations.

In Hong Kong, as Dan explains, "speakers were from the Rape Crisis Centre, Migrant Workers organizations, LGBT groups and the Transgendered community, the League of Socialist Democrats [a grass roots/blue collar political action group] and from various political organizations or parties who are active in standing up for victim rights." When I inquired on the demographics of each march Dan emphasized that participants were mainly activists from the various groups mentioned above. As well, there was a fair bit of diversity in age: while the majority of participants were in their twenties or thirties a significant number were older. At the first march, approximately 25 per cent of participants were men. Importantly, a significant number of participants were migrant workers. In Hong Kong, as Dan explained, "there are about 200,000 foreign domestic workers. The treatment of these workers has been an issue for a long time. They are a vulnerable population so they have a vested interest in the issue [of sexual exploitation]." Asked to reflect upon what people wore at the walks he attended, Dan commented: "Every SlutWalk that I have seen in Hong Kong I've not seen anybody wear anything that I would consider, for lack of a better word, 'slutty' or provocative. There wasn't much skin showing at all. I think maybe some people wore a bra over their shirt; one or two people wore a negligee over their clothes. You didn't see anything overtly sexual. I'd say that was one of the most remarkable things about SlutWalk." Asking him to reflect more upon the differences between his experiences of SlutWalk and how the movement was represented in the media, Dan remarked:

> One is that it was more diverse. Second it was not an issue of privilege. And third would be the fact that the degree of sexualisation of SlutWalk was miniscule compared to the consumer society and what you see on television, on film, at the beach. You have a neo-liberal society criticizing the social justice movement for being sexualized when it's really not; at the same time, the same society promotes the sexualisation of minors.

Dan went on to comment "that if you look at the photographs I took (in contrast to mainstream media representations), we had a mixer, and we had some straight people, some GLBT people, expats, Asians and so forth."

Dan's comments effectively discredit the commonly-held assumption that SlutWalk is a movement solely about and for young, educated women, or in the words of Wente, "graduate students in feminist studies who have run out of things to do." Dan's statements also undeniably challenge popular descriptions and representations of SlutWalk participants as, again to borrow from Wente, "nubile young women in thigh-high cut-offs and tube tops."

The same can be said of the SlutWalk Singapore movement. When asked to describe who was most involved in their movement, one organizer explained: "We put out a call for organizers and it happened that the punks came in. I think that is what is unique about us ... it was very much about the punk scene. The punks really came out because this is a good cause. They started coming on board. The first year we had a lot of punks." She explains further:

We sent out emails to different organizations and asked, are they affected by rape culture, do you feel like this something you would like to contribute on? But I must say it was hit and miss because the language at the time was extremely new. Whether it was a women's shelter, whether it was an organization for disabled people ... I emailed tons of people and only three got back: GLBT, migrant/domestic workers, and women's groups.

Significantly there was no university involvement or student participation in the Singapore SlutWalk Movement. In Singapore, as one respondent explained "there are no student movements as you see in North America (the war movement, the rape movement). The last one was in the fifties, 250 people were thrown into detention without trial and that sedimented [sic] the laws and standing up for a cause." As well, there are no gender or women's studies departments at Singapore universities; one university does offer a minor in Gender Studies but as one respondent explained: "I don't know anyone taking it." When I asked them who attended their events, one respondent emphasized that "they always have a diverse group of people." These comments, in detailing the wide range of organizations contacted, the absence of student involvement, the importance of the punk scene, and finally the diversity of individuals who attended their events, challenge the accepted interpretation of who organizes and attends SlutWalk events; they are not all women, students, young, or privileged.

"CAN WE JUST GET OVER THE WORD AND TALK ABOUT THE MESSAGE?"/"WE HAD TO DO SOMETHING OUT OF THE ORDINARY TO GAIN MEDIA ATTENTION. TO RISE ABOVE": SLUT TALK AS "RESONANCE AND DEFIANCE"

A criticism central to the inaugural SlutWalk in Toronto was its use of the term slut. As discussed in earlier chapters, for many the word slut was problematic because it betrayed a lack of sensitivity to how the word is interpreted and used in different historical and cultural contexts. Given the contentiousness of the term/concept of slut in public and media, discussions on SlutWalks, and the controversy the word generated as the movement went global, I was particularly interested in exploring how the word slut and the concept of slut-shaming was taken up in an Asian context.

I opened my interview with Dan by asking him to reflect upon what he perceived as the central goals of the Hong Kong SlutWalk movement: "Part of the unspoken goal of [Hong Kong SlutWalk] was to raise consciousness, to provoke people to think about the issues [of slut-shaming/victim-blaming and rape culture], to educate or enlighten them to the issue and to motivate them to take some action, to speak out." When I asked Dan why he became involved with the SlutWalk movement in Hong Kong he explained: "It just really resonated with me. Having been involved in national security I've dealt with police a lot. I am very aware of some of some of the abuses and travesties of justice that go on." He elaborated:

Originally I was helping out [one of the organizers] and as I learned more, I become more interested and read the criticisms and I did not think the criticisms reconciled with my personal experience and my critical reading of the media coverage, and I saw certain political and rhetorical lines

127

about stigmatism of certain groups: red flags that told me there was something else going on here.

Asked to explain further, Dan emphasized that:

> it was the representations—the misrepresentations of Slut-Walk—that were the catalyst for me to get more involved … I do see, whether it started this way or not, a civil war within the feminist movement. I also saw it as a classist type of environment. Even in Hong Kong, the more elite media, the more elite police tend to be more critical and dismissive of the movement, than perhaps the grassroots.

Discussing more specifically the use of the word slut Dan commented:

> SlutWalk falls in a post-modern social movement. Obviously, we had to do something out of the ordinary to gain media attention. We have to rise above. So how do you do that? How do you do that in a non-violent way? I think it's a valid technique, it worked well. [Yet] it can be coopted. They're thinking how can it be used against you?" The term nigger has become very controversial. Queer has become controversial. Perhaps with the term like queer, you're seeing a trajectory, where it was being reclaimed and there is some backlash against this. Slut is being used in different ways. Some people use the term slut because they've slept with a lot of people; some because they enjoy a particular activity; they enjoy sex. Some people use it in those contexts but the media does not make the extensions behind that. The migration of the term is a political migration. It has a certain resonance; it has certain defiance against the mainstream controlled society.

Another useful aspect of the SlutWalk debate, Dan explained further, "is that it identified for some people the incongruence of their thinking. Teach 'don't rape' rather than 'don't get raped.' How to perceive things? It seems to me that part of the problem is when you start to examine the issue of consent and the power involved there, it raises other uncomfortable issues about the way a patriarchal society is organized."

Concluding the interview, I asked Dan to reflect upon the impact of SlutWalk in Hong Kong:

> I think it had an impact in making it visible in the media, bringing some visibility to the issue. I think in that context it has planted a seed, it's been in discourse, and now people have something they can point to, a sort of sign or symbol. I think one of the more important things is the documentary base to point back to. Because quite often when you want to criticize power, people say "Where is your evidence?" Well, if no one is documenting, then there is no evidence. It may not seem important, but let's start to document the process. So SlutWalk should not be seen as an end necessarily, but as building a foundation. But will something come after SlutWalk? Maybe, I don't know. The issues are not going away. Perhaps the tactics might need to change, especially as the media or authorities become adept at absorbing our demands.

Significantly, with my Singapore respondents it was precisely "the sex positive message of SlutWalk" that motivated them to become involved. When I asked why they used the term slut, one organizer explained:

> We were not concerned that the word slut is not as common in Singapore. We have different, colloquial words like "chicken." It's a synonym for prostitute. And also "village bicycle" means everyone has ridden you before. It is a common word for slut. However "village bicycle" is specific for the region. If you say it in Laos people wouldn't get it.... When we decided upon the word slut, it was strategic. We wanted to introduce a new idea. It was strategy ... we wanted to be in solidarity with the international movement. To get people talking about the word slut and its contemporary use in Singapore. It did

manage to spark a debate just over the word itself which was our intention as well.

She went on to explain: "With people discussing that maybe we should call [SlutWalk] something else—it caused tension. It's a good tension. It is a healthy discussion. I just see the value of it. It was like, can we just get over the word and talk about the message?" Later in the discussion, one respondent discussed how the use of the word slut and the overall discussion on slut-shaming and rape culture got people talking about these issues:

I think the reason rape culture is used is because the majority of people don't think of people they know. So when asked in Singapore if there's a rape culture, they think there's no such thing. [Yet] women are being raped everywhere.... We wanted to tell people that it has happened in Toronto, and in other countries. It's happened in Singapore. We have found evidence of it happening in Singapore.

Another respondent commented:

[The concept of] of victim-blaming is more credible in a way, but not [yet] slut-shaming. I work with sex workers, sex workers get raped but they don't get to go to the police because they know what is going to happen to them. You know [you will not be believed] if you look a certain way. If you're dressed decently, if you're a virgin, and assaulted [you are more likely to be believed].

Speaking more generally on the activism of SlutWalk Singapore one respondent explained: "I didn't see it as a movement that would have legal changes. I saw it as a way to blast out our message." Another woman commented:

Every time we do stuff, we got encouraged. There are a lot of people coming back to us. They come to events, and we do a retrospective. We do a follow-up where people throw out suggestions. It has been very encouraging reaching out to [our] communities. Really amazing! Double PhD holders who said thank you for doing this. "I didn't know I was raped until you gave me the vocabulary." I feel very, really emotional now. Really encouraged we've been getting our message out loud.... [It] is amazing, really amazing!

For both Dan in Hong Kong and the group of SlutWalk organizers in Singapore, their use of the word slut was "strategic." Well aware of how contentious and controversial the word slut is, particularly in an Asian country, they nonetheless consciously used the term because they saw it as the most effective and powerful way to, in their words, "blast out their message," "gain media attention," "provoke people to think and talk about the issues," "raise consciousness," "introduce a new idea," "spark a debate" and show "solidarity with the international movement." The word slut made possible "a good tension; a healthy discussion."

CONCLUSION

These interviews from Hong Kong and Singapore powerfully challenge and effectively correct many of the misconceptions of the SlutWalk movement, particularly as it developed in so called non-western contexts. The organizers and attendees of SlutWalk marches and events in Hong Kong and Singapore were anything but homogeneous or privileged. Punks, sex workers, migrant workers, and grassroots activists were involved as were members from LGBT communities and individuals from various political organizations. They were young and old, men and women, students and workers. Though cognizant of the controversy surrounding the word slut particularly in non-western contexts, the organizers strategically used the term to meet the needs of their particular community and fulfil the goals of their specific SlutWalk movement. Most impressive, in my view, was how each SlutWalk developed, grew, and flourished in response to the unique challenges and possibilities of their specific cultural locations. With marches illegal in Singapore, they set up consent workshops and martial arts classes. In Hong Kong, SlutWalk organizers turned to the large and established activist networks of their country to mobilize support and increase visibility. These SlutWalks were anything but derivative: they did not simply duplicate or replicate western SlutWalks as is often assumed, but rather created unique and vibrant movements of their own. Each SlutWalk has a rich and robust history and now, entering their fourth year with many events planned, they have a promising future as well. Indeed, they have outgrown—and outlived—the original SlutWalk.

WORK CITED

Wente, Margaret. "Embrace your inner slut? Um maybe not." *The Globe and Mail*. Globe and Mail. 12 May 2011. Web. 10 December 2014.

Mapping the SlutWalk Paradox

Challenges and Possibilities of Using Raunch in Transnational Feminist Politics

AMANDA D. WATSON AND CORINNE L. MASON

THE PORTRAIT OF THE SLUTWALKER, albeit unrepresentative, easily comes to mind: able-bodied, scantily clad, and "war-painted." This chapter explores what Watson has elsewhere called the "SlutWalk paradox": the clash between resisting the sexual policing of women's bodies through raunch, and appealing to the masculinist and heteronormative media gaze. By analyzing SlutWalk's use of raunch, this chapter argues that while SlutWalk wrongly assumes that all women experience slut-shaming and victim-blaming similarly, it is also a platform that generates possibilities to shift discourses on violence against women and girls in real ways. For example, the concepts of "slut-shaming" and "rape culture" have been popularized in the "post-SlutWalk" period, now rife in media accounts of girl tragedies, including the deaths of Amanda Todd (Dean) and Rehtaeh Parsons (Hodge "RIP"). Here we argue that while marking a significant success in changing mainstream discourses, the terms "slut-shaming" and "rape culture" are themselves exclusionary, relying on racist ableism, and thus, further complicating the im/possibilities of SlutWalk (and raunch culture more generally) as an anti-violence platform. In order to present raunch as a contested strategy that forecloses some possibilities of agitation against violence, while simultaneously giving access to others, we first explore the concepts of slut-shaming and rape culture. Second, we interrogate raunch as an anti-violence tool and then detail feminist challenges to the SlutWalk movement. Finally, we present evidence of a discursive shift around mainstream reporting

133

of rape culture post-SlutWalk. We conclude with discussion of what this means for future incarnations of the movement and for anti-violence activism more generally.

SLUT-SHAMING AND RAPE CULTURE

"Slut-shaming" refers to "the practice of criticizing a woman for engaging in certain sexual behaviors outside of traditional gender roles, whether it be actual or presumed based on her manner of dress, speech or personality" (Amanda B.). In 2006, popular blogger Alon Levy used the word to describe an online argument between two bloggers, wherein one woman shamed the other for her sexual behaviour. Levy explained that the meaning of the word slut is of less consequence than its implication that women who fall outside of traditional expectations of femininity be socially punished. The practice of slut-shaming explicates a sexual double-standard, and, as it refers to a conventional gender performance that is tied to whiteness and Christianity, it folds whiteness into proper, moral sexuality. As demonstrated by popular culture responses to Taylor Swift's dating record (Davis), Miley Cyrus' duet with Robin Thicke (Yates), Kristen Stewart's infidelity (Lang), and Rihanna's Twitter account (West), slut-shaming is a pervasive and powerful tool used to discipline women's sexuality. Slut-shaming is also now a popular topic in the blogosphere, and has recently been discussed most prominently in the context of cyberbullying, which we explicate in a later section of this chapter (see Dean).

The mainstreaming of slut-shaming in popular discourse has made way for discussions of rape culture, wherein the sexual violation of women's bodies by men is made acceptable, and even encouraged, by virtues of misogyny and competition. Rape culture allows sexual assault and rape to go unacknowledged and unpunished. When women are sexually assaulted they are deemed deserving or "asking for it." Jill Filipovic explains that in rape culture, while most people may publicly denounce rape, the well-established right-wing family ideal promotes "an extremist ideology that *enables* rape and promotes a culture where sexual assault is tacitly accepted" (17). According to arts-based project blog *Force: Upsetting Rape Culture*, rape culture includes "jokes, TV, music, advertising, legal jargon, laws, words and imagery, that make violence against women and sexual coercion seem ... inevitable."

IS RAUNCH CULTURE AN ANTI-VIOLENCE TOOL?

As a resistance tactic to slut-shaming and rape culture, raunch is used as a tool for women to claim bodily and sexual agency while also calling attention to masculinist objectification in provocative ways. The Toronto police's slut-shaming and victim-blaming discourses that initially sparked SlutWalk were largely met with raunch as resistance. In the context of the SlutWalk, both the reclamation of the term slut and the (sometimes assumed) expectations for "slutty dress" at rallies can be understood as raunch. The term raunch is used both positively and negatively in reference to women's sexual expression in the public sphere. In a 1994 article published in *Esquire* magazine, Tad Friend derogatorily characterized women's pro-sex aims, popularized by the likes of Naomi Wolf and Susie Bright, as "do-me feminism." Of course, the concept termed "do-me feminism" was meant to insult and depoliticize the pro-sex, inclusive, and pro-choice ethos of some feminisms in the 1990s. Friend's angle denied the richness of turn-of-the-century feminist politics that destabilized status quo liberal feminism. It castigated and skewed the emergent "third wave" feminist energies of the 1990s that saw feminist aims pluralized and diversified—particularly by women of colour, poor women, sex workers, and transgender persons who called attention to various women's subjective and localized experiences of oppression that had been previously folded into white women's experiences with gender inequity (see Zeisler 113).[1]

Ariel Levy, with her book, *Female Chauvinist Pigs: Women and the Rise of Raunch Culture*, became a polarizing figure in the debate over the collective attitudinal shift toward celebrating the sexually explicit, which she terms "raunch culture." Invoking *Girls Gone Wild* and *Sex and the City,* Levy refuses the link between "scantily clad" and claims to freedom. She finds "depressing" the ways in which girls and women are encouraged to sexualize themselves to fit the trope of the modern, empowered woman (44). For Levy, performances of raunch by (heterosexual, white, rich, thin, able-bodied, conventionally attractive, blonde) women resembling porn queen Jenna Jameson at the height of her career, hotel heiress and business mogul, Paris Hilton, and *Sex and the City* character, Samantha Jones, are representations and performances of a conventional version of female sexiness. For Levy, they are also, therefore, a form of seeking social approval—itself a "crucial criterion for hotness" in our culture (33). She goes so far as to argue that raunch culture is in fact *anti-feminist* because it's "inherently commercial" (30); that "the emergence of a woman-backed trash culture is a rebellion *against* the values of feminism, egalitarianism, and antimaterialism" (44-45). Given the influence of raunch on consumption practices and the link between pleasure and materialism, Levy maintains that expressions of raunch are not progressive. "Raunch culture isn't about opening our minds to the possibilities and mysteries of sexuality. It's about endlessly reiterating one particular—and particularly commercial—shorthand for sexiness" (33).

For others, especially some postfeminists (for example, sex educator and former stripper and porn actress, Annie Sprinkle), engagement with raunch is about shifting the sexual paradigm; raunch celebrates a particularly assertive feminine sexuality, re-jecting the still-popular notion that women should be pursued by men, or that only heterosexual expressions of sexuality are publically acceptable. It takes forward the orgasm-seeking femi-nist campaigns of the 1970s (see Koedt; Hite), as well as radical pro-sex and anti-racist art and activist organizing by women of colour,[2] continuing advocacy for women's sexual pleasure against patriarchal and white supremacist dictations of what is appropriate. In popular culture, this unabashed feminine sexuality is typically represented by (young, white, blonde, thin) pop stars like Christina Aguilera (*Dirrty*), Ke$ha (*We R Who We R*), and, most recently, Miley Cyrus (*Wrecking Ball; We Can't Stop*)—each star immensely popular for asserting their sexual desires in lyrics, choreography, and provocative clothing (and, of course, by too-often appropriating Black and Indigenous cultures). These stars reject some (though not all) of the restrictive norms of traditional femininity dictated by popular culture that we see repeatedly in extremely high-grossing romantic comedies like *Hitch* and *He's Just Not That Into You*; in these films, women who stray far from traditional feminine dress and behaviour, away from beauty ideals and toward women's career success, for example, end up unhappy and need to be reformed by the end of the film. Therefore, expressions of raunchy sexuality (for example, Ke$ha's "hot and dangerous" sexuality and unapologetic attitude in the video *We R Who We R*),[3] that do not ask for permission and are not necessarily directed at an object of desire or toward a monogamous partnership might be understood as radical, or at least resistant.

In 2012, upon the death of Helen Gurley Brown, longtime editor of *Cosmopolitan* and author of *Sex and the Single Girl,* Helaine Olen wrote an article entitled "Failure of Do-Me Feminism" for *Forbes* magazine. Olen argued that as much as Brown advocated for single women's sexual pleasure, and against the inevitability of marriage, especially for women without the privileges of class and higher education, her pleasure-guided vision for feminism depoliticized women's issues, and ultimately could not change the status quo. Maurine Dowd shares Olen's critique of what Dowd calls "fun feminism" or "bimbo feminism": a movement that gives "intellectual pretensions to a world where the highest ideal is to acknowledge your inner slut" (qtd. in Greer 9).

Using raunch as a strategy, as SlutWalk does, runs the risk of, as Levy puts it, "perverted" notions of liberation and empowerment related to provocative dress (200). As Meghan Murphy claims about her own experience at SlutWalk for *Rabble*: "While these issues seemed very feminist to me, I was hard-pressed to find anyone actually talking about feminism." Suggesting that choice rhetoric (especially around clothing) was more prevalent at the event than a structural critique of rape-culture, Murphy claims that she saw more aversion to feminism than an alignment with feminist politics. Calling SlutWalk's employment of raunch culture "funfeminist" (in contrast to the ubiquitous ugly feminist killjoy stereotype), Murphy argues that it is easy to get attention, but harder to do the work of feminism.

The debate over whether raunch is good or bad for feminism is polarized. At one extreme, Ariel Levy calls it feminism's failure, "a testament to what's still missing from our understanding of human sexuality" (198), and a "desperate stab at free-wheeling eroticism in a time and place characterized by intense anxiety"

(199). On the other, sex-positive and sex-affirming feminists like Annie Sprinkle, who mobilized raunch in her workshop *Sluts and Goddesses* in 1991, argue that the celebration of women's sexuality in the public sphere is key to liberation. Feminists who theorize pro-sex movements while criticizing popular versions of raunch culture, like Jack Halberstam in his 2011 blogpost, *The Summer of Raunch*, fall somewhere in between.

To claim raunch is to use it with all of its failings. The ways in which raunch has been employed and rejected from within and outside of the SlutWalk movement tells of the complexity of feminist responses to victim-blaming and slut-shaming discourses, particularly in terms of inviting a mainstream masculinist gaze, and erasing structural divisions among and between women through the assumption that anyone can claim to be a "slut," that we all "know" what a "slut" looks like, and that we all have equal access to performing "sluttiness" (and only in the confines of a rally with a start and end time, often urban location, and with security "protection"). In reckoning with this tension, we conceive of raunch as a powerful and slippery feminist practice since it both resists and re-inscribes expectations of femininity, whiteness, able-bodiedness, and feminism simultaneously, while further capturing historical and contemporary debates and divisions within the feminist movement. Given its complexity, raunch is caught between the language of women's empowerment and feminism's destruction, depending on how it is used, by whom, and at whom it is directed. Acknowledging its complexity, we understand "raunch" to mean the Western, typically white, able-bodied expression of sexuality associated with skin-baring and feminized dress, and pursuing sex outside of the confines of conventional arrangements like heterosexual monogamy that ultimately leads to marriage.

STRATEGIC RAUNCH: FROM RIOT GRRRLS TO SPICE GIRLS

Somewhere in between Levy's disavowal of raunch culture and embracing raunch in the face of "do-me feminism" critiques may lie possibilities for using raunch as a powerful tool. In the early 1990s, strategic raunch hit the punk scene in Washington, DC and the Pacific Northwest in the form of Riot grrrls—organized feminist punk rockers with overtly political aims and anti-sexist messaging. Often associated with the beginning of the third wave, Riot grrls confronted issues of sexism, among them rape and sexual abuse, scribbling SLUT and WHORE across their stomachs in denunciation of society's confinement of women's sexual expression (Ziesler). Chided by mainstream media as vengeful and frightening, and further distorted because of their refusal to associate with main-stream media outlets, their movement was chilled by pop icons of the late 1990s, who paired the notion of independence with consumption, high heels, thinness, and intentional naïveté. Andi Ziesler, founder of *Bitch* magazine and author of *Feminism and Pop Culture*, writes on how Riot grrrl transitioned, albeit ironi-cally, into the sugar-coated girl power of the late 1990s embodied by the Spice Girls. Rather than subverting the image of the pinup girl, Ziesler explains, the Spice Girls, created by Simon Fuller, sold pinup femininity as what women "really, really want." Raunch expression moved from the realm of the punk underground to the iconized celebrity realm of commercial pop.

The line between what constitutes strategic raunch and what is directed toward the male gaze has since been blurry, with feminist and anti-feminist commenters weighing in on a slew of pop culture events and icons, both in favour and against women's overt sexual expression (Friedman; Halberstam "Summer"; Levy; Zeisler). The SlutWalk movement was formed in these muddy waters; in the context of, for example, women improving their career prospects by attending university at higher rates than men, and still being instructed to ward off potential attackers by self-policing their dress and behaviour. While women in the music industry are en-couraged to strip for the cover of *Rolling Stone*, women and girls in the suburbs of Toronto are punished for wearing short skirts.

TALKING SLUTWALK:
FEMINIST CHALLENGES TO THE MOVEMENT

For many in the feminist blogosphere, SlutWalk has come to represent a major and well-documented failure of mainstream feminism to be intersectional by employing a particular form of raunch as an anti-violence resistance tool. Almost immediately following the call-out for "slutwalkers" in Toronto, feminists questioned the expectation to leverage raunch as resistance via "slutty" dress at the event, as well as the meaning of the term slut, and the possibility of reclaiming "slut" for different women across lines of race, class, and ability (Women of Hamilton Against Patriarchy). In the words of Harsha Walia, SlutWalk represented, for many women, "the palatable 'I can wear what I want' feminism that is *intentionally devoid of an analysis of power dynamics*" (emphasis our own).[4]

One of the most notable and circulated responses to SlutWalk, "An Open Letter from Black Women to the SlutWalk," traces the historical institutionalization of understanding Black women's bodies as "sexual objects of property, spectacles of sexuality, and deviant sexual desire" ultimately maintaining that their bodies are already always understood as inherently rapeable, on "the auction block, in the fields or on living room television screens." For Black women, anti-violence organizing has meant fighting racists stereotypes of the "slut, jezebel, hottentot, mammy, mule, sapphire."[5]

Tracing another racist and colonial lineage, many Indigenous women and allies argued that the reclamation of the term slut obscures the histories of colonialism and current genocidal occupation of unceded territory that has relied on the stereotype of the "squaw." Squaw is a derogatory word used to dehumanize Indigenous women, imbued with insulting meaning like "dirty," "easy" and "lazy." For Kim Anderson, this negative construction of Native womanhood is an imaginary that is "ingrained in the North American consciousness" and is not only internalized by Indigenous women, but overshadows violence committed against them when they seek justice (267). Andrea Smith argues that Indigenous women are considered "rapeable" through the construction and treatment of Native women as squaws. She argues that Indigenous bodies are marked by their so-called "sexuality perversity"—as popularized by colonial narratives—and these racist and sexist stereotypes deny the dignity and worth of Indigenous women. The construction and circulation of the squaw stereotype permits some men to commit violent acts of hatred against them without consequence. As Walia writes for *Feministing*: "The systemic ideology that upholds the colonial disposability of

Indigenous women's bodies and lives has normalized the tragedy of thousands of missing and murdered Indigenous women across this country." For many women of colour, Indigenous women, trans individuals, sex workers, and women with disabilities, the use of raunch vis-à-vis the reclamation of "slut" was impossible, even if they ultimately supported the anti-victim-blaming and anti-violence messaging of SlutWalk.

Transnationally, the reclamation of the term slut is complicated at best. In Singapore, SlutWalk was organized around a discomfort with the reclamation of the term. Suggesting that one did not have to utilize raunch or identify as a "slut," participants were told by organizers that they need not "wear sexuality on your sleeve," or "vamp it up." Instead, organizers in Singapore asked protesters to "come as you are—whether in T-shirt and jeans, fishnets, in a sari, in a jacket, or in a tudung (hijab)" (Gwynne 177).[6] In London, a march within the SlutWalk march called "Hijabs, Hoodies, and Hotpants" emerged as a rejection of the reclamation of the term slut and also the proliferation of raunch in the movement. As Lim and Fanghanel's research demonstrates, Hijabs, Hoodies and Hotpants participants were critical of rape discourses, while providing a wider "contestation of racist, Islamophobic, sexist and classist discrimination, especially as it takes place around the materiality of dress" (214). In India, the 2011 SlutWalk organizers used the term "besharmi morcha," or "shameless protest," to expand the appeal of the march, and to speak to the Indian context (Kapur 12). According to one participant in SlutWalk Dehli, participants received a message before the event urging them to dress "modestly." Since the trope of "besharmi" (shame in Hindi) was employed, few people "dressed as 'sluts'" which, for some, "did not challenge the notion of the 'good woman'" prevalent in India (Borah 416). Following on the heels of a local protest called Pink Chaddis (in which women sent pink panties to a right wing Hindu organization that blamed the victim of a recent sexual assault on her being in public), Kapur argued that SlutWalk represented a Western-imposed reclamation of the term slut, even though it was replaced with shame in some instances, and was unhelpful for local feminist concerns (such as laws that do not protect women from rape).[7]

Women with disabilities have a differently estranged relationship with raunch and the term slut. Jennifer Scott maintains in "Thoughts on SlutWalk from a Wheelchair" for *Ms. Blog* that the term slut was never hers: "While women all over the world are waiting for people to stop seeing them as sex objects, women with disabilities are still waiting to be seen at all." The assumption that women with disabilities are, or should be, asexual or non-sexual conceptualizes individuals as objects of pity, rather than as desirable. This means that they are not endowed with the capacity for "sluttiness." Since women with disabilities are at a higher risk of violence globally than women without disabilities, including sexual violence (WHO), for Scott, it is not the word "walk" that excludes her from the movement (although for some women with disabilities, the language, logistics, and parameters of various rallies have been exclusionary). It is, rather, the lack of attention paid to the intersections of disability and gendered sexual violence in SlutWalk that is of most concern.

Importantly, feminists also criticized the police presence at Slut-Walks, especially in Toronto (see Women of Hamilton Against Patriarchy). Since the "slut-shaming" comments that sparked the movement came from the Toronto police, the presence of police offers for "protection" at the event is puzzling. For women of colour, Indigenous women, queer, genderqueer, transgender and transsexual individuals, women with disabilities, immigrant women, previously incarcerated women, homeless women, and sex workers who are particularly vulnerable to police, judicial, and state-sponsored violence (including the lack of credibility of supposedly "inherently rapeable" persons when making claims to the criminal justice system), the collusion of the movement with security forces reflects the way in which SlutWalk was built around the privileged "white activist subject" (Gordon).

EMPTY PLURALISM: FROM SLUTWALK TO FEMEN

SlutWalks have taken place in Canada, the United States, the United Kingdom, Australia, India, Brazil, Singapore, Israel, South Korea, Poland and beyond. Amazed by its popular appeal, some feminist bloggers agree with Jos Truitt, remark that, "SlutWalks is one of the best things to happen to feminism in decades." But it is clear that as the SlutWalk platform has been taken up globally, participants and organizers have had different relationships to the reclamation of "slut" and the use of raunch to resist slut-shaming and victim-blaming. While the original SlutWalk has responded to critiques by adding language of inclusivity and global diversity, it has failed to respond to the ways in which SlutWalk has been taken up globally *at home*. That is, while SlutWalk is now global, it continues to fail to be *transnational*. With an opportunity to build coalitions of women across borders in the interest of ending violence against women and girls, SlutWalk attachment to the term slut and lack of attention to power and difference has meant that the movement embraces what Mohanty calls "empty pluralism." Without attending to asymmetrical power relations between the North/South, in particular, the movement fails to think transnationally domestically. As The Association of Filipinas, Feminists Fighting Imperialism, Re-feudalization, and Marginalization claim, the term slut has become integrated into languages and cultures through colonialism and imperialism, and has built systems of power on the exploitation of women's bodies that SlutWalk fails to address. If ending violence against women, slut-shaming, and victim-blaming globally is the ultimate aim of SlutWalk, it must attend to the "structurally racist and sexist US society, as well as transplanted cultures from our families' countries of origin," and the manifestations of racist, classist, ableist, and gendered violence globally.

In some ways, raunch as a tool of resistance in SlutWalk is not that different from that leveraged by the activist group FEMEN, although many feminists have rejected FEMEN's strategic use of raunch. In 2008, a group of young women in Ukraine called FEMEN deployed raunch in a series of topless and bikini-clad protests against sex tourists. Garnering international attention, FEMEN has since expanded its protest sites, goals, and headquarters (to Kiev and Paris), aiming to "fight the Patriarchy in its three manifestations—sexual exploitation of women, dictatorship, and religion" ("Femen Activists"). The group has been the centre of huge controversy over their tactics, from anti-Muslim extremism to questionable financing practices. In 2013, FEMEN announced "topless jihad day," triggering a group of young Muslim women to form Muslim Women Against Femen. The Muslim group launched a Facebook page featuring women holding signs reading such slogans as "FEMEN does not represent my freedom," "Do I look like I need imperialists to free me?" and "Femen can't tell me what I can and can't wear" (Nelson). Assembling around the hashtag #Muslimahpride, the response by Muslim Women Against Femen was picked up by a *Huffington Post* poll that asked which organization "has feminism right?" As a relatively shocking and explicitly anti-Muslim example of raunch-as-tactic, FEMEN exemplifies how raunch fails to escape racist underpinnings, regardless of how it might be helpful for shifting other discursive formations around (white) women's bodies. Made overt by FEMEN's conventionally attractive, thin, young, able-bodied front-women, FEMEN represents a narrow strand of feminism that is not only exclusionary but precludes transnational and intersectional efforts.

The lack of attention paid to the power and privilege associated with raunch tactics in the SlutWalk movement has also relied on Islamophobic messaging, albeit while attempting to be inclusive. Lim and Fanghanel claim that in this smaller bloc of the march, that Muslim women's bodies were positioned as anti-thesis to the "slutty dressed" women in miniskirts who walked in the main march. Speaking to a group of people who marched in this offshoot, Lim and Fanghanel reveal discursive schemes employed by some who rejected the reclamation of the term slut. As the authors suggest, the claim made by a marcher that "even Muslim women who are veiled get raped" functions to situate the veiled Muslim female body as little more than a figure to claim that "rape has nothing to do with what you wear," rather than agents in their own understanding and experiences of sexual violence and the meaningfulness of the term slut to their participation.

IM/POSSIBILITIES: LANGUAGE AND NEWS MEDIA

Since the first Toronto SlutWalk in 2011, the terms "slut-shaming" and "rape culture" have circulated widely in popular news media. While keyword searches turn up coverage of the SlutWalk itself, news media outlets have also begun to use these concepts in framing other stories. Before the original Toronto SlutWalk in April 2011, major Canadian daily newspapers covered the issue of slut-shaming six times. After April 2011, slut-shaming was covered in 50 articles.[8] While the SlutWalk did not create the language of slut-shaming, we suggest that the coverage of the movement has aided in the mainstreaming of the language of slut-shaming in response to rape culture. While we maintain that raunch functions in SlutWalk as racist and ableist, while also being underpinned by neoliberal choice and even anti-feminist rhetoric, the ability of the movement to gain mainstream coverage via raunch culture has had positive and feminist effects. As a platform, the SlutWalk movement has opened up possibilities for re-framing coverage of violence against women and girls.

Most recently, popular news media coverage of "sexting" and cyberbullying use the term slut-shaming. While not all coverage of cyberbullying includes information or analysis on the connections between misogyny, sexual violence, and slut-shaming, where the gendered implications of online harassment are considered, we are seeing more connection being made between online harassment and victim-blaming. For example, media coverage of Rehtaeh Parsons (who died as a result of a suicide attempt after a digital photo depicting a brutal sexual attack was circulated at school and on social media) often uses the terms slut and slut-shaming to describe the way she was harassed online, and continues to be harassed postmortem (Hodge "RIP"). *The Globe and Mail* printed an opinion editorial written by Elizabeth Renzetti who carefully quoted a Facebook post by Parsons' mother claiming that because her daughter's attackers had a "slut story" she was seen as a "slut," and thus deemed deserving of being raped and all the violence that followed by way of the attackers' distribution of the photos. Asking "Is all this slut-shaming and vile video-sharing any worse than it ever was?" Renzetti's editorial is one of many mainstream media responses that employed the term slut-shaming and discourses of victim-blaming to resist violence against girls understood as "slutty" and "asking for it."

In October 2012, a white 15-year-old girl from Port Coquitlam, British Columbia died by suicide after posting a YouTube video called *My Story: Struggling, bullying, suicide, and self-harm.*

Using flash cards, Amanda Todd told the story of her being blackmailed, bullied, and assaulted. After the video had gone viral and police launched an investigation into her suicide, BC Premier Christy Clark called for a national discussion on criminalizing cyberbullying (Fowlie). But as cyberbullying became a common discursive thread in the coverage of Todd's death (see Szalavitz), a debate emerged, even in mainstream reports, over whether the reason for her death might better be termed systemic sexism (Hodge "Bullying"). Feminist blogs, such as *Feministing* (Shireen), SACE, and *Hook and Eye* (Morrison), explain that the de-gendered language of "bullying" disguises how Amanda Todd was a victim of slut-shaming, victim-blaming, and misogyny. In Todd's case, the language of slut-shaming and victim-blaming was front and centre as news outlets tried to interpret her tragic death (see Wolf).

From commentary in the *National Post* (Newcomb) and *The Gazette* (Sklar) about cyberbullying, to a *Calgary Herald* (Fowles) report on a new course at the Vancouver School of Economics called "The Economics of Sex and Love," to discussion of *Twilight* actress Kristen Stewart's infidelity in the *Ottawa Citizen* (see "One night with Lainey"), "slut-shaming" has emerged as a buzzword to describe victim-blaming that centers on women and girls' sexuality. Yet, as critical race feminist bloggers have pointed out, the way in which "slut-shaming" is used in mainstream news continues to obscure the intersections of race and gender in women and girl's experience of slut-shaming. Mirroring the failures of the SlutWalk, the mainstream focus on victim-blaming in relation to Amanda Todd and Rehtaeh Parsons has meant that claims to "this is what rape culture looks like" are, in fact, a white-washing of women's varied experiences of interpersonal and state-sponsored violence and victim-blaming. While important for anti-violence movements, the hyper-visibility of Todd and Parsons in mainstream media coverage has meant that violence against racialized women and girls continues to go ignored. For example, according to critical race blog *Gradient Lair*, conversations around rape remain white, even though both black men and women in the U.S. have an asymmetrical relationship to rape culture and the criminal justice system, which purports to support survivors of gendered violence. In the Canadian context, in particular, the visibility of "slut-shaming" in relation to cyberbullying does little to explain ongoing violence against Indigenous women and girls nationally. As Jiwani and Young's research articulates, Indigenous women and sex-workers are slut-shamed and understood as deserving of violence in Vancouver's Downtown Eastside, and yet the main-streaming of slut-shaming has not made this violence more visible to the mainstream. In fact, the hyper-visibility of young, white women works to further marginalize the most marginal, and the mainstreaming of slut-shaming in public discourses by way of the popularity of the SlutWalk movement globally does not necessarily result in meaningful change for most bodies; it can actually serve to normalize or neutralize social conditions.

CONCLUSION

We have attempted to consider the ways in which SlutWalk has been a successful movement, a site of controversy, and an on-going transnational dialogue on women's bodies, sexuality, and persistent violence perpetuated against women and girls. Here we have shown how SlutWalk's use of raunch is complicated, as it resists slut-shaming while employing a strand of feminism that has foundations in white supremacy and able-bodied activism. As revealed by Slutwalk's offshoot marches and rebranding globally, raunch is not a tool that can be taken up by women universally. Holding on to feminist critiques of Slutwalk, this chapter also explored the ways in which mainstream media coverage of "raun-chy feminism" helped to bring feminist critiques of rape culture, particularly slut-shaming and victim-blaming, into mainstream discussions of girl tragedies. Taking seriously the possibilities for raunch-y feminism, we also mapped the ways in which particular girl tragedies (read: white, able-bodied) were publicized over others in relation to raunch-induced public dialogue on rape culture in North America.

Feminists who are critical of SlutWalk call for a "re-branding and re-labeling process" (Black Women's Blueprint) that goes beyond simply adding inclusive language to websites and call-outs. Perhaps in an effort to respond, SlutWalk Toronto now sells T-shirts that claim "Stop Policing Our Bodies" and list "victim-blaming, heterosexism, misogyny, slut-shaming, cissex- ism, patriarchy, racism, ableism" as "many of the intersections that support and condone sexual violence." As intersectional feminist blogger Haifisch Geweint notes in *A Brief History of SlutWalk Racism*, such initiatives can read like an attempt not to appear racist, rather than a genuine effort to reconceptualize the movement. Whether SlutWalks around the world (but par- ticularly white, Western incarnations) are able to contend with and sufficiently respond to these critiques remains to be seen, as do the real impacts of SlutWalk's discursive contributions to the experiences of gendered violence across lines of race, class, sexuality, and ability. Yet, as some mainstream publications shift their reporting style on violence against women and girls to reflect the sexist context of slut-shaming and victim-blaming, especially in a context where raunch has gained the SlutWalk movement mainstream media attention, naming rape culture gives future feminist movements something concrete around which to rally.

ENDNOTES

[1] While exploring various strands of postfeminism is beyond the scope of this chapter, the so-called postfeminist and "do-me" at- titude popularized in mainstream media in the 1990s and 2000s, however superficially by anti-feminist journalists like Tad Friend and Danielle Crittenden, embraced the pursuit of sexual desire over formally political aims. Denouncing the "man-hating" "se- riousness" of feminist struggles before them, young women of the 1990s were seen as lustful, light-hearted, and individualist (Zeisler). Journalist Jennifer Weiner laments what she calls the "do-me" feminist manifesto: "A lot of us just want to go spray paint and make out with our boyfriends and not worry about oppression." [2] See, for example, "Our love is militant" collaborative photograph (Shash, Kidane, and Khan). [3] True to "do-me" feminist critiques, Ke$ha's lyrics simultaneously resist sexual policing while affirming the apolitical pro-materialist campaign—her "going h-h-hard" with "hot pants" and "glitter" is intentionally in opposition to "being so serious."

[4]Walia echoes what Mohanty and other critical race feminists have argued: the assumption that all women share experiences of patriarchy ignores the ways in which women are stratified by race, gender, class, sexuality, disability, and global systems of power including colonialism and imperialism.

[5]Please refer to the introductory chapter for a detailed discussion of Black Women's Blueprint and their critique.

[6]Gwynne suggests that the cultural climate of xenophobia was also a major target of the movement. In statements made about local incidents of sexual violence, Gwynne maintains that there is an assumption that because of low sexual violence crime statistics (the government does not collect them), the general populace is quick to blame foreigners for committing rape as equally as they blame women for being dressed "provocatively" or for being drunk. In Singapore, racism targeted at Bangladeshi men, in a context of large numbers of foreign workers, intersects with patriarchal beliefs about women's sexuality.

[7]Like Borah, Kapur maintains that SlutWalk ignores the post-colonial context of India, especially the figure of the "good woman" in the context of struggles for independence. Kapur argues that the intersections of local patriarchies, nationalisms, and histories of colonization meant that women were represented as needing their honour and chastity protected in coverage of the SlutWalk.

[8]A database of major Canadian daily newspapers, which included *The Toronto Star, The Montreal Gazette*, and *The Vancouver Sun,* was searched.

WORKS CITED

Anderson, Kim. "The Construction of a Negative Identity." *Gender and Women's Studies in Canada: A Critical Terrain*. Ed. Margaret Hobbs and Carla Rice. Toronto: The Women's Press, 2013. 269-279. Print.

Association of Filipinas, Feminists Fighting Imperialism, Re-feudalization, and Marginalization. "Women of Color Respond to SlutWalk: 'The Women's Movement is Not Monochromatic.'" *Bermuda Radical*. N.pub. 1 Oct. 2011. Web. 1 Sept. 2013.

B. Amanda. "Slut Shaming," *Know Your Meme*. N.pub. 2 Aug.

2013. Web. 29 Aug. 2013.

Black Women's Blueprint. "An Open Letter from Black Women to the SlutWalk" *NewBlackMan (in Exile)*. N.pub. 23 Sept. 2011. Web. 1 Sept. 2013

Borah, Rituparna. "Reclaiming the Politics of SlutWalk." *International Feminist Journal of Politics* 14.3 (2012): 415–421. Web. 2 Sept. 2013.

Crittenden, Danielle. *What our Mothers Didn't Tell Us*. New York: Touchstone, 1999. Print.

Davis, Allison. "The Taylor Swift Slut-shaming Continues." *New York Magazine*. 28 June 2013. Web. 4 Sept. 2013

Dean, Michelle. "The Story of Amanda Todd." *The New Yorker*. 18 Oct. 2012. Web. Sept. 13 2013

"Femen Activists Jailed in Tunisia for Topless Protest." *BBC News Africa*. 12 June 2013. Web. 1 Sept. 2013.

Filipovic, Jill. Offensive Feminism: The Conservative Gender Norms That Perpetuate Rape Culture, and How Feminists Can Fight Back." *Yes Means Yes: Visions of Female Sexual Empowerment and a World Without Rape*. Ed. J. Friedman and J. Valenti. Berkeley, CA: Seal Press, 2008. 13-28. Print.

Fowles, Stacey May. "Are Origins of Love Found In Our Bank Accounts? Book Explores Motivations for Romance, Sex." *Calgary Herald*. 16 Mar. 2013. Web. 8 Sept. 2013.

Fowlie, Jonathan. "After Amanda Todd's Death, Christie Clark Says New Laws May Be Needed to Combat Cyber Bullying." *Vancouver Sun*. 13 Oct. 2012. Web. 1 Sept. 2013

Friedman, Jaclyn. "In Defense of Going Wild or: How I Stopped Worrying and Learned to Love Pleasure (and How You Can, Too)." *Yes Means Yes*. Ed. J. Friedman and J. Valenti. Berkeley, CA: Seal Press, 2008. 313-320. Print.

Friend, Tad. "Feminist Women Who Like Sex" *Esquire Magazine* (1994). Print.

Geweint, Haifisch. "A Brief History of SlutWalk Racism." *Haifischgeweint*. N.pub. 12 May 2013. Web. 20 Nov. 2013

Gordon, Joanne. "Birthing a Movement? Negotiating the Mother Subject through Activist Mama Zines." Unpublished paper. University of Ottawa, 2013. Print.

Gradient Lair. "Why the Rape Joke Conversation Remains a

White Conversation." *Gradient Lair* N.pub. 8 June 2013. Web. 20 Nov. 2013.

Gwynne, Joel. "Slutwalk, Feminist Activism and the Foreign Body in Singapore." *Journal of Contemporary Asia* 43.1 (2013): 173-185. Web. 3 Sept. 2013.

Greer, Germaine. *The Whole Woman*. London: Transworld Publishers, 1999. Print.

Halberstam, Jack. "The Summer of Raunch." *Bully Bloggers*. N.pub. 16 July 2011. Web. 1 Sept. 2013.

Halberstam, Jack. *Gaga Feminism: Sex, Gender, and the End of Normal*. Boston: Beacon Press, 2012. Print.

Hite, Shere. *The Hite Report on Female Sexuality*. Toronto: Publishers Group Canada, 1976. Print.

Hodge, Jarrah. "Calling It Bullying Doesn't Do Amanda Todd Justice." *Huffington Post*. 13 Oct. 2012. Web. 1 Sept. 2013.

Hodge, Jarrah. "RIP Rehtaeh Parsons: Victim of Victim-blaming," *Gender Focus*. N.pub. 9 Apr. 2013. Web. 4 Sept. 2013.

Jiwani, Yasmin and Mary Lynn Young. "Missing and Murdered Women: Reproducing Marginality in News Discourse." *Canadian Journal of Communication* 31 (2006): 895-917. Web. 13 Sept. 2013.

Kapur, Ratna. "Pink Chaddis and SlutWalk Couture: The Postcolonial Politics of Feminism Lite." *Feminist Legal Studies* 20 (2012): 1–20. Web. 6 Sept. 2013.

Koedt, Anne. *The Myth of the Vaginal Orgasm*. New York: New York Radical Women, 1968. Print.

Lang, Nico. " 'Trampire': Why the Public Slut Shaming of Kristen Stewart Matters for Young Women." *Huffington Post*. 4 Sept. 2012. Web. 4 Sept. 2013.

Levy, Alon. "Slut Shaming." *Abstract Nonsense*. N.pub. 4 Nov. 2011. Web. 1 Sept. 2013.

Lim, Jason, and Alexandra Fanghanel. "'Hijabs, Hoodies and Hotpants'; Negotiating the 'Slut' in SlutWalk." *Geoforum* 48 (2013): 207-215. Web. 4 Sept. 2013.

Mohanty, Chandra Talpade. *Feminism without Borders: Decolonizing Theory, Practicing Solidarity*. Durham: Duke University Press, 2013. Print.

Morrison, Aimee. "Amanda Todd: The Problem Is Sexism, Not

the Internet." *Hook and Eye* N.pub. 17 Oct. 2012. Web. 20 Nov. 2013

Murphy, Meghan. "Link Round-Up: Feminist Critiques of Slut-Walk." *Feminist Frequency: Feminist Conversations with Pop Culture*. N.pub. 16 May 2011. Web. 1 Sept 2013

Nelson, Sara. "Muslim Women Against Femen: Facebook Group Takes On Activists in Wake of Amina Tyler Topless Jihad." *Huffington Post UK*. 4 May 2013. Web. 1 Sept. 2013

Newcomb, Sarah Sweet. "Another Story of Small-town Slut-shaming." *National Post*. 16 Apr. 2013. Web. 20 Nov. 2013.

Olen, Helaine. "Failure of Do-Me Feminism." *Forbes*. Forbes Magazine. 14 Aug. 2012. Web. 1 Sept. 2013.

"One night with Lainey: Celebrity gossip maven meets Ottawa fans." *The Ottawa Citizen*. 4 August 2012. Web. Sept 8, 2013.

"Rape Cutlure." *Force: Upsetting Rape Culture*. 2012. Web. May 5, 2014.

Renzetti, Elizabeth. "Rehtaeh Parsons Shows Connectedness has Driven Us Apart." *Globe and Mail*. 12 Apr. 2013. Web. 1 Sept. 2013.

Sexual Assault Centre of Edmonton (SACE). "Amanda Todd and the Degendered Language of Bullying." *SACE Blog*. N.pub. 19 Oct 2012. Web. 1 Sept. 2013.

Scott, Jennifer. "Thoughts on SlutWalk From a Wheelchair." *Ms. Magazine Blog*. Ms. Magazine. 11 Oct. 2011. Web. 1 Sept. 2013.

Shash, Nabil, Luam Kidane, and Janaya Khan. "Our Love is Militant." *Soulful and True*. N.pub. 2012. Web. 20 Nov. 2013

Shireen. "On Slut-shaming, Victim Blaming, and Sexuality Bullying," *Feministing*. N.pub. 4 Nov. 2012. Web. 1 Sept. 2013

Sklar, Alissa. "Opinion: Parents, Educators Need To Be More Proactive In Dealing With Online Sexual Exploitation," *Montreal Gazette*. 22 Apr. 2013. Web. 20 Nov. 2013.

SlutWalk Toronto. 2012. Web. 8 Sept. 2013

Smith, Andrea. *Sexual Violence and American Indian Genocide*. Boston: South End Press, 2005. Print.

Szalavitz, Maia. "The Tragic Case of Amanda Todd." *Time*. 16 Oct. 2012. Web. 20 Nov. 2013

Truit, Jos. "Slutwalk redux with Rebecca Traister and Feministing writers." *Feministing*. Web. 20 July. 2011.

Walia, Harsha. "Slutwalk—To March or Not To March." *Feministing*. N.pub. 18 May 2011. Web. 1 Sept. 2013

Watson, Amanda Danielle. "The SlutWalk Paradox." *Ottawa Citizen*. 17 Aug. 2012. Web. 1 Sept 2013

Weiner, Jennifer. "Beating Swords into Bustiers—Is 'Do Me' Feminism the Future?" *Philly.com*. 3 Mar. 1994. Web. 20 Nov. 2013

West, Lindy. "Rihanna Does Whatever She Wants with Her Vagina and For Some Reason That's A Problem." *Jezebel*. N.pub. 17 May 2012. Web. 4 Sept. 2013.

Wolf, Naomi. "Amanda Todd's Suicide and Social Media's Sexualization of Youth Culture." *Guardian*. 26 Oct. 2012. Web. 1 Sept. 2013

Women of Hamilton Against Patriarchy. "Dear Hamilton Slutwalk Organizers." *Tumblr*. 30 May 2013. Web. 1 Sept. 2013

World Health Organization (WHO) and the World Bank. *World Report on Disability*. Geneva, Switzerland: World Health Organization Press, 2011. Print.

Yates, Clinton. "Miley Cyrus and the Issue of Slut-Shaming and Racial Condescension," *Washington Post*. 26 Aug. 2013. Web. 4 Sept. 2013.

Ziesler, Andi. *Feminism and Pop Culture*. Berkeley, CA: Seal Press, 2008. Print.

This Is What a Feminist Looks Like

An Understanding of the SlutWalk Movement through Internet Commentary

NORAH JONES AND MARGARET K. NELSON

A S THE SLUTWALK MOVEMENT addressed its core issues of rape culture and victim-blaming, it also incited a wave of commentary on the topics of female sexuality, the reappropriation of language, and the inclusivity of the feminist movement. Controversies about these issues—central to feminist debate for generations—now take place on the wide stage of the Internet. In an analysis of that wider discourse, focused specifically on SlutWalk New York City, we suggest that SlutWalk generates an overarching unity that allows the discordant voices of feminism to have their say while expressing commitment to a common cause.

SlutWalk New York City took place on October 1, 2011. The event attracted 3,000-4,000 participants and involved a march and a rally featuring music and speakers. Following the walk the Internet blossomed with commentary. The analysis in this chapter relies primarily on a random selection of 50 websites (and the attached commentary) from the first 200 items that emerged from a Google search using the words "Slutwalk NYC."[1] The 50 websites represent a variety of different forms, including personal blogs, Facebook pages, and social media sites like Tumblr or Flickr. In what follow, all comments and blog quotes are left in their original form; we did not correct grammar, punctuation, or spelling.

CENTRAL ISSUES OF DEBATE

Re-claiming Female Sexuality; Resisting Objectification
While being clear about being their anti-*rape* position, protestors

showed a desire to be certain that their message was not anti-*sex*. On the SlutWalk New York City website, organizers claimed that the "fight for a culture without rape" is a fight for "sex positivity," "body positivity," and "sexual freedom" and they stated explicitly that "[t]here is room in the world for an aggressively sex-positive feminism, and SlutWalk embodies the best of it."[2] At the event itself, pro-sex messages were prevalent with many participants carrying signs reading "consent is sexy" while other marchers wrote the phrase on their half-naked bodies. Nevertheless, the meaning of female sexuality became a contentious issue of subsequent Internet commentary and evoked earlier debates about sex and the objectification of women.

Some individuals posting comments in response to SlutWalk NYC drew on a quite traditional, liberal feminist ideology as they employed the rhetoric of choice and personal control to describe their sexual identities: "The SlutWalk is all about us reclaiming our own bodies. Our right to decide what we want to do with our own bodies. Not the state, not other people, not right wingers."[3] Others expanded the pro-sex message into what appeared to be a more radical feminist vein to include a broader definition of sex, citing queer sex in opposition to standard heterosexuality which they understood to be male-dominated sex:

A SlutWalk goal of mine is to normalize and broaden our conceptions of female sexuality, male sexuality, trans sexuality, etc. in all their diversity and potentiality, and to not reflexively vilify sex as "evil" or reduce it to the most petrified, uptight, TAUGHT (as opposed to natural) "male" standard of attack-penetrate-flee. Male sexuality is not more legitimate than female sexuality. Straight sex is not more special than queer sex.[4]

The word slut became part of the effort to reclaim female sexuality as posters on the Internet noted that the word itself appeared to contain a prissy condemnation of female sexuality. These posters drew on what were assumed to be common experiences of slut-shaming emerging from sexual behaviour and dress: "So many of us know how it feels to be shamed, ridiculed, or cast aside because we violated another person's definition of acceptable sexual behavior"[5]; "Anyone can be a slut. The most respected, powerful woman can be degraded down to nothing because of what she's wearing."[6] In addition, commenters suggested that SlutWalk New York City itself could be understood as an occasion for women to end these incidents and participate in a movement "for women to feel free to express their sexuality without 'slut-shaming.'"[7]

As some posters discussing the NYC event drew on a broad range of feminist viewpoints to celebrate female sexuality through SlutWalks, others argued a quite different point. They suggested that by dressing in provocative and sexually explicit clothing, protestors were participating in misogynistic structures that objectify women. These individuals claimed that the SlutWalks themselves actually supported the rape culture that the movement purported to fight because they put forth individual, rather than collective, responses to rape culture and allowed (or even reinvigorated) that culture:

> Individual solutions that focus on women's behavior—whether in celebrating a behavior that conforms to male fantasy in the affirmation of slut, or in instructing women to dress appropriately and avoid strange men (most rapes happen between acquaintances and/or in relationships with men!), are flip sides of the same problem.[8]

In the same vein, some argued that dressing provocatively propagates the message that women are only valuable in a sexual context. Furthermore, they argued that such clothing buys into rather than resists the objectification of women and is a special problem when it is combined with what some perceived to be too much emphasis on female sexuality, especially among young children. As one individual wrote, "Pagents in the south dress 5 years olds like 'sluts' and it is becoming more and more popular. Recently, one of these children was outfitted with false breasts. There is work to be done. Slutwalks are not the way to do it."[9]

Some posters even argued that presenting women in a sexual manner was anti-feminist because it went against how earlier feminist protestors fought not to be understood only through the lens of sex. "Does anyone else see how this is doing nothing but setting the women's movement back and makes absolutely no sense?"[10] Similarly, some argued that the protestors' skimpy clothing de-legitimized their voices:

> I think the name takes away from the intent, as does the code of dress. Who is going to take a woman seriously that is standing in her underwear, in public, yelling about being a slut? Yes, it is against the law for her to be accosted, despite her behavior, but it certainly brings her down as a respectable human being worthy of being taken seriously in other aspects of her life.[11]

Others further argued that the advice that the Toronto police officer gave was relevant and legitimate: "If you walk into a biker bar and get beat up, whose fault is it? If you dress up like a prostitute, why do you believe you should be respected?"[12] In so doing, this set of commenters disputed the position of the organizers who claimed that rape is never a result of any action taken by the victim. In an interesting response to this set of concerns, one commenter located those concerns within the historical context of second-wave feminism, with which she appeared to agree:

> Second-wave feminists, in my experience, have tended to take a less sex-positive, more male-resistant stance, which I get and I dig and I accept. Because when you've been oppressed by a male sexist society that milks you for your "sexiness," before throwing you to the wind, I understand the protective resentment to sexuality, as you've perceived it.[13]

In short, on one side commenters responding to issues raised about SlutWalk NYC drew on a variety of feminist perspectives to argue women's rights to express and control their own sexuality and thereby to transcend the virgin/whore dichotomy. On the other side, commenters argued from diverse perspectives that the sexual expression displayed at SlutWalk was problematic: In representing themselves as sexual beings, Slutwalk participants were participating in their own objectification, trivializing their concerns, and putting themselves at risk. While the former group believed the method of SlutWalks was essential to its message, those on the other side thought that the provocative dress was a poorly chosen method used to draw attention from the "real purpose" of ending a culture that supports rape.

Reappropriation of the Term Slut

The issue of the "real purpose" of the movement also emerged around the use of the term slut in the title of the event in New York City, as was the case elsewhere. The debate about this issue echoes other historical moments of reclamation of derogatory terms for minority groups.

Those in favour of the attempt to reappropriate the word explained it as "taking back derogatory terms for sexual liberalization."[14] As one person said, "A term only has the power to harm if it is used as a derogatory term. When you own it, it isn't offensive anymore."[15] Others noted that using the term wasn't just about taking the negative connotation out of one word, but was also about exposing a system that creates and continually uses language that demeans women and vilifies them for having sexual desires: "I wanted to ridicule it, I wanted to suck the venom out of it, I wanted to be confrontational and unapologetic for owning my sexuality, I wanted to turn the word on its head, and expose why it exists in the first place."[16] Still others argued that using the term would denude it of its power to be divisive. Commenters like this believed that feminists had to find ways to resist divisions based on whether the sexual behaviour one engaged in was perceived as being appropriate by others:

> Feminists have yet to effectively challenge the way women are split into the respectable and the disreputable. As long as that split remains, it will encourage the dehumanization and disposability of women framed as "sluts" and "hos," while encouraging other women to be complicit in order to hold onto their "respectability."[17]

Another poster noted that when women were engaged in name calling, they were all at risk of being the victims of patriarchy:

"None of us are made any safer by making the distinction between the 'good feminists' and the 'sluts.' When we make that distinction we can easily throw ourselves under the patriarchal bus."[18]

Commenters on SlutWalk NYC repeatedly emphasized that they should be focusing their efforts on fighting forces that seek to divide them instead of fighting each other. In fact, some argued that the SlutWalk moniker, despite its controversial nature, could actually be a force for just this unification: "Our organizers wanted to tap into something that was powerful and transnational, something that obviously resonated with a lot of people"[19]; "Almost every woman out there has been called a slut at some point in her life. She's probably called another woman a slut, too. Because so many women know what it feels like to have that word thrown at them, the SlutWalk phenomenon has caught fire."[20]

On the other side of the reappropriation issue, many posters felt that the term slut either couldn't or shouldn't be reclaimed. Some commenters made arguments using previous reappropriation situations as evidence against the title, noting that there is a difference between reclaiming a word for use within a minority community and publicly protesting under that title (Gamson): "Well we could always re-name Gay Pride 'Fag Walk.'"[21]

In an argument similar to those who claimed that by wearing sexy clothing women were risking their own objectification, some opponents to the term argued that in adopting the language of oppression, women were defining themselves by an over-sexualized, misogynistic standard:

> This ancient curse will not go away just because a few women think it's okay to reclaim the status of "slut." When we reclaim that status as being our own, we have just bought into the depiction of women as bitches, whores and sex slaves who are nothing more than chattel to be bought, sold and exploited; and we will continue to be raped, tortured and killed at an ever increasing rate, as human life becomes cheaper and more expendable with each passing moment.[22]

In an even more dismissive way, some posters declared that the term couldn't be reclaimed because no one should be proud to claim inclusion in that category:

> Furthermore, I don't want the word slut to be a good thing. Yes, I think women should be able to sleep with as many men as they want, whether it's a low number or a high number, because that's their choice and yes women actually enjoy sex. BUT I do think there are many women out there called "sluts" who DO give women a bad name. The woman who sleeps with a man because he bought her dinner. Or he treats her like a jerk but she still sleeps with him to try and win his attention. Those are not positives.[23]

Indeed, this commenter suggested that some women do still deserve the word slut, but insisted also that the word should be reserved for those who trade sexual favours for affection or material rewards. In so doing, the writer is challenging the more common application of the term to someone another believes is engaging in "too much" sexual activity.

Finally, in another echo of the debates about sexuality and provocative clothing, some commenters argued that the issue of reappropriation was irrelevant to, and less important than, the "true purpose" of the movement. One poster wrote, "Instead of perpetuating a terrible word and making it 'trendy,' focus on ways from preventing rape. I just see all of this backfiring, even though it's being done with good intentions."[24] And another said, "It's unfortunate that Slutwalk's become a movement that seems to be 'claiming' the word slut. The original impetus was stronger than that."[25]

Posters who believed that the name was problematic found inspiration in the way that SlutWalk events in other places had been presented with quite different language. One poster pointed out that, "They changed the name in New Delhi and many other places around the world, which shows how the message resonates, but not the moniker."[26] Others argued that changing the name was a solution that took the reappropriation issue out of the protest altogether: "Today I went to the first Bristol (UK) slutwalk—the people organising it also didn't really want to reclaim the word 'slut' and so in the publicity and on the blog the word is crossed out, a visual which I think sends a strong message."[27] Comments like these seek to remind the reader that the overall goal of the movement is more important than the issue of language. For these posters, debates about language are missing the point.

Inclusivity: Women of Colour Feminism

To some commenters, language itself represented the key issue of inclusivity. The organizers of the NYC event appear to have been extremely concerned about including all women. In a video produced before the event, they explained their motives and encouraged participation: "A big third-wave feminist thing is inclusivity and benevolent interest in all stripes of justice-seekers be they gay, straight, trans, female, male, many races, ethnicities, ages, and abilities. That's cool."[28] Both in this video and on other occasions some of the organizers mentioned their own non-normative social location. In so doing, they emphasized the perceived importance of having a wide variety of feminists participate in the event: "I'm a queer woman of color, and I think it's important to put my voice into the feminist movement because queer women of color are often overlooked or marginalized."[29]

This call did not satisfy everyone. Black Women's Blueprint's letter[30] spoke from a historical perspective that suggested there was a racial significance to the term slut that a simple event (or even a series of events) could not eliminate: "We don't have the privilege to play on destructive representations burned in our collective minds, on our bodies and souls for generations."[31]

Three blog posts within the sample were specifically written about this letter (HipHopWired, The Huffington Post, and the Ms. Magazine blog). Comments on these articles highlighted the contentious issue of race with both support and criticism of the Black feminists' letter. Those who agreed with the letter's critique of the movement's name sarcastically claimed that the majority of organizers were white and therefore ignorant of the privilege that participation in this event assumed: "Of course these white, priviliged, oh so open-minded and progressive girls live on another planet and would never understand."[32] Comments like these frequently minimized the efforts put into creating the protest. "It's a lot easy for giddy college girl 'activists' of more privileged ethnicities to pull this off than black women."[33] Additionally, they compared the walk to what they deemed the more productive and important work for feminism. As one protester wrote, "This event will not stop the criminalization of black women in New Orleans, nor will it stop one woman from being potentially deported after she calls the police subsequent to being raped."[34]

On the other side of the debate, those who disagreed with the Black feminist critique of the event argued that the protest had universal relevance and that women of colour should add their voices to it, rather than detracting from it. Some of those who disagreed trivialized the complaints of women of colour and urged them not to divert attention to the issues of race: "Give me a break. This isn't about race. If you want a 'space' in the SlutWalk movement, quit complaining and make one"[35]; "Ok black people, if you wanna get involved in the slutwalk, get involved. Don't turn it into a 'woe is me, black people are excluded again' symphony. This is about people not how does asian, blacks, indians, and hispanics, middle easterners fit into this equation, good grief!"[36] Some even became quite hostile as they suggested that the focus on race undermined the unity of feminism: "I thought that the Slutwalk was because all women were included in the officer's stupid comment, so are the 'black' women somehow not women, or do they claim special professional victim status not enjoyed by women who are not 'black'? How's this—if you want to claim status as a woman, just join in and march; if you prefer to be 'black', just stay home and whine."[37]

Although they restate the ideal that the SlutWalk movement was an inclusive one, the actual tone of these comments often contradicts that ideal in its open anger and hostility toward the notion of racialized people having distinctive concerns that need to be addressed in separate forums. Other, less hostile comments emphasized the idea that the Black Women's Blueprint was not speaking for all Women of Colour. While the nature of anonymous Internet debate prevents us from knowing the details of commenters' identities, several comments criticizing the letter were prefaced by claims of racialized identities.

More frequent than hostility, however, were comments that were either conciliatory or stressed that racial discussions were beside the point as the discussion circled back to the idea that the "real message" of the movement was anti-rape and anti-victim-blaming. In fact, organizers responded directly to the Black Women's Blueprint by reiterating their focus on inclusivity:

> Focusing SlutWalk NYC on sexual violence in all communities is to provide a safe space for everyone affected, and in particular marginalized populations who have felt disconnected from this particular movement, to speak out against victim blaming. I do understand the critiques of SlutWalk based on racial privilege and agree that, as a white organizer, I need to continue to investigate my own unearned privilege. It has been extremely important to us at SlutWalk NYC that people of color who have issues with SlutWalk feel comfortable approaching us and engaging in these important dialogues.[38]

CONCLUSION

The most obvious finding of this analysis is that almost every aspect of SlutWalk NYC engendered disagreement. Conflicts extended from who felt comfortable participating to what protestors should be wearing to the name of the event itself. Blog posts and comments clearly came from multiple sides of every issue. Every opinion generated voices in support and in opposition, and no clear winners or losers emerged from these debates. Indeed, this is not surprising: the Internet allows for both dialogue and debate.

Some of the comments about SlutWalk represent the most problematic of the possibilities created by the Internet. As many have noted, because online discussions are mostly anonymous, they often produce "a state of loss of self-awareness, lowered social inhibitions, and increased impulsivity" (Kabay). Whereas in person people censor themselves so as to avoid unpleasant consequences, in online settings people often engage in extreme rudeness and spiteful behaviour (Suler). Occasionally this was true in the debates considered here, especially around issues of race and inclusion.

The comments about SlutWalk also represent the best the Internet has to offer. In contrast to those who argue that anonymity creates rancorous debate, some argue that anonymity promotes a *democratic* debate because it places all participants on an equal footing (Papacharissi). Indeed, some studies of political discourse in online communities suggest that civility emerges when a collective base ideological belief in democratic principles informs the behaviour of commenters (Hill and Hughes). And this seems true of much of the online commentary on SlutWalk: often the disagreements remained remarkably respectful, with what can be defined as "collective politeness, with consideration for the democratic consequences of impolite behavior" (Papacharissi 10).

Beyond mentioning disagreements handled with both rancor and civility, we want to note two other findings that can be drawn from this analysis. First, we find that even though the SlutWalk movement is a recently developed manifestation of feminist protest, the conflicts represented in the contemporary commentary echo differences in feminist theory that have been present within the larger feminist movement since its inception (Jaggar and Rothenberg). As noted, these disagreements revolve around debates concerning the sexual empowerment of women versus the objectification of women, about the importance of language and reclaiming derogatory terms, and about whether one group of leaders could speak on behalf of others. The persistence of these debates suggests that they are not easily resolved; indeed, they may never be resolved within feminism. Even so, we might note that the most hostile comments came around the issue of separation on the basis of race or ethnicity. In the second wave of feminism, both issues of race/ethnicity and sexual orientation were divisive; today, only the former seems to be especially problematic.

Second, and perhaps even more significantly, in spite of overt disagreement on the Internet, the discussion about SlutWalk New York City contains a strong thread of comments that dismiss the debates as being irrelevant, a waste of time, and a distraction from the *real* purpose and importance of the event. Almost all posters agree on the central goal of enacting and spreading an anti-victim-blaming, anti-rape culture message, even though there is extensive controversy about how best to accomplish this goal. Evaluated from the perspective of this common agreement, Slutwalk NYC can be seen as an interesting and inspiring representation of today's feminist movement—a movement that is evolving with young activists leading the charge. The difference between contradictions arising within this movement and earlier contradictions that arose within feminism as a whole is that those earlier disagreements broke groups apart. Ideological differences developed different brands of feminism, such as anti-pornography feminism, multicultural feminism, and pro-sex feminism. Although not all feminists believe in, or support the SlutWalk movement, many of the conflicts that do exist today can co-exist under the SlutWalk banner.

Of course it is possible that with the future developments, this movement will identify a clear ideological stance on all of these contested issues and that participants who disagree will break off from the movement to create their own groups. However, in the immediate aftermath of the SlutWalk New York City event, the dialogue about the event centered on a common identification with the underlying ideology of a movement designed to end rape and to do so in a form that sent a strong message that the victims of rape could not be blamed for their victimization. The shared ideological commitment suggests that the SlutWalk movement provided a rare opportunity for discussion about contentious issues without fundamental dissension about one significant, or "real," message. As such, the discussion allows modest hope for a future of feminism that continues to redefine itself through the acknowledgment of uncomfortable differences and as well as a celebration of shared understandings.

ENDNOTES

[1]The first author also made observations at the SlutWalk New York City event. For a fuller discussion of the methods, see Jones.
[2]http://perrystreetpalace.wordpress.com/2011/10/01/slutwalk-nyc/
[3]http://www.encyclopedia.com/video/IEhxr4-Yhqw-we-are-slut-walk-nyc.aspx
[4]http://persephonemagazine.com/2011/09/persephone-pio-neers-slutwalk-nyc/

[5]http://www.csmonitor.com/Commentary/Opinion/2011/0613/
SlutWalk-protests-A-dress-is-not-a-yes

[6]http://toronto.ctv.ca/servlet/an/local/CTVNews/20110403/
slut-walk-toronto-110403/20110403/

[7]http://msmagazine.com/blog/blog/2011/09/27/should-black-wom-
en-oppose-the-slutwalk/

[8]http://msmagazine.com/blog/blog/2011/09/27/should-black-wom-
en-oppose-the-slutwalk/

[9]http://msmagazine.com/blog/blog/2011/09/27/should-black-wom-
en-oppose-the-slutwalk/

[10]http://www.huffingtonpost.com/2011/09/29/nyc-slutwalk-con-
troversy-_n_987736.html?ir=Black%20Voices

[11]http://www.oa6.net/slutwalk-nyc-october-1-2011-updates.html

[12]http://www.huffingtonpost.com/2011/09/29/nyc-slutwalk-con-
troversy-_n_987736.html?ir=Black%20Voices

[13]http://persephonemagazine.com/2011/09/persephone-pio-
neers-slutwalk-nyc/

[14]https://scandalousmuffin.wordpress.com/tag/slutwalk-nyc/

[15]http://www.huffingtonpost.com/2011/09/29/nyc-slutwalk-con-
troversy-_n_987736.html?ir=Black%20Voices

[16]http://persephonemagazine.com/2011/09/persephone-pio-
neers-slutwalk-nyc/

[17]http://msmagazine.com/blog/blog/2011/09/27/should-black-
women-oppose-the-slutwalk/

[18]http://msmagazine.com/blog/blog/2011/09/27/should-black-
women-oppose-the-slutwalk/

[19]http://persephonemagazine.com/2011/09/persephone-pio-
neers-slutwalk-nyc/

[20]http://www.csmonitor.com/Commentary/Opinion/2011/0613/
SlutWalk-protests-A-dress-is-not-a-yes

[21]http://joemygod.blogspot.com/2011/10/nyc-slutwalk-2011.html

[22]http://msmagazine.com/blog/blog/2011/09/27/should-black-wo-
men-oppose-the-slutwalk/

[23]http://msmagazine.com/blog/blog/2011/09/27/should-black-wo-
men-oppose-the-slutwalk/

[24]http://msmagazine.com/blog/blog/2011/09/27/should-black-wo-
men-oppose-the-slutwalk/

[25]http://msmagazine.com/blog/blog/2011/09/27/should-black-wo-

men-oppose-the-slutwalk/
[26]http://persephonemagazine.com/2011/09/persephone-pione-ers-slutwalk-nyc/
[27]http://msmagazine.com/blog/blog/2011/09/27/should-black-wo-men-oppose-the-slutwalk/
[28]http://persephonemagazine.com/2011/09/persephone-pione-ers-slutwalk-nyc/
[29]http://www.encyclopedia.com/video/IEhxr4-Yhqw-we-are-slutwalk-nyc.aspx
[30]Please refer to the introductory chapter for a detailed discussion of Black Women's Blueprint and their critique.
[31]http://hiphopwired.com/2011/09/30/black-women-critici-ze-slutwalk-organization/
[32]http://www.huffingtonpost.com/2011/09/29/nyc-slutwalk-con-troversy-_n_987736.html?ir=Black%20Voices
[33]http://www.huffingtonpost.com/2011/09/29/nyc-slutwalk-con-troversy-_n_987736.html?ir=Black%20Voices
[34]http://msmagazine.com/blog/blog/2011/09/27/should-black-wo-men-oppose-the-slutwalk/
[35]http://www.huffingtonpost.com/2011/09/29/nyc-slutwalk-con-troversy-_n_987736.html?ir=Black%20Voices
[36]http://www.huffingtonpost.com/2011/09/29/nyc-slutwalk-con-troversy-_n_987736.html?ir=Black%20Voices
[37]http://www.huffingtonpost.com/2011/09/29/nyc-slutwalk-con-troversy-_n_987736.html?ir=Black%20Voices
38http://persephonemagazine.com/2011/09/persephone-pione-ers-slutwalk-nyc/

WORKS CITED

Gamson, Joshua. "Must Identity Movements Self-Destruct? A Queer Dilemma." *Social Problems* 42.3 (1995): 390–407. Print.

Jones, Norah. "This is What a Feminist Looks Like: An Under-standing of the Slutwalk Movement through Internet Commentary." Senior Project. Middlebury College: Sociology and Anthropology, 2011. Print.

Hill, Kevin A. and John E. Hughes. *Cyberpolitics: Citizen Activism in the Age of the Internet.* Rowman & Littlefield Publishers, Inc.,

1999. Web. 2 Jan. 2014.

Jaggar, Alison M. and Paula S. Rothenberg. *Feminist Frameworks: Alternative Theoretical Accounts of the Relations between Women and Men.* New York: McGraw-Hill, 1978. Web. 2 Jan. 2014.

Kabay, M. E. "Anonymity and Pseudonymity in Cyberspace: Deindividuation, Incivility and Lawlessness versus Freedom and Privacy." Paper Presented at the Annual Conference of the European Institute for Computer Anti-Virus Research (EICAR). 8 (1998).Web. 2 Jan. 2014.

Papacharissi, Zizi. "Democracy Online: Civility, Politeness, and the Democratic Potential of Online Political Discussion Groups." *New Media & Society* 6.2 (2004): 259–283. Print.

Suler, John. "The Online Disinhibition Effect." *Cyberpsychology & Behavior* 7.3 (2004): 321–326. Print.

An Open Letter to Sinéad O'Connor and Miley Cyrus on the Topic of Sluts, Constrained Choices, and the Need for Dialogue

MAY FRIEDMAN

D EAR SINÉAD AND MILEY,
Forgive me if I am being overfamiliar but I couldn't
resist the opportunity to write to you both in response
to your controversial public dialogue in the fall of 2013. I'm sure
the details are seared on your memories, but just in case, permit
me to recap the highlights.

Sinéad, as you no doubt recall, in response to Miley Cyrus citing
you as an influence, you chose to publicly express your concern
for her behaviour in the video for her song "Wrecking Ball," suggesting that the nudity and suggestive sexuality of the video were
put forth in an effort to satisfy Miley's male handlers and were
pandering to a male audience. Specifically, you stated that you were
"...extremely concerned for you [Miley] that those around you
have led you to believe, or encouraged you in your own belief, that
it is in any way 'cool' to be naked and licking sledgehammers in
your videos. It is in fact the case that you will obscure your talent
by allowing yourself to be pimped, whether it's the music business
or yourself doing the pimping." You suggested that you offered
support, Sinéad, "in the spirit of motherliness and with love."

Miley, I'm sure you remember that you met Sinéad's concerns
head on by providing a screen shot of tweets she had made while
in the midst of a mental health crisis in early 2012. Responding
to your thoughtful intervention (that's sarcasm, honey), Sinéad,
sent you several more strongly worded letters.

While the controversy was titillating and while no one loves an
online catfight more than me, I'm not writing just to pore over the

grubby details of your altercation. Rather, I'm writing as someone who was dissatisfied with both of your positions and also the overwhelming response, online and offline, to the ideas that you each represent. While it's an obvious oversimplification to reduce your position, Sinéad, to "humorless maternal feminist" and yours, Miley, to "oversexed twerking teenbot," I'm going to suggest that there isn't a lot of overlap between your points of view. I write here, then, in an effort to build bridges between your positions, to explicate the complicated continuum between a wholesale celebration of sexual agency and a reflective awareness of sexual violence. I also write to remind us that there is "no correct way to be a feminist, no seamless narrative to assume and fit into..." (Walker xxxi).

Perhaps it's best if I tell you a bit about myself before I go any further. I write as a defender of women's sexuality and sexual agency. I also write as a strong supporter of the SlutWalk movement which began in the spring of 2011 and has catalyzed a global response to the problems of slut-shaming, and the inadequate and victim-blaming responses to violence against women. This movement argues that "while 'slut' and related terms remain powerful disciplinary mechanisms for regulating women's sexual behavior, particularly among young women, such terms also are being subverted and reclaimed" (Flood 95).

Now, you may be wondering what on earth a few open letters on Facebook and some inflammatory tweets have to do with a global feminist movement, but permit me to suggest that there are parallels. One of the (many) challenges that arose from your dialogue is the way sexuality is presented as binary, as either totally empowered or deeply dangerous. Indeed, the reactions to your debate, but also to Miley's sexual renaissance more broadly, suggest that this binary is alive and well. SlutWalk engendered similar responses. Some folks felt that the performance of public sexuality and nudity which arose for (some) people at (some) SlutWalks was inappropriate and instead staged a spectacle for the male gaze. Others suggested, correctly, that the privilege of mounting a slutty exhibition is reserved for particular bodies over others. (I note that the same critique of normative beauty standards, and of the capacity to be a "bad girl" based on privileged social location, has generally been overlooked in the responses to Miley—but more on that later!) I'm not unaware of the critiques of SlutWalk. The concept fell short for some women of colour (though it is significant that there was a fairly robust uptake of the movement in the global South). The focus on violence against women resulted in some SlutWalks, whether through malice or inattention, becoming unsafe for trans folks. And the whole concept of a "walk" may betray ableist thinking. In other words, SlutWalks showed all too well that, "in the contemporary moment, 'slut' functions for some as an impossible space, the space of contradictions that cannot be resolved in language, theory or practice; the source of conflict between generations and feminisms; a trap and a dead end" (Attwood 244).

In the aftermath of SlutWalk's inception and the many million words that have been written about it since, I think that the vigorous dialogue which has emerged from the movement may be its greatest legacy. Despite the many ways that SlutWalk fell short, it accomplished something truly extraordinary in its capacity to decry sexual violence while simultaneously celebrating sexual expression. As a core mandate, this was an amazing accomplishment, particularly for a "movement" that largely began with the hasty outrage of five or six feminist undergraduates.

I think that some of the backlash to Miley's' burgeoning sexuality (including your own critiques, my dear Ms. O'Connor) may come from similar ideological positions as those aimed at SlutWalks. We ask: "Can we uphold sexual agency while deploring sexual objectification of women and girls?" (Carr 34). We fear that any expression of sexuality will be exploited, that our empowered passion will instead be taken over as someone's masturbatory tool. We fear that the expression of our sexuality in the first place comes from a tarnished position, that we merely bare our tits and lick our lips because we've been taught so well that this is our limited and most reliable currency, and notions of desire and autonomy are buried beneath the weight of a life's worth of gender socialization. On the most visceral level, we may fear that Constable Sanguinetti was right, that by dressing "like sluts" we will provoke attack, that, no matter how unfair and unsubstantiated the claim that dressing "nice" will keep you safe, the only control we can wrest back from the chaos of sexual violence is the illusion that by reducing our desirability we will also reduce our likelihood of victimization.

We are right. And yet—we are also wrong. We learned young that sex gave us power, but many of us learned even younger that it felt (forgive my French) fucking great as well. We had our innocence stripped bare, but that loss of innocence included lessons about the illusory nature of safety no matter how we dressed—lessons that, paradoxically, gave us back the right to wear what we damn pleased. We are mindful that we engage in performance and spectacle, but sometimes we enjoy the role of director rather than merely puppet actor. Finally, we learned early and often to use our sexuality to make our lives easier—and for this we do not deserve to receive blame. Purvis writes that "feminists not only realize their implicatedness in power structures, but they also recognize the workings of systemic power, including aspects of resistance" (105). Within the imperfect patriarchal world in which we dwell, feminist empowered living needs to include acknowledging and manipulating systemic power. It means using every tool in your belt, and it needs to include MacGyvering some of those tools to make them uniquely yours. Which is to say: Miley, if you want to drop trou, have at it. But be clear that you're BOTH pandering to sexist stereotypes that mean we all listen to your song way more now that you're licking construction equipment and ALSO that you might be turned on by the sensual pleasure of that heavy chain between your legs. And frankly, if it feels good and gets you what you want in a world that has little respect and few options for young women (even those as privileged as you, dear Miley), then I'd say you're doing a damn fine job.

Okay, Sinéad, I hear you shaking your head. I'm referencing a global movement that chooses to harness sexuality (among other things) to address inequality and social change, transformations that you have allied with strongly in your own history of activism. Given that "there is still relatively little space for the notion of a sexually desiring, active and empowered female sexuality, at least one which is not defined entirely by the narratives of mainstream pornography" (Flood 105), how can I possibly suggest that Miley's flagrant sexuality is in aid of anything other than Miley—or more problematically, the men who you think control her? As you wrote to Miley: "They will prostitute you for all you are worth, and cleverly make you think it's what YOU wanted."

I'll grant you that it's somewhat difficult to view Miley's performance in "Wrecking Ball" as a transformative feminist moment. Likewise her booty-shaking activities at the 2013 Video Music Awards cannot immediately be categorized as activism. At the same time, however, I think there is something deeply radical in expressing visceral female sexuality. As I've discussed above, Miley's choices are thoroughly constrained by the limitations of how, as a young attractive woman, she can get attention. No doubt her managers were, if not actively encouraging her coming of age, at least delighted to see her head in such a provocative direction. And yet I'm not sure I see her as a helpless victim.

Some of the backlash, not necessarily expressed in your letters, Sinéad, but articulated elsewhere in the shoals of the Internet, responded to the shame of Miley undermining her position as a role model for young women. As the mother of young children who are very invested in pop music, I'm not immune to the concern. Yet the heart of this concern does not seem to rest on fears of exploitation but rather a thinly masked fear of sexuality itself, suggesting that, "for teenage girls in particular, the term 'slut' props up a sexual double standard, marks female sexuality as deviant, and works to control girls' behavior and social positioning" (Attwood 235). I'm not convinced that seeing a young woman enjoy herself sexually is any likelier to harm my children's view of sex than it is to teach them to play with wrecking balls and sledgehammers in their spare time. Indeed, I wonder if seeing a "role model" who has embraced her sexuality might be somewhat inspiring as they come to terms with their own incipient desires.

In particular, your repeated use of the word "prostitute" in both verb and noun form in your letter, Sinéad, concern me deeply in their supposition that sex work is not worth our respect. If we come from a position that honours sex work as labour, we arrive at a more nuanced response to Miley, one which sees the ways we use sex and sexuality as bargaining chips or work for pay as calculated choices, and, sometimes, as choices that may neatly align with our desires. This response considers "some younger women's view that sexual display and activity are modes of empowerment" that, dependent on social capital and other currencies, some women "can use their sexuality to gain attention and influence without it then being used against them" (Dow and Wood 30).

Miley, I'm catching your smug grin, so let me be clear that all of my arguments above are not to say that I don't have any concerns at all about your performances. I'm concerned that you've taken on dance moves invented by women of colour and prevalent in racialized communities yet it's only thanks to you, skinny white chick, that "twerking" is now a household word. Speaking of skinny, I'd be a lot happier if a happy, sexy fat chick was on top of that wrecking ball, or at least if there were popular representations of female sexuality (outside of niche porn fetishes) that celebrated a greater diversity of shapes and sizes. This is one of the things that made SlutWalk so revelatory to me: the visual impact of so many different bodies, naked and clothed; fat and thin; black, brown and white; scarred, smooth, hairy, droopy, pert or creased—it felt like coming home. Carr writes that "women in bikini tops have marched next to women in burkas, students marched alongside grandmothers and nuns, and significant numbers of men have participated in the events" (26). I acknowledge that some people felt left out, that despite the diversity of the gatherings, some SlutWalks nonetheless felt like exclusive spaces. As feminist spaces, SlutWalks have a responsibility to work out these kinks, to talk and argue and fight and cry to understand the impacts of this movement, both good and bad. Without minimizing the impact of some of the limitations of the movement, SlutWalk did present a space that challenges the sanitized and ultimately deeply normative type of sexuality that you represent, Miley. If I want my kids to react to your video, I want them to roll their eyes at yet another skinny white girl getting naked. And I want them to wonder why no one ever yells at Robin Thicke.

Let me be clear, however: I hope my children would have a similarly critical lens toward your Hannah Montana years, during which you were the poster child for normativity. It's notable to me that you, Sinéad, were not terribly concerned about what happens to a young girl held captive by Disney. I'm much more worried about the impact of the Disney princess cartel than Miley's naked butt.

Having said all this: Miley, your response to Sinéad's letter doesn't earn you many points. You were a mad-phobic, sanist lout to present her screen shots. You are defending your choice to colour outside the lines a little bit these days but you're doing so by pointing to someone who has the passion and life experience of having scribbled. This is not how the world heals. We do not begin to unpack the margins of difference by pointing to our own particularities with pride while simultaneously pointing and laughing at others. Let me be clear: the problem is not that you weren't "nice," Miley. In case I haven't been explicit enough, I like you best when you leave "nice" behind, when you let Hannah Montana go all Sandy-at-the-end-of-Grease-hotpants and begin to push outside of what's expected of you. Sinéad built an incredible career and weathered massive controversy out of her choice not to do what was expected. So while she has no right to ask you to conform (or to suggest that you would never knowingly choose to publicly express yourself in sexual ways), you have even less right to point and mock her decent, responsible attempts to seek help in the midst of a crisis. I see no shame in your naked booty, but about your response to Sinéad's letter, I say shame on you.

Okay, okay, enough with the shame and judgment. I can see I've managed to offend both of you despite my lofty goal of building bridges. I'm not going to sway you toward a third way by judging any more than your public condemnation of one another created a path toward understanding and dialogue. I'm reminded of Hogeland's words: "We neither agree to disagree nor do we disagree; instead we evade. We foreclose the real conversations feminists must have about politics, conversations that could help us clarify our positions, conversations that could help us work more effectively both together and separately" (quoted in Purvis 108). What are the "real conversations" we must have in order to work together rather than against one another?

In order to move forward, I think you—and I—need to take a lesson from the best (and rarest) sites of activism and learn how to act as critical, loving allies. Rather than assuming we already understand the rationale behind anyone's actions, we need to ask more questions and provide fewer answers. We need to stop asking Miley to be the perfect young pop star, stop expecting Sinéad to be the quintessential proto-grrrl, stop expecting Slutwalk to be the perfect movement. Rather, we need to note the ways that we are all constrained by much larger forces, and we need to start allying with one another to push back against those forces. We would do well to remember that "to insist on a united position on a feminist issue such as SlutWalks is to fall back on a piece of history that we *should* unlearn: the assumption that feminism is better off when it speaks with a singular voice. This assumption overinvests in media logic at the expense of political creativity and diversity, yet its temptations are real and ongoing" (Dow and Wood 39). In other words, it's okay—perhaps more than okay, perhaps obligatory—for us to use very different tactics. We come from very different positions with different strengths and challenges, from different spaces of oppression and privilege. We need to simultaneously use our best and strongest tools and also—and this is the hard part—learn to listen to one another when we learn that *our* path to social transformation may have inadvertently bumped into or sidelined someone else's. These are tender moments: our good intentions are called out and we may quickly jump to outrage and defensiveness. Yet if we can move instead toward openness—open hearts and minds and ears—we might find that we can grow.

The Slutwalk movement is at an interesting crossroads. In many places the movement has ground to a halt. In 2014, as of this writing, there are fewer and fewer cities hosting SlutWalks than in years past. At the same time, relatively unlikely locales—such as Hong Kong, whose SlutWalk is examined in detail in this book—maintain their commitment to SlutWalk as an appropriate tool to speak back to sexual violence and victim-shaming.

Maybe some SlutWalks have shut down because of the critiques put forth; perhaps all that defensive energy and hurt feeling resulted in organizers just giving up and stomping off rather than doing the hard work of sticking around to "fix" it. Or maybe, in the face of many of the critiques of the movement as exclusive and founded on privileged social locations, some SlutWalkers learned that it would be unethical to move forward, that the movement had its moment but cannot be manouevered into what we need for a truly feminist uprising. Likely both outcomes are true in different jurisdictions with different populations and different controversies.

As I said above, however, SlutWalks made us talk. They made us try to understand one another better than we had before and they pushed us out of our comfort zones in so many ways beyond the simple double-take of seeing bare nipples on College Street. I am not saying they always succeeded, but in all the outrage and defense there was nonetheless a sharing of positions that was important for feminist movements to be robust and realistic. They got us to ask whether "any feminist action [can] effectively represent the diverse experiences of all women?" (Dow and Wood 34) and forced us to confront the tensions of our divergent answers head on. The best of these dialogues began with open minds and hearts and may have begun to build quiet bridges between activists, feminists, and others.

Your dialogue fell well short of this goal, but don't misunderstand me. In a world that reduces us to our silos so completely, the notion of any overlap between you, Miley and Sinéad, is already interesting and important. I hope that beneath the vitriol and rhetoric there is some room to open your hearts to one another's positions, since there is, at the core, some deep consistency. Fundamentally, you are both showing that we do the best we can with what we have—and who can argue with that? If instead of censure we let Miley know that we're here if she decides that she wants a different tool than sex—and that we're equally happy and supportive if she doesn't—isn't that a feminist moment? If we hold Sinéad in her moment of crisis and applaud her courage for asking for help, doesn't that action contribute to social transformation? To me, truly feminist principles would allow us to view each other making choices, and also to understand the deep inviolable stories told *about us* that constrain our capacity every day. This might sound like hippy shit, but I think that as two talented women who are swimming upstream (at least in some respects) we have more to admire than to deride.

But that's just my two cents. In the spirit of non-judgment I'll cheerfully admit that I know nothing about either of you, really. You could be as humourless as you're portrayed to be, Sinéad, and perhaps you really are in the grip of some terrible deviance, Miley (there's that sarcasm again!). In either case, I wish you both well. I hope you are able to make happy and healthy choices, including the choice to define what happy and healthy mean to you. I hope you find friends, lovers, and allies who cherish you in all ways. And I hope your minds have inched open a crack to consider how we must learn freely from one another, to consider one another's truths, to grow and sway in the wind instead of sitting rigid and concrete.

With all my best wishes to you both,

May

WORKS CITED

Attwood, Feona. "Sluts and Riot Grrrls: Female Identity and Sexual Agency." *Journal of Gender Studies* 16.3 (2007): 233-247. Web. February 10, 2012.

Carr, Joetta L. "The SlutWalk Movement: A Study in Transnational Feminist Activism." *Journal of Feminist Scholarship* 4 (2013): 24-38. Web. January 29, 2014.

Cyrus, Miley. "Before Amanda Bynes.... There was...." *Twitter* (@mileycyrus). 3 October 2013, 11:53 a.m. Tweet. October 10, 2013.

Dow, Bonnie J. and Julia T. Wood. "Repeating History and Learning From It: What Can SlutWalks Teach Us About Feminism?" *Women's Studies in Communication* 37 (2014): 22-43. Web. May 10, 2014.

Flood, Michael. "Male and Female Sluts: Shifts and Stabilities in the Regulation of Sexual Relations Among Young Hetersexual Men." *Australian Feminist Studies* 28.75 (2013): 95-107. Web. May 10, 2014.

O'Connor, Sinéad. "Open Letter to Miley Cyrus." *Facebook.* 3 October 2013. Web. October 10, 2013.

Purvis, Jennifer. "Grrrls and Women Together in the Third Wave: *NWSA Journal* 16.3 (2004): 93-123. Web. March 6, 2014.

Walker, Rebecca. *To Be Real: Telling the Truth and Changing the Face of Feminism.* New York: Anchor Books, 1995. Print.

Halt! Don't Do What You Want
With My Body

RAUSHAN BHUIYAN

I DO MOST OF MY TRANSFORMATIVE WORK through my feelings. That's why I need to be with others who understand that so much of how I navigate liberation work is with feelings. Clichéd as it sounds, I have always felt a sense of "rightness" when I listen to the voice of my gut. That voice is not a hunger grumble or a belch about to be burped, but that voice has saved my skin on many occasions when injustice was about to be or was being done. Whenever I feel uncomfortable, the voice of my gut is the voice that says, "Leave," "Get out of here," or "This space is no longer serving you." Nowadays I listen to my gut, because when my emotions run astray, my gut has my back. Listening to my gut affirms my feminism as an embodied feminism, and like the innards of my human flesh, my feminism is just as messy. Listening to my gut is why I ended up leaving the space of SlutWalk Toronto in the summer of 2012. This text is a testament to my experiences as an organizer of a SlutWalk protest.

My personal reasons for joining the SlutWalk team were no different from why many people join social justice protests. Plain and simple, I figured it would feel liberating to partake in transformative work that had the potential to shift the current tide of public dialogue about violence against women, particularly when it came to the issue of whether certain modes of women's dress made women more "rapeable." I admired the group that came together to organize SlutWalk because they were a group of self-identified women who wanted to flip the script of conventional discourse on how to avoid getting raped. Unlike the sentiment of previous women's marches organized around violence against women, which had more of a grieving tone, I was attracted to the cheeky, fresh undertone of the SlutWalk space. I caught a snippet of this undertone at the first march where a protester in the crowd cried, "We wouldn't have to defend if you didn't learn how to attack!" It was a straight to the point ethic, like nothing I had heard before.

When I decided to take part in organizing the second SlutWalk in 2012 in Toronto, I was already very much aware of the critiques of the action. But I am a feminist and I wanted to see for myself what this organizing would look like, both because I have a stake in it and because I personally don't want any feminist movement to be exclusively by and for privileged bodies and identities.

Despite the growing number of organizers of colour that I had the pleasure of speaking with, SlutWalk as a global phenomenon was and is still seen to be born largely of the efforts of white women feminists. The only time I saw images of people of colour at a SlutWalk event was when said organizers had to make use of their diversity in photos. But people of colour are not your diversity photos to be wantonly selected like nail polish at Trade Secrets for a special occasion. People of colour are real people with real struggles and feelings and it is a damn shame that they are always underrepresented in protest imagery. It simply enraged me that whenever it was brought up that I was an organizer with SlutWalk, people would squint and say, "Really? But isn't that just for white women? What is a woman of colour doing at a SlutWalk? Don't you feel all alone there? There are people of colour organizing with SlutWalk?" It would enrage me, because there were so many of us! As the outreach organizer, I had the chance to engage in discussions and meetings with fellow organizers of SlutWalk in many different countries. And most of them were not white. So why did popular representations of the movement depict it as such?

I was particularly moved by the fact that a SlutWalk protest had tried to take place in Mumbai, India, at the end of 2011 but was promptly shut down by Mumbai police services. Where was the extensive coverage of that? Why was solidarity not claimed with the organizers of the Mumbai SlutWalk? Again, why weren't people of colour represented as organizers and participants at Slut-Walks? Were they hidden? And if so, why? Why is it that Internet readership collectively cheers the activism of the Gulabi Gang, but then fails to acknowledge and recognize the presence of people of colour, particularly women of colour, in countercultural women's movements? Is the Gulabi Gang, a group of South Asian women handing out punishments to rapists, more palatable to a North American audience than a first- or second-generation woman of colour organizing something like SlutWalk? Again, why were women of colour so easy to erase in SlutWalk's narrative?

It makes you wonder who benefits from the ways countercultural protests are presented to a mainstream audience. And the simultaneous erasure and putting up on a pedestal of women of colour at these sorts of events not only reinforces the stereotype of the disappearing, silent, docile brown woman, but also centers the activism by white women as the only type of reform effort worthy of institutional attention. Why are some voices in feminist action heard over others? Why are North American audiences interested in countercultural issues always so willing to congratulate a white ally for saying seemingly profound things that organizers of colour have been saying for decades? Who is palatable and who is not? What happens when someone who is not palatable flips the script of what is expected of them? We are told that liberation can be found if we work together in solidarity, but what do you do when the people with whom you are trying to build a sense of solidarity partake in your oppression?

I had a tough time putting the 2012 march together. It was emotionally and physically draining, to say the least, and I departed with a sour taste in my mouth from the important political discussions that were bypassed in favour of arranging the technical details of the march. While I understood the intensity and importance of logistics in planning any event, what must be understood as well, and never forgotten, is that political discussions are also logistical. Politics are the foundation upon which other actions are built. They cannot come second. What bothered me was that it took outside criticism to really make SlutWalk organizers wake up about the lack of an intersectional approach, while there were many people within our organizing body who had been voicing critiques of privilege since the beginning. I was also troubled by the fact that, despite my feelings telling me to leave the SlutWalk space in earlier phases of organizing, I stayed put. I stayed because I believed that the tough task of transformative work would happen when I helped to educate the more socially privileged organizers about how different people were impacted by particular discourses of violence against women. And that's not healthy. That's not something people currently organizing social justice-based protests should be doing because it inevitably leads to irreparable burnout.

Being in the SlutWalk space has made me question the kinds of pressures that are assigned to bodies of colour in organizing spaces. Why are bodies of colour always doing the majority of the grunt work? Why are people of colour not sufficiently represented in images of countercultural protests? What is going on in organizing spaces that results in bodies of colour routinely having to leave the spaces in order to take care of themselves? Why are people of colour more often turning to fellow people of colour to organize? What does that mean for questions of solidarity and organizing across borders and boundaries?

We should be telling organizers to try their hardest to remain accountable to each other. And when that gets to be too tricky to handle, people should have the means to leave the space and make room for other people who can be more accountable. I cannot stress this point enough. Many South Asian women like me have been taught since babyhood to always be the receptacle of care for others. Broadly speaking, we have never been taught to say no or that something doesn't feel right because doing so would be directly contradicting the cultural socializations of South Asian femininity. But South Asian women are not everyone's caregivers. They are their own people and it is worth all the effort to unlearn the default temptation to care for others, Buwa/Ayah syndrome you could call it, and start to learn to care for ourselves. There's a lot that goes into to organizing a countercultural protest event like SlutWalk. And all this effort won't be in vain if organizing teams were to forgive themselves and each other when they have been wronged.

Having said this, even before that kind of forgiveness happens, there has to be visible recognition that someone has been wronged. South African revolutionary Steve Biko said that in order to have a genuine conversation about oppression with your oppressor, your oppressor must first have a conscience. There can be no accountability if there is not the initial recognition that an injustice has been committed. This will be a tough measure to implement in some SlutWalks where, although there is the outward acknowledgement of working within interlocking systems of oppression, genuine engagement with an anti-oppressive, critically intersectional approach within the organizing group remains to be seen. We should already be an inclusive space and the fact that we even have to have this conversation is a mark of how we are not a safer, anti-oppressive space for everyone.

Organizers who start to feel that they are being silenced need to be told by people around them that they should refuse to waste their energy adding extra sparkle to other people's learning curves. Particularly organizers who are people of colour: you need to know that you are magic and that everything you touch will be better by having you in it. However, if that thing you have touched has bitten you and is draining you, you need to cut the head off that snake and live your own adventures. It is not your obligation to help others. It is not your obligation to stress yourself so others can benefit. You need to be selfish with your magic and conserve it as much as you can. Only then, when people's feelings are genuinely honoured, can we truly carry out transformative work.

Single Mothering in Rape Culture

Confronting Myths and Creating Change

SHANNON SALISBURY

WHEN THE FIRST SLUTWALK was organized in Toronto in 2011, it caught my attention. Having worked in campus-based anti-sexual violence for years, I was upset but not surprised to hear that a police officer's advice to law school students was "Don't dress like a slut" (Anderssen "Toronto Police"). This idea that women's choices are responsible for men's violence against us is an old one, and continues to be used to both excuse the behaviour of those who sexually assault women and to vilify us when we are assaulted. We're told the police are supposed to protect us from those who would do us harm. We're told that the criminal justice system can't work to effectively prosecute perpetrators if victims don't report. And we're told this entirely without irony, while officers tell young women that how we dress or what we do will make us complicit in our own assaults.

I reacted to the report of this officer's blunder with defiance. I was initially thrilled to see others had organized SlutWalk to protest sexual shaming in general and this officer's statement specifically. I shared in the feeling of "YEAH! WOMEN GETTING MAD" (Murphy). I thought action was appropriate and justified. I believe in speaking out publicly against rape culture, and I'm committed to challenging the social and political institutions which reinforce the ideology that victims and survivors are responsible for others' actions.

But, something didn't sit right. I was, and continue to be troubled. As much as I like the idea of sexual liberation activism in principle, the "reclamation" of the word slut is profoundly uncomfortable for

184

me. When I gave myself the time to push up against my discomfort, I realized that my status as a single mother renders the identity of slut as my default. I realized that it is privilege that allowed me to consider the word slut as an identity that gives me power. It led me to wonder about the cultural messages my children are internalizing about sexuality in general, and their place in the world as sexual adolescents. Finally, it left me wondering what I could do to counteract those messages, to provide the children and youth in my life with an alternative narrative of consent.

SINGLE MOTHER, SLUTTY MOTHER, BAD MOTHER

In my early twenties, I went back and forth between casual sexual hook-ups with friends and acquaintances, and extended periods of celibacy. When I felt like having sex, it was never difficult to find a partner. I'd have sex and never think anything of it. Had an event like SlutWalk taken place in the late '90s, I'd have gladly called myself a slut, playfully, using it to describe my identity as a woman who enjoys having sex without emotional or social constraints. I would have owned that word without a second thought. As an early adopter of the Yes Means Yes approach to campus sexual assault prevention, I believed sexual liberation was an integral piece in the liberation of women. As I dealt with my own history of sexual violence, I believed that we could upset the gendered power imbalance through a revolution of sexual enthusiasm.
And then I had kids.

> slut
> whispers its way into my head
> i wear a scarlet s on my chest,
> rolling my shoulders in shame to hide it
> s for single mother
> s for (presumed) sexual
> s for slut
> no ring on my finger, no man in sight
> two little people to shelter and feed
> s seared into my flesh before my belly even grows
> you can't even be sure it's yours, they tell him

185

concerned parents that they are
if I open my legs for him, I must for everyone
do your children have the same father?
i'm not even sure they have the same mother
why do you want to know?
do you ask that to parents who are married?
will the answer change how you treat me, them?
do yours?

There's no longer space for me to comfortably call myself a slut. It's not something that opens up my opportunities for liberation, as it has become my assumed default. Even my children's principal has asked me, as diplomatically as possible, if my children have the same father, as if not sharing the same parentage would somehow be the reason there was a school-based issue with one of them. By not fitting into the compulsory heterosexuality-laden model of the traditional family, single mothers pose a threat: we don't belong to one man, so we must be open and available to any man.

Because of this open availability, we are useful only for sex, and nothing else. A quick Google search of the words "single mother slut" brings up 1.8 million results. While some of the hits are from sources critiquing the assumptions in connecting the three words, the majority speak directly to the perceived sexual availability of the single mother, and how long-term dating is out of the question. When I started trying to date[1] as a single mother, I didn't know that connecting with people would be so difficult. I was naive to the idea that I was a new member to an exclusive club in which casual sex was the only thing people wanted from us. I lost count of the men who would tell me they were only interested in sex from me, as they had no interest in "raising another man's children." I suppose I could be thankful for their frankness, for not wasting my time. Still, there's only so much of the idea of single mom as sexual conquest I can take, even when those men were honest about their intentions.

This idea of slut as a default identity is further complicated by issues of race and class, discussed in the "Open letter from Black women to the Slutwalk" by Black Women's Blueprint.[2] This critique acknowledges that the ability to safely call oneself slut without repercussion is a privileged context, one that needs to be heard and understood (B.).

The single mother, for all of her sexual availability, is judged for making bad choices with her life. So many contemporary social evils have been placed at the feet of working-class and poor single mothers.[3] The lack of a present male role model is used as a reason for the vulnerability of teenaged girls to sexual violence: with only one parent in the home, there is little time to teach "desirable values" (Strouse, Goodwin, Roscoe: 574). Young children of all genders are seen as at-risk in single mother-led homes, as sexual predators target us as a way of getting access to our children (Lanning).

Blaming single mothers for the violence that happens to our children is not a historical artifact. As recently as 2011, the *New York Times* published an account of an 11-year-old Texas girl who was repeatedly sexually assaulted by more than twenty boys and young men in her community. The first question one resident asked was, "Where was her mother? What was her mother thinking? How can you have an eleven-year-old child missing down in the Quarters?" (McKinley). No one asked, "What were those boys thinking?" No. Where was her mother. The child was criticized for dressing much older than her age, for wearing make-up, and for spending time with older boys—another clear sign that her mother wasn't paying enough attention to prevent her child from being raped. It's also clear that the child herself, even at eleven, was seen as complicit in the crimes committed against her.

At eleven years old, my daughter was riding her bike to school in downtown Toronto. While stopped at a corner, waiting for the light to change, two men on the sidewalk started to loudly discuss her sexual availability. Now, I was with her when it happened, and I made sure to get her across the street and away for them as quickly as possible, but when I shared the experience with other women later that day, I was surprised by one reaction. "Maybe if you didn't let her didn't dress provocatively, it wouldn't have happened." Never once had I even mentioned what she was wearing, but I, like the mother of the child in Texas, was to blame for my child being targeted. And my child, like that child, was not innocent.

INNOCENCE AT THE EXPENSE OF UNDERSTANDING?

How we approach anything to do with sexuality and children is, at the very least, complicated. We want to keep our children small, to believe they are too innocent to understand the rougher parts of the world. We want to keep them safe. We react with shock and horror when "sexy" Hallowe'en costumes and dolls are marketed to our little girls; we want them to be seen (and for them to see themselves) as more than just sexual objects. In the efforts to legitimately keep our youngest people out of the adult world of sexual objectification, though, I think we may end up doing more harm than good.

When we think to ourselves, "Please don't let my daughter turn out like that" (Colby) upon seeing young women experimenting with their sexuality, we reinforce the dichotomy of good and bad behaviour and appearance. We're saying that some girls and women are more at risk of being seen as sexual objects (and are therefore more at risk of sexual violence) than others. And as much as we deny that anyone asks to be harassed or assaulted, deep down inside, we actually do think that how one dresses announces one's intentions and availability regardless of that person's explicit consent. This is well-illustrated by the enforcing of dress codes that target adolescent girls whose prom dresses are deemed too revealing (Holmes), or whose yoga pants are too snug: "By declaring that women are responsible for controlling men's behaviour, the school is sending the message loud and clear: if men are 'distracted' by you, or worse, it's your fault for not dressing the way you're 'supposed to'" (Angyal).

I wish I could say I'm immune to this reaction. I wish I could say that I don't cringe when I see my young adolescent daughter wearing clothes that draw attention to her body. I find myself in a constant internal battle, wanting to protect her from those who would interpret her cut-offs and yoga pants as an invitation to harass her, but also wanting her to feel confident in her body and the choices she makes in clothing it. I hear my mother in my head: it's not you I don't trust, it's everyone else I'm worried about. In wanting to spare her the ugliness of the world, though, am I keeping her in the dark?

By claiming that we want to I keep our children innocent, we run the risk of their being ignorant. They are already learning early on how to ignore consent, and how to reinforce the construct that it is girls' and women's responsibility to keep themselves safe from harassment and sexual violence. I once worked with a Grade 7 class, teaching a health unit on harassment and safety. After spending one period working in groups to define the words consent, respect, and boundaries, and a follow-up class examining case studies of harassment, I asked the students to complete a homework assignment in which they would reflect on what actions they thought could prevent sexual harassment. The majority of students chose "dressing appropriately" as their focus, mirroring the words of the police officer who triggered the SlutWalk action. It had never been mentioned in class, no one had suggested it as an option in the case studies, but because of its ubiquitous presence in our lives, this was a concrete reality for these twelve-year-old students.

This perpetuation of the mythology surrounding sexual violence is in part a result of our attempts to put our children's innocence above their understanding. This innocence leaves young people extremely vulnerable. By high school, most students feel they know what they need to know about the mechanics of sex (assuming it's heterosex). It's the messier, interpersonal parts they feel they don't know nearly enough about (Flicker et al.). They feel they're not getting opportunities to talk about healthy relationships, communication, and how to handle break-ups. They don't feel emotionally supported, by school or family, when it comes to their discussions of sexuality.

Young people also have significant gaps in their understanding of the impact of intoxication on the ability to provide consent. There are still Canadian students who are surprised that an intoxicated person cannot legally give consent to sexual activity (Anderssen "No Means No"). In a February 2013 Angus Reid poll commissioned by the Canadian Women's Foundation, 23 per cent of Canadians between 18 and 34 stated they believe a woman "can provoke or encourage sexual assault" when she is drunk (Canadian Women's Foundation). There seems to be something about a young woman drinking that leads others to believe she is worthy of less respect.

In a 2007 study by Young, McCabe, and Boyd, adolescents

were given scenarios in which a female character was drinking. Participants perceived the young woman as more sexually available under two conditions: when she was seen as very drunk and the young man in her acquaintance was not drinking at all; and when she was somewhat drunk and the young man was very drunk. The authors determined that while we generally feel a level of sympathy for women when they're in vulnerable positions, the specific sort of vulnerability that occurs when a young woman has consumed alcohol seems to trigger antipathy in those around her: "if victimized, she gets what she deserves because she knowingly disregarded the traditionally appropriate behaviour designated for girls" (236).

Young people don't feel empathy for young women who are drunk and who are sexually assaulted. They are less likely to step into a situation where a young woman is drunk, because they don't feel she is worthy of safety. This study explains the bystander inaction when Jane Doe was sexually assaulted at a party in Steubenville, Ohio. It explains similar events happening to Rehtaeh Parsons in Dartmouth, Nova Scotia. Both women were drunk. Both were sexually assaulted and photographed in the process. Both were harassed after the fact through social media. Both were shamed by their peer communities because in being drunk at a party with boys, both had asked for it.

Just after Rehtaeh Parson's suicide, @username1397, a graduating high school student living in Dartmouth, contacted me via Twitter to engage in a conversation. I had critiqued what I saw as inaction on the part of Cole Harbour High School in addressing the sexual violence and ongoing harassment that led to Parson's death earlier that week. This student admitted to having received the infamous photograph. Not knowing it was child pornography, they deleted it from their phone without reporting it. This student's feedback on the situation as a whole is useful: "Jr. Highs need to be taught about drinking, drugs, bullying and empathy needs to be taught on day one of primary. Issues like this slip through."

BUILDING A CULTURE OF CONSENT

Empathy needs to be taught on day one of primary. How simple an idea is that? Could that one small thing teach very young children that we all have value, change the way we see each other as adolescents and adults? It might. Some studies on adolescent sexual violence suggest that empathy may be a factor that works in conjunction with other factors to increase or decrease sexual violence: "Empathy ... may exert inhibitory control when decision making is compromised by other situational risk factors, such as intoxication, anger, or anxiety" (Tharp et al 8).

Empathy is the starting point for change, but we also need to recognize that because of sexism, because of racism, because of capitalism and colonialism and the idea that some people have more worth than others for a whole host of intersecting reasons, we need to talk about power: who has it, who doesn't, and why. And we need to do it much earlier than high school. Part of how we do this is in how we talk about who we value. It's far easier for us to feel empathy for family members: mothers, sisters, aunts, cousins. But this, as Edwards argues, sets all of us up for failure: when we tell our children that certain kinds of people deserve better treatment, "that implies those who are not family are subhuman and therefore deserving of their own victimization." How can we address rape culture with children and youth? First, we need to talk to kids: "We need to stop behaving as if it's all a terrible problem out there, and start talking about it with each other and with our children" (Tutu, Lief, Abdulali). We need to talk about consent explicitly, but we also need to model it. If a young child doesn't want a hug, show respect for that, and offer a handshake or a wave as alternatives. Give children opportunities to exercise consent and negotiation so they can use these skills with their peers as they get older. We also need to question the gendered expectations that are placed on children, and provide our kids both a refuge from, and an alternate narrative to, the essentialist arguments that leave boys doing one thing and girls doing another.

We need to give our children space to develop the confidence they need to speak up and act when they witness sexual harassment or assault. It takes bravery to stand up against a group of peers and call them out for their abusive behaviour. We also need to listen, and recognize that our children's social lives are complex. One of the scariest things for many parents is the unknowable threat of social media. Many have no real understanding of the online lives of their children, and may be quick to limit or restrict their children's access after any incidents of harassment or misuse. Our children's fear of this knee-jerk reaction leading to social isolation makes many young people less likely to disclose if something serious happens to them online or via their cell phones (Strauss). Understanding the importance of the connections our children have with peers online may help mitigate our protective reactions, and may help our children feel safer disclosing to us without fear of (further) loss.

We need to work with our schools and our communities to support work that may be in progress. Because of ongoing pushback against comprehensive sexual education programs, school administrators and government leaders don't hear the voices of parents who want to work collaboratively to ensure all children grow up feeling safe and valued. Advocating for up-to-date educational materials that address issues of healthy relationships, gender roles, and power will help to ensure that students have access to the knowledge they feel they are currently missing.

Finally, we need to not be afraid that talking to our children about rape culture will rob them of their innocence: "You do not lose innocence when you learn about terrible acts; you lose your innocence when you commit them. An open culture of tolerance, honesty and discussion is the best way to safeguard innocence, not destroy it" (Tutu, Lief, Abdulali).

ENDNOTES

[1]The dating narratives to which I refer in this chapter are with men. While I also dated women over this time, I never felt as though the "single mom as sexually available" trope was the focus in those interactions, whereas it has been a common feature in introductory dates with men.

[2]Please refer to the introductory chapter for a detailed discussion of Black Women's Blueprint and their critique.

[3]This seems to happen less often when affluent women choose single parenthood, which would imply that economic privilege may protect some single mothers from assumptions of both availability and poor parenting.

WORKS CITED

Anderssen, Erin. "No Means No—But Does Yes Mean Yes?" *The Globe and Mail*. 14 Apr 2013. Web. 20 Nov 2013.

Anderssen, Erin. "Toronto Police Officer Offers Inappropriate Safety Tip." *The Globe and Mail*. 17 Feb 2011. Web. 20 Nov 2013.

Angyal, Chloe. "This is how you teach rape culture to 12-year-olds." *Feministing*. n.d. Web. 20 November 2013.

B., Lutze. "Why I Won't Call Myself a "Slut."" *Salon*. N.p., 22 Oct. 2013. Web. 16 Nov. 2013.

Black Women's Blueprint. "An Open Letter from Black Women to the SlutWalk." *Facebook*. N.p. 23 Sept. 2011. Web. 16 Nov. 2013.

Colby, Scott. "When did kids' Halloween costumes go from scary to scandalous?" *The Toronto Star* 28 Oct. 2013. Web. 20 November 2013.

Edwards, Stassa. "Thinking about the Steubenville Rape and Raising a Son." *Ms. Magazine Blog*. 18 Jun 2013. Web. 17 Nov 2013.

Flicker, Sarah, Susan Flynn, June Larkin, Robb Travers, Adrian Guta, Jason Pole, and Crystal Layne. *Sexpress: The Toronto Teen Sex Survey Report*. Rep. Toronto: Planned Parenthood Toronto, 2009. Web. 17 November 2013.

Holmes, Elizabeth. "For Prom, Schools Say 'No' to the Dress." *The Wall Street Journal*. 29 Mar 2012. Web. 20 Nov 2013.

Lanning, Kenneth V. *Child Molesters: A Behavioral Analysis for Professionals Investigating the Sexual Exploitation of Children*. 5th ed. National Center for Missing and Exploited Children. 2010. Web. 20 Nov 2013.

McKinley, James C. "Vicious Assault Shakes Town." *The New York Times*. 8 Mar 2011. Web. 20 Nov 2013.

Murphy, Meghan. "We're Sluts, Not Feminists. Wherein My Relationship with Slutwalk Gets Rocky." *Rabble*. N.p. 16 May 2011. Web. 16 Nov. 2013.

Canadian Women's Foundation. "One in five Canadians thinks a woman encourages sexual assault when she is drunk." 2013. Web. 20 Nov 2013.

Strauss, Susan L. *Sexual Harassment and Bullying: A Guide to Keeping Kids Safe and Holding Schools Accountable*. Lanham, MD: Rowman and Littlefield Publishers, 2012. Print.

Strouse, Jeremiah S., Megan P. Goodwin, and Bruce Roscoe. "Correlates of Attitudes toward Sexual Harassment among Early Adolescents." *Sex Roles* 31.9-10 (1994): 559-77. Print.

Tharp, Andra T., Sarah DeGrue, Linda A. Valle, Kathryn A. Brookmeyer, Greta M. Massetti, and Jennifer L. Matjasko. "A Systematic Qualitative Review of Risk and Protective Factors for Sexual Violence Perpetration." *Trauma, Violence, and Abuse* 14.2 (April 2013): 1-35. Print.

Tutu, Desmond, Jacob Lief and Sohaila Abdulali. "To protect our children, we must talk to them about rape." *The Guardian* 26 April 2013. Web. 17 November 2013.

User (username1397). "@middle_ladle I'm a grade 12 student, so I don't think it could benefit me in any way. Jr. Highs need to be taught about drinking, drugs" 11 Apr 13, 5:53 p.m. Tweet.

User (username1397). "@middle_ladle and bullying and empathy needs to be taught on day one of primary. Issues like this slip through." 11 Apr 2013, 5:55 p.m. Tweet.

Young, Amy. M., Sean E. McCabe, and C.J. Boyd. "Adolescents' Sexual Inferences about Girls Who Consume Alcohol." *Psychology of Women Quarterly* 31. 2007. Print. 229-240.

Sluthood & Survival

A Reflection on the Merits of Reclamation

TRACY B. CITERONI

I AM CONFLICTED about the SlutWalks. A colleague in Gender Studies approached me to lead a discussion of them on our campus in the fall of 2011, and my initial inclination was to say no. I knew very little at that point and was, frankly, hesitant to dive into what seemed a contentious debate. I did lead that (fairly spirited) discussion and as a consequence of the research I conducted to prepare for it, as well as the fruitful exchanges that followed, I developed a more complicated and nuanced understanding of the SlutWalk phenomenon. In this essay, I examine apparent tensions in attempting to reclaim the term slut and employ it in the service of gender justice. I utilize an auto-ethnographic lens to illustrate how these tensions may play out for individual persons committed to the cause but unable to fully embrace the tactic. I use my own experiences and difficulty in becoming a champion of SlutWalk to raise questions about the wisdom and efficacy of assuming that a resignification of the term slut is possible (or even desirable) for all victims or potential victims of sexual assault. I also question its revolutionary potential. I suggest we accept SlutWalk as a novel approach to organizing rather than an end in itself. Our movement can benefit from the imagination and flexibility of a protest like SlutWalk as we confront ever more challenges in the quest to reduce and eliminate sexual violence in our communities.

SLUT SOLIDARITY

SlutWalk invites people of all backgrounds to participate in a playful display of our collective outrage over sexual violence and the further mistreatment of victims by law enforcement professionals, health care providers, journalists, coworkers, family, friends, neighbours, acquaintances, bystanders, or strangers. The message is clear. No one "asks for it" or deserves it, regardless of what they wear, what they do, or what they say. The theatrical nature of the protest events aims to defuse persistent distortions of the nature of sexual violence. It is in this sense a brilliant strategy. SlutWalk effectively mocks ignorant notions about victims of sexual violence. Protesters had/have so much to be furious about. SlutWalk unleashed this anger and channeled our deep and abiding hunger for gender justice. It also activated (inadvertently) long-standing disagreements about how to achieve the justice we crave.

Some women attending marches held signs that said, "This is what I wore the night he raped me." Some scrawled words, often just "SLUT" and in one case "SuperSlut," directly on their clothing or skin. Why self-label with one of the most derogatory and oppressive sexist insults? One aim of SlutWalk has been to reclaim, resignify, and destigmatize the term slut as a slur against women who have been sexually assaulted. The goal is to empty the word of its disparaging meaning, to embrace it as emblematic of women who are in control of and unashamed of their sexuality. If we boldly claim sluthood ourselves, the thinking goes, we can preempt and defuse accusations that our sexuality is dangerous, not our own, that our variously adorned or naked bodies incite violence in helpless and hapless men who can be taken over by hormonal urges at any moment. This stance seems particularly appealing to a generation of young feminists that has come to consciousness during the so-called Third Wave and others who carry the mantle of sex-positivity.

We have witnessed a range of tactical uses of the term slut by a variety of people as a consequence of the SlutWalks. Whether the term sticks, whether people incorporate it into their everyday lives, whether the practice spreads, may tell us something of the success of the campaign for reclamation. Another measure of progress in the struggle against victim-blaming regards how pervasive and comprehensive the reclamation may be across social groups.

As someone who does not embrace the slut label, I imagine the difficulty others may have in doing so. As a sociologist, I question the true promise of SlutWalk as a revolutionary movement.

SOME OF US ARE MORE SLUTTY

As is to be expected in any social action or movement, there is not perfect unity in the message of SlutWalks or the experiences of people involved. Some feminists want to reclaim the term slut and others do not. We cannot agree on what would signal a successful rescue of the term. Even if feminists and allies accept the salvaged term, meaningful victory may be dependent upon outside others also seeing sluts in a new light.

An intersectional feminist approach facilitates consideration of how "sluthood" is fraught with danger for women who embody certain social identities. Structural divisions among women dictate that some are less able to exercise power in claiming a "slut" identity. Being called a slut differently taints women of colour, poor/working class women, queer women, ethnic women, migrant women, disabled women, trans women, women of the global South, and women with sexually transmitted infections/illnesses. The label does not hold the same meaning or consequences across these groups. To be blunt, when some of us write "SLUT" on our chests, observers may simply nod in silent affirmation. "Of course you are a slut. Tell us something we don't know." The slur remains intact from the perspective of those who would employ it to discredit and dismiss many of us.

Some women have the cultural capital to successfully reclaim sluthood, or at least to keep the stain of its stigma from deeply or permanently marking them. They likely have the financial resources, education, racial identity, and other symbols of status to augment their position as women and legitimate their claims to sexual power. They exercise power relative to other women, a privilege available to them by virtue of their position within intersecting dimensions of inequality. It works as a low-risk, fleeting tactic to gain awareness for a cause. For these women, the successful deployment of sluttiness may be seen as creative, empowering, playful, and even sexy. For others, a claim to being slutty further degrades their social standing, marking them as low, dirty, and worthless. SlutWalk assumes a consequential agency not readily available to all of us.

Is the undoing of the stigma reliant on the claiming of the label by someone who is not already seen as a slut? If it only works when "normal" and "respectable" women adopt it, I question its value as a liberation strategy. This is at best a partial reclamation that benefits women who were already at low risk of suffering the indignities of sluthood. People may look at the "unlikely slut" and question their preconceptions about sluttiness. Or they may see her as a humourous exception that would never be relegated to the slut category but gains even more respect for being willing to wear the label to make a point. This is akin to the reaction many people have when they see a conventionally handsome, mainstream man wearing a "This is what a feminist looks like" t-shirt. It may be read as a demonstration that "normal" and "respectable" people can be feminists, a claim which may further marginalize those feminists who are already seen as social outcasts.

These are age-old divisions, activated anew with the SlutWalk movement. Gender justice has never been a uniform, linear progression of enlightenment forces. As ever, some people are positioned to take better advantage of new opportunities than others. Some feel more at home in the movement. Who feels at home with the SlutWalks? Who revels in their newly claimed sluthood? Who feels (again) marginalized by them/it? We need research to answer these questions. We need to hear a proliferation of stories from people at the center of the movement as well as those grappling with it from the outside or at the margins.

Is SlutWalk an effective activist strategy? It was successfully organized and garnered media attention, neither of which is a small feat. One could argue their use of patriarchal symbols to bring attention to a feminist cause is something of an activist coup. Whether the actions translate into effective social change, how the images of marches are consumed, the lasting impact of SlutWalk, remain to be seen. The issue I want to raise here is whether a feminist claim to sluthood takes power away from or undermines those who would use slut pejoratively. A successful reclamation would do so. In addition, it would keep people from blaming women who are victims of sexual violence. It would challenge a patriarchal culture that objectifies and subordinates women. It would help to dismantle the social/sexual hierarchies that make some groups of people more vulnerable to rape.

DISIDENTIFYING AS A SLUT

I did not attend a SlutWalk event. I might have participated in one on our campus, but our students declined to organize a march. Much of what I know about them comes from media accounts, online articles, and exchanges on blogs. I have read with interest the ongoing debates about the suitability and effectiveness of utilizing the master's insult to challenge our collective subordination. I have discussed with colleagues, students, and friends their reactions to SlutWalks. All available information reinforces the fact that there is imperfect harmony around the concept and no neat resolution to the conflicts embedded there. I share my own thoughts and experiences here as illustration of one type of struggle with SlutWalk.

I do not embrace a slut identity for myself. While I applaud the personal freedom some may feel by doing so, and admire the solidarity emerging for many at SlutWalk actions, I do not feel a sense of belonging with them. I have serious doubts about the value of SlutWalks as a collective liberation strategy. I wrestle with my own positionality and my views have continued to develop as I challenged myself to engage with the movement. I even wonder if my resistance to embracing slut as part of my identity stems from rightful feminist critique or deep-seated fear. After all, though the word my mother used was "hussy" the message instilled from a very young age is the same. Perhaps I am apprehensive to put in jeopardy the middle class gains I have made in my climb from less-privileged, small-town girl to tenured professor. Even writing this essay feels in some ways like a risky outing of those parts of me that run counter to my achieved status. Regardless of the potential flaws in my own relationship to SlutWalk, legitimate doubts remain.

Having contracted a high-risk strain of HPV that later developed into cervical cancer squarely places me in the slut camp. Cervical cancer is a slutty cancer. When I was first trying to make sense of my diagnosis in 1999, I picked up a pamphlet from the waiting room at the cancer center where I would have my treatment. Two of the few risk factors listed for cervical cancer were "sexual activity at an early age" and "multiple sexual partners." Reading this irritated me and I wondered aloud to my then-husband how many newly diagnosed women felt chastened by it. Despite my feminist resistance to shaming, I did feel inadvertent pangs of regret. I wondered what I had done to give myself this life-threatening disease and how I could have prevented it. Women with cervical cancer often work hard to escape the implicit accusation in that list of risk factors. Imagining myself at a rally lofting a sign that reads "I am a proud slut!" or scribbling the word "SLUT" on my chest provokes bewilderment more than deliverance.

I know women with cervical cancer who report enduring moral accusations from family, friends, and others as a consequence of popular sexist stigmas regarding sexually transmitted infections. They struggle with the ignorant notion that women have brought on cervical cancer due to "immoral" sexual behaviour. Increasing public awareness of HPV as the cause of cervical cancer only seems to have exaggerated such responses. Some women have even been told that their cancer is punishment for their sins. In the United States, we have witnessed a backlash against HPV vaccines, with the root of opposition being a conviction that access to the vaccine may give young women permission to be slutty. The weight of these judgments on women struggling through a cancer diagnosis and treatment cannot be understated.

While this did not happen to me, I have to wonder whether my "cover" as a white, middle class, (at the time) married, college professor somehow inoculated me from such insults. I vividly recall the unprompted reassurances I received from doctors, nurses, residents, and medical students on my team that I had "done nothing wrong." Which of course communicated to me that some women had done things wrong. Were they bigger sluts than I was? Did social privilege exempt my sexual history from moral scrutiny? I was constantly made to feel that I was an exception. With an illness that disproportionately afflicts poor women and women of colour, this treatment and these messages distanced me from my fellow sufferers. I was seen as a "respectable" woman whose potential death from cervical cancer at a relatively young age would certainly be unjust, a tragedy, and a fluke. Still, all efforts to exonerate me simply reinforced how cervical cancer is seen as a slutty cancer.

The fact that I may have contracted my high-risk strain of HPV as a consequence of repeated sexual assault from the ages of ten to twelve only compounds the slut factor. I was not violently accosted by a stranger, you see, as I had learned would happen in "legitimate" cases of rape. I was bullied into sexual acts by an older boy whose primary mission in life was to terrorize me. This experience eroded my personal boundaries in such a way that left me vulnerable to the encroaching sexual desires of others for many years to come. Coming to sexual maturity was fraught with pain and uncertainty for me. I fail to see the liberatory potential of reclaiming sluthood in that narrative thread.

I have no pride in suffering from cervical cancer. I have no pride in succumbing to the violent whims of that older boy. I have no pride in spending too many years of my life alienated from my own sexual self and vulnerable to the dominating desires of others. Nor do I aim to develop any. I have survived and in small ways transcended, but I have done so by rejecting the very notion of a slut. To me, there is no such thing as a slut. The term's only purpose is to exercise patriarchal power to demean, shame, and control women. The last thing I want to do is imprint the oppressor's reckless charge on my finally healing body-self. I have rarely enjoyed the level of sexual agency celebrated by SlutWalk.

Even if I were able to suspend my own experiences of cervical cancer and sexual assault, trying to do so in order to feign belonging only takes the movement so far. It would be an empty gesture. My playing along for the sake of the movement would not advance the cause. It is an incomplete camaraderie, a partial strategy. Still, I am part of this movement and I am angry, as I am sure were all of the people who turned out for the SlutWalk events. I want to forge bonds with others to challenge sexual violence. Is there room for my palpable fury in the space of SlutWalk? Does rejecting the label preclude me from expressing my solidarity? How is slut play balanced with rage?

SlutWalk is a march of solidarity. But must one accept the reclamation to express that solidarity? Can SlutWalk be a simple effort to point out the ridiculousness of common accusations against victims of sexual violence?

SOLIDARITY AND LIBERATION

Apart from my individual resistance to embracing the label, I also wonder about the SlutWalks as a fruitful expression of wrath concerning sexual violence. What is the potential and what are the limits of this specific strategy? We must confront the problems of inequality in the movement and resolve the tension between individual identity claims (whether or not one can buy in) and the need for the strategy to be collective. One person cannot accomplish this alone, but we cannot have unity of message and complete participation either. Where is the appropriate equilibrium?

I applaud the imaginative response of the SlutWalk organizers to such a foul and baseless piece of "advice," and I celebrate the solidarity against injustice they inspired around the globe. They mobilized a global wave of resistance. They employed artistic energy and endorsed a playful sexuality. They successfully drew media attention in an age when social movements struggle to gain the public recognition they so deserve. They inspired people who may never have considered themselves feminists to find common cause with those of us who do, joining forces to decry hackneyed ideas about sexual violence. Some argue that the zany theatre of such gatherings can change people's minds and attract new recruits to the movement. One writer on *Feministing* called the SlutWalk a potential "gateway drug" (Truitt). The SlutWalks provided a vibrant space in which the people who attended could speak truth to power and do so in a creative way that engaged the public in meaningful discussions about sexuality, injustice, and violence.

SlutWalk is not the first attempt to rescue the term slut from the clutches of patriarchy. It is, in fact, part of a pattern of reclamation begun more than twenty years ago. Attwood points to a group of texts published in the late twentieth century that share "...a positive re-evaluation of sexual promiscuity and/or sex work through a mobilization of the 'slut' persona" (235). She recounts the history of the term and analyzes various arguments in the ensuing debate over the purpose and worth of such reclamation.

Attwood recalls the Riot Grrrl habit of writing the word slut on their bodies at performances as an act of transgression. Riot Grrrls meant to flout conventional policing of their bodies, lay claim to their sexuality, as well as provoke conversation and debate. She documents a proliferation of uses of the term slut with the advent of the Internet and the rise of alternative online media. She concludes, "Whether our focus is the way 'slut' is used to police women's behaviour, the significance of sluttiness in popular culture, or its appropriation in mainstream and subcultural practices, an understanding of the ways it might unite or divide us as women and as feminists is crucial" (244).

What differentiates SlutWalk from previous attempts is their reclamation of the slut label in union with a collective protest against sexual violence. This deployment of a sexist slur has the potential to put into stark relief the double standard routinely applied to women's and men's sexuality. It can, as many have claimed, serve a liberatory purpose for those women who freely embrace the mantle of sluthood. Individual women who proudly call themselves sluts come out of the shadows, release shame, and proclaim control of their sexual selves. SlutWalk, however, represents a first attempt to politicize the term and to organize under its banner in the service of gender justice.

Several questions point to likely limitations of this strategy. First, does the rightful claim to slutty behaviour inadvertently confine us to a stereotypical dominant straight masculine sexuality? Is being a slut about women getting to exercise sexual power much the way men have done? If so, our liberatory project appears to be trapped within a structure of unequal power relations. Further, the absence of deconstructive discourse reinforces a heterosexist gender binary. Claims to "no strings emotion free sex" abound in popular culture and online forums. In an analysis of *Sex and the City*, Gail Markle questions whether "the sexual double standard has been replaced with an equal opportunity sexual freedom." (46) Such a goal seems to echo the patriarchal privileges of hegemonic masculinity and may also invoke neoliberalism.

As self-proclaimed sluts, what do we mean to communicate and accomplish? If our primary gain in sluthood is adopting sexual practices that were marked as the domain of men then we find ourselves in an equally constricted place. A simple inversion of sexualized gender hierarchy is no liberation and certainly does not reflect the full spectrum of sexual expression and exploration. In Lamb's words, "feeling emboldened sexually is not the same as empowered" (qtd in Gavey 719). If sluthood is part of a broader feminist project, we need to carefully elucidate the ways in which being a slut liberates us from sexist practices rather than reinscribing sexual privilege (albeit inverted) within an undisturbed hierarchy. We must not conflate desire and pleasure with empowerment. We have more conceptual work to do to make that clear. Perhaps this is an instance in which we should put down the master's tools (Lorde).

Second, does the use of the slut trope serve to minimize the incidence or repercussions of sexual violence? The answer to this question requires empirical investigation. While I embrace the meaningful exchanges brought on by the SlutWalk phenomenon, I do wonder what those outside the movement see/hear/feel/think in response to a march. I would inquire whether the protests have precipitated a cultural shift and in what direction. We know that officer Sanguinetti will not likely utter those hateful words in public again, nor will any of his colleagues in Toronto or elsewhere. But will they stop thinking that women dressing "like sluts" invite assault? Will men hesitate to rape? Will communities refrain from blaming a woman for being raped? Preliminary evidence points to some danger in individual deployment of a slut identity. Young girls who had embraced the slut label to proclaim their sexual empowerment reported in interviews that they "ended up losing control of the label when their peers turned it against them" (Tanenbaum qtd in Valenti). We need to investigate, document, and understand the broader consequences of exposure to SlutWalks.

Third, does making the link between sexuality and violence communicate acceptance that they are related? I have serious doubts about the linking of playful/powerful sexuality and violence. We can empower ourselves and each other to feel confident and comfortable in our sexuality, to not live in fear of being called a slut or being assaulted. However, doing so will not in and of itself protect us from or reduce sexual violence at large. This may be another case for putting down the master's tools (Lorde).

We must unlink sexuality from violence. Even if the SlutWalk strategy works to liberate individual women from shame and regret, it may not work to curb sexual violence. Social structures that make some people vulnerable to attack and others likely to assault remain intact regardless of what women choose to wear or how they act. The same argument that serves to uncouple our sexuality from the sexual violence visited upon us leaves the latter unbroken. No matter how free we feel to dress as we like, love as we like, and indulge in carnal pleasures to our hearts desire, we are still at risk of being raped. Reclaiming the word slut and enacting a confident sexuality does not protect us from assault. Neither does it help to unfasten our sexuality from the violence visited upon our bodies. How can we extend SlutWalk beyond the protest action and connect it to ongoing efforts to combat sexual violence?

FROM STREET THEATRE TO SUSTAINED SOCIAL ACTION

We should be careful not to ask too much of SlutWalk. We must accept it for what it is, an inspired but limited strategy to confront inaccurate, oppressive claims about sexual violence. We need to think of it as a situational technique. In that case, it has been hugely successful. It is a collective public strategy, emerging to confront a specific threat. As such, it also offers a model of flexibility and the chance to embrace the slut label at some moments and let it fall away at others. It makes our movement more supple.

SlutWalk gives us a model to follow, arising in reaction to a specific attack, more than a comprehensive movement in and of itself. SlutWalk organized to make a statement and garner media attention, to stick up for every person who has ever endured sexual violence and public rebuke for bringing on their own suffering. The organizers and walkers are one manifestation of the larger movement to eliminate sexual violence in our communities. Slut-Walk properly shames those who would lay the blame on victims of sexual assault. I am grateful to SlutWalk for provoking exactly the kind of discussions we are having. We need more outrageous, ingenious social actions to do the same, and we need to make sure their influence extends to the broader movement itself.

We must harness the energy of the SlutWalks to reinvigorate, draw more attention to, and encourage new activists to contribute to ongoing attempts to reduce sexual violence and support those who have been assaulted. If a playful celebration of women's sexuality brings new people to the movement, I am all for it. But we need to remember that it does not stop there. Our bodily integrity, emotional health, and in some cases our very lives depend on it.

WORKS CITED

Attwood, Feona. "Sluts and Riot Grrrls: Female Identity and Sexual Agency." *Journal of Gender Studies* 16.3 (2007): 233-247. Print.

Truitt, J. "SlutWalk Redux with Rebecca Traister and Feministing-Writers." *Feministing*. N.pub. 22 July 2011. Web. 16 December 2013.

Gavey, Nicola. "Beyond 'Empowerment'? Sexuality in a Sexist World." *Sex Roles* 66 (2012): 718-724. Print.

Lorde, Audre. "The Master's Tools Will Never Dismantle the Master's House." *This Bridge Called My Back: Writings by Radical Women of Color*. Ed. Cherríe Moraga and Gloria Anzaldúa. New York: KitchenTable/Women of Color Press, 1983. 94-101. Print.

Markle, Gail. "'Can Women Have Sex Like a Man'? Sexual Scripts in *Sex and The City*." *Sexuality and Culture* 12 (2008): 45-57. Print.

Valenti, Jessica. "What Makes a Slut? The Only Rule, It Seems, Is Being Female. *The Guardian*. 23 June 2014. Web. 23 June 2014.

Loud, Proud, Fat Slut

MORRISA SILVERT

BEING FAT HAS ALWAYS AFFECTED every part of my experience. I have been large since the day I was born, and grew
up with awareness that I was a giant compared to most kids
my age. I was the only fat kid in my class from nursery school
until high school. I was tormented for my weight by kids in all
the grades, as well as ostracized by members of my own class.
For many years during this time, one of my only friends was a kid
who was slightly chubby. We were excluded, together; we spent
a lot of time at each other's houses talking about how much we
hated our bodies. When my friend hit puberty she got tall and
thin and left me behind in the short fat dust. As a loyal fat-hater,
I helped her in her mission to become more popular, which aided
my own quest to have a popular friend to prove to me that I was
worthy of friendship. When she "hooked up" (the most perfect
of vague phrases) with some guy we knew, she asked me to tell
some of the girls in our class. I did this one night at a pre-teens'
party at our local house of religious worship. I started an awk-
ward conversation with some of the girls by casually calling my
friend a slut for giving the boy a hand job. This seemed like the
perfect way to say this because of course if my friend was a slut
who "hooked up," then she was pretty enough for someone to
want her to touch them, and therefore she was really awesome
and cool and you should want to be like her too. When I called
her after the party to say I told two of the more popular girls
who would surely spread the word, she said "Well don't call me a
slut when you tell people!" I was so surprised that she didn't see

slut as a good thing that I promised not to call her that anymore, without any explanation.

When SlutWalk came around and I heard about people trying to breathe new life into the word, it resonated with me because of that experience of trying to make my friend popular. Suddenly I became aware of all these people expanding upon the idea I once had when I was twelve and then quickly suppressed because of shame. We were talking about having control of our bodies, loving our bodies, and consensually experiencing pleasure with other people. In this redefinition of the word, being a slut means having ultimate authority over your body, including having sex with yourself and embracing the fact that you may never want to have any sexual experiences, ever. After attending SlutWalks in both Toronto and Hamilton, I finally found the emotional capacity to co-organize these protests in Hamilton, where I now live.

I started my post secondary education at York University in Toronto in 2006, where I lived in Vanier Residence. I was lucky to live on a floor in Vanier full of wonderful, friendly people. In fact, our floor was such a community that the university chose to do their residence tours there to make a good impression on prospective students. We always kept our doors open, so we were constantly in and out of each others' rooms. We also spent a lot of time eating and hanging out in the common room—a room that was right by the elevators on every other floor. At the opposite end of the floor, and in the same spot on every other floor, was the room of the Don—the older student who got paid to encourage inclusivity and make sure no one died. Residence was glorious. For many reasons, I felt that I had a home in which I could thrive, not merely exist. I am still friends with the majority of these people, and for that I am lucky and grateful.

I have spent so long dissociating from the following memories that I have trouble recalling the details beyond some snippets of impressions and images. It takes time to remember—I have to go back and put myself in my mind's eye of Vanier Residence at York University in 2007, and I have to remind myself to take deep breaths to stay calm so I can focus and record. I've wanted to write out the entire story for a long time. It was my second year of university and that year a bunch of my friends remained in the residence from first year. I didn't have a roommate that year but was next door to one of my best friends who I had met the year before. The events happened during Frosh Week and everyone still had their name tags on their doors.

Every Thursday was pub night. We tended to start drinking early in the afternoon on pub nights, so by midnight I was wasted and exhausted. One night, I remember I went to my room for something, but once I saw my bed I decided to lie down. I thought, fuck it, I'm going to sleep. I suddenly remembered I had not locked my door. I groaned and tried to figure out if I would really be in danger. Was it worth the risk just so I would not have to get up? I did feel safe enough; this place had been my home for so long that I trusted I was safe. However, I was raised a girl, and this means that I always think about how "you never know" and "well if it turns out I am not safe, I will be so mad at myself for being lazy and not getting up to protect myself." So I got up and locked the door, scurried back to bed and leapt in.

At around 4:00 a.m. I woke up and, still kind of drunk, realized I needed to use the bathroom. I stepped out of my room and in the dimness of the safety lights I saw a girl wandering down the hall, staring at the doors. I can't remember what I said to her. I hope it was something caring, not just a "What's up?" but it was probably the latter. She told me she was looking for the Don's room. I thickly registered that this was strange, since everyone knew where the Dons' rooms were, but I pointed it out to her then headed into the bathroom. While I was in the stall I heard someone pounding on a door—a sound you get used to identifying in residence—so I went to investigate. It was the same girl thumping on the Don's door. Again, I cannot remember what I said to her, and again, I hope it was something more sensitive than "What are you doing?" I usually ask a lot of questions, to the point that some people get annoyed by my curiosity. This was the first time I can remember not asking for more information, either to see if I could help or to appease my curiosity. She told me she needed to talk to the Don. I told her to call the "Don-on-duty" pager number that the Dons took turns monitoring at night. She asked me what the number was, and I said I didn't know but to check the common room, that it was posted in there. She asked me where the common room was, and again I thought how it was strange that she didn't already know, but I just pointed her in the right direction and went back to bed.

The next morning I jumped out of bed at the sound of loud banging on my door. I looked out my peep hole and saw a cop. These days, I would definitely be wary of opening a door to a cop, but I opened my door for him. He told me that there had been a sexual assault the night before and asked me if I had any information. I said no. I asked him if it was rape. He nodded quietly and said, "We think so." What alarmed me was that even he looked sad, and I had never before seen a cop who let their face betray their emotions.

It turned out that two men had snuck into the building with an extremely drunk person who lived in the building under the pretense of helping their "friend" to bed. The two men, Justin Connort and Daniel Katsnelson (the latter changed his last name to Kaye before he was sentenced in an attempt to "start over"), then prowled the building, finding female door tags and turning the handles to see if the doors were unlocked. It feels good to have names for these people, the people who so drastically affected my world. In their trials, the men admitted to breaking into five unlocked rooms and raping women in two of them. Both women had been sleeping. I think Connort and Katsnelson lied, and that they actually broke into more rooms. They broke into my friend's room—the room right next to mine. My friend was in her room, but so were two of our male friends. The rapists quickly left, and the accounts they gave in court of breaking into rooms do not match any of my friends' accounts. I have probably spent hundreds of hours agonizing over the thoughts, "Did they try my door handle? Would I have been assaulted that night if I had not locked my door?" It shouldn't have mattered that these women's doors were unlocked. Of course they left their doors unlocked! They were in their home—we all left our doors unlocked!

During his trial, Katsnelson said that he hoped that the victims learned something positive from this: to lock their doors. When I read that statement in the news reports in 2011, it launched me into rage and panic. How dare he place the blame on the victims? I have not committed an act of violence since I was a very young child, but that statement was enough to make me want to break his face.

I am consistently awed by the strength and power of the survivors. These women had the courage not only report, but to face the attackers in court to tell their stories. This is an extremely brave act in a world where the vast majority of sexualized violence is not reported due to fear of retribution or being accused of lying. I don't know these women, but I am so incredibly proud of them, and I know many people who are also awed by their strength. If these women ever feel safe enough, or are so inclined to speak publicly about what happened, I will be the first to tell them how much I respect that decision.

Before there were any details beyond "something like rape happened last night," news spread throughout our campus. I heard countless variations of the accusation that, since it had been pub night, these women must have led the men into their bedrooms. I was enraged by these accusations, I wanted to scream at everyone "Who the fuck cares if she let him (them) in? Even if she had, and then she said no, it doesn't mean what happened was ok!" But I couldn't. Not knowing the terms "rape culture," "slut-shaming," or "victim-blaming," I did not know what to say to stand up for these women without incoherently screaming and sobbing.

Almost immediately after the rapes occurred, the head Don and a cop walked around Vanier Residence, trying to make sure that everyone's doors were closed and locked. Mine was wide open—in fact, many people on my floor had their doors open. For me, keeping my door open was important so I could see if anything fun was going on that I didn't want to miss, and to talk to my floor mates and friends as they walked past. The head Don and the cop told everyone that from now on they had to keep their doors locked at all times. I told them that under no circumstance would I be doing this. The last thing we needed now was for everyone to be shut up in their rooms, not paying attention to what was going on. Residence is a community—we needed to know each other, to be able to check in on each other, to make friends and include everyone, and to help anyone who was unhappy or unsafe. Eventually the Don and cop left, saying something along the lines of,

"We will see about this." I propped open my door again, as widely as possible. I would have kept that door open regardless of what they threatened me with. Later that week, the head Don saw me in the lobby of the building and told me that she and the cop had decided to give me special permission to keep my door open. As time passed, it seemed like fewer and fewer people continued to lock their doors, and when I walked around my floor, I was still able to check in on my floor mates and say hello.

I forgot all about the girl I had run into in the hallway that night until a few days later when I was talking to my Don. She told me that she had been the Don-on-duty that night and had gotten the call from the survivor around 4 a.m. Something clicked and I realized it was that girl—the girl wandering around the floor was one of the survivors. I felt sick. Of all times, why did I choose to keep my big mouth quiet? Why hadn't I helped her, asked if she were ok, offered to get the Don-on-duty number for her, offered to stay with her? I realize that even if I had done those things, it wouldn't really have been any help to her. There was nothing I could have done at all, but I still felt immensely guilty that I hadn't been more helpful, and terribly guilty that possibly the only reason I didn't get assaulted that night was because I let fear get to me and I locked my door.

Years later I heard about SlutWalk and I felt immense relief, although I was reluctant to attend as I was still suffering from survivor's guilt from that night. Luckily my younger sister talked me into going. As we descended onto Queen's Park the day of the protest, I felt electric goose bumps running all over my body. I looked at all the women, some naked, some covered from neck to ankle, bearing signs of protest that said things like "I was nine—did I deserve it?" That first walk was overwhelming, empowering, triggering, joyful, and painful in the deep achy way that is the start of healing. Because of this, I don't have many solid memories from that day. Mostly I remember images and feelings, such as briefly meeting up with a good friend and her child, my niecey-nephew. The toddler was bundled up in a stroller and they were going to meet with a few other moms. I also remember being swept up in the crowd of protestors, but feeling safe instead of panicked. Mostly I remember milling about,

reading people's powerful signs with declarations of body autonomy and decrying victim-blaming and slut-shaming. I bumped
into two more friends, one of them a man, and was excited to
find out that they too were feminists, which led to us spending
a lot of time together since we all lived in the same area. There
were hundreds of people there that day. After assembling, we
marched to police headquarters. Speeches were given, including
one by Jane Doe, a rape survivor who successfully fought the
Toronto Police, causing safety audits of how the force handled
sexualized violence. She talked about healthy consent, and got
us all laughing by reiterating how important and awesome it is
for people to have hot consensual sex.

The first SlutWalk Hamilton was similarly overwhelming, even
though there were fewer people (Hamilton is much smaller than
Toronto). I attended the protest with the two friends I had bumped
into at SlutWalk Toronto, as well as some of their friends who I
would become extremely close to. Two of these friends held signs
that decried the shame unloaded on them while their rapists were
not judged. I had never met anyone that I knew had been raped. I
felt nauseated. I wanted to cry—for them, I told myself at the time,
but as I came to acknowledge my own assaults, I would realize
that I wanted to cry for me, too. Jane Doe was a speaker for the
first Hamilton SlutWalk, and I spoke with her at the after-party.
I was really nervous, as I usually am with people whose strength
overwhelms me. I told her that since the Toronto walk, every time
I had "hot consensual sex," I had thought of her. This made her
burst into laughter, and for a moment I felt an intense connection
with her. I still think about her a lot.

That first march went from Hamilton City Hall to police headquarters. A lot of things happened that day that I don't feel safe
including here because they deal with interaction between the
police and the organizers, and demands that were made but were
never met. Communication between the organizers and the police
got very personal, and if I wrote about it here I truly feel that I
would be putting those organizers in danger. Through various
avenues, especially the sexual misconduct between several police
officers (that year, Kevin Dhinsa, and more recently, Derek Mellor)
and the civilians they were working with, many of the SlutWalk

Hamilton organizers feel wary talking to police, let alone about them. And that is really the point: the people who are supposed to protect us terrify us.

One thing that did happen as planned was that attendees were invited to come to the front of the crowd and share their stories of survival. Person after person came up to declare their stories through a megaphone: one woman spoke about her special needs son being assaulted by a caregiver; another woman spoke about waking up in a hotel room after being drugged and raped, and then hearing from male acquaintances that if they knew they wouldn't get caught, they would do it too. My friends gave testimonials of surviving rape and stalking and continual harassment. At the core of many of the testimonials were the common experiences of being disbelieved, blamed, shamed, and being unwilling or unable to report. This is the rape culture we live in. During all the testimonials, I tried to convince myself to go up and share. I was sweaty and shaky and my stomach felt fiery—a sensation I always feel during times of anxiety and potential. Finally, I found myself walking up and taking the megaphone. I unleashed my story of the York University rapes. I gave as many details as I could pluck from my racing thoughts, and talked until I was hoarse. By attending SlutWalk, I felt like I was finally doing something about what had happened at York. SlutWalk enabled me to begin unburdening myself from survivor's guilt, and turning rage into the empowerment needed to fight against patriarchy. I was cheered by the crowd every time I faltered or paused, and elicited shouts of "Shame!" when I told the most sickening parts. When I was done, I felt calmer, but with a different kind of rage. I had opened up about what had been agonizing me for years. It was truly the start of fighting back.

When I arrived at the second SlutWalk Toronto in 2012, the first thing I noticed, as in previous SlutWalks, was the abundance of topless and otherwise unclothed women. They all seemed so free, like they felt safe surrounded by one thousand allies, and proud of their bodies. The more topless women I saw the more I wanted to peel off my shirt and bra and loudly proclaim, "Look at my beautiful fat body! Look at the curves, and the muscles, and all the wonderful flesh that protects me! And you know what? This is here for ME to enjoy! Maybe you can enjoy it too, if I want you to, but it is here for ME." Finally, I tore off my top and bra, and while I did not proclaim any of those things, I certainly felt them. I marched through those streets and felt protected by the allies around me. Others smiled at me and our voices rose loudly together. While this was happening, I realized my picture was frequently being taken in a short amount of time. I knew that as a fat woman, and maybe the fattest topless woman there, I was a source of intrigue for photographers. I calmly let it happen. My body is beautiful and if people wanted to photograph it, that was fine with me. Later, I saw some of these photos online. A lot of people commented on them, and what surprised and touched me most was that none of them were negative. In fact, all but one were deeply positive comments about my strength and beauty, and words inspiring others to feel good about their bodies, too. The one commenter that was not overly positive, but not negative to me, said they were confused about my gender. This was not bothersome to me at all because I love and appreciate gender fluidity, and it excited me that I could be seen as androgynous. However, many people immediately jumped to my defense, some saying I am a beautiful woman, and others asking why naming gender even matters. I loved that—because it doesn't matter, and I am proud to have been the catalyst for someone to learn.

During the second SlutWalk Hamilton, I was ready to be a volunteer, but not to co-organize. I was a marshal that year— the buffer between cars and marchers— as well as the head cheerleader. Me—a cheerleader! As a kid I could never understand the ideology behind cheerleading. Why dance around and yell when you can get right in there and play the game? I kept giggling to myself when I thought of myself as a cheerleader, but I was excited to yell those feminist chants. I even got my own bullhorn; it was so heavy that by the end of the day I could barely lift my arm! We marched through the streets, yelling phrases and slogans in unison, catching the attention of people walking past. We had some of the classics like "Hey mister mister, get your hands off my sister" and "Hey hey, ho ho, the patriarchy has got to go!" But one of the most powerful chants was Hamilton-exclusive. There is a strip of bars and clubs located near downtown Hamilton called Hess.

As this is an area designated for heavy drinking, it has become a space where people are unsafe because perpetrators of sexualized violence are routinely excused for their behaviour. Therefore the chant was: "Hey, Hess, a dress is not a yes!" As we walked through Hess, chanting, yelling, and singing, we watched the puzzled faces of people on patios, and it felt good to disturb them. At the end of the march, we assembled in a parking lot and used the bullhorns to invite people to come up and share their stories. That year we saw an older man, a man none of the volunteers had noticed at the beginning of the march, walk up through the crowd to the bullhorn. I caught the eye of the head organizer and we both grimaced, preparing ourselves to have to confront this man. What he said still affects us today: He had been sitting on a patio enjoying a drink when he heard and saw us coming. He read our signs. He joined in. He was so touched and impressed by our organizing that he felt compelled to join and congratulate us for bringing awareness to such an important issue.

SlutWalk Hamilton 2013 was the first time that I was a co-organizer. I was certainly not the head organizer, and I am eternally grateful to Nikki Wilson, Lauren Charman, Jenna Purnell, Ashleigh Patterson, Quinn Jones, and Christine Hughes for allowing me the opportunity to be involved in something so amazing. I did not even realize how much passion I had until the planning was well under way. I was overwhelmed and astounded by how much work there was to do. One thing that complicated our planning was being harassed by a local group of MRAs—people who claim to be mens' rights activists, but are anti-woman, anti-feminist, and aggressive. Their ideology is that because women abuse men, women are terrible people who, at the very least, do not deserve respect. Because our names were out there, these men were able to find us online and attack us personally. One of our organizers was so tormented that she dropped out of organizing and did not feel safe enough to attend the protest. I did, however, manage to learn a lesson from the MRA. One day, a few weeks before the protest, Jenna and I wandered the city putting up flyers. We came across an MRA poster that was clearly posted high enough to prevent any "average" sized woman from ripping it down. The poster was inflammatory, triggering, and awful. Jenna and I, who are both short, were enraged. With her consent, I grabbed her around the thighs and hoisted her as high as possible so that she could tape one of our posters over theirs. We felt amazing, and congratulated ourselves on getting back at the MRAs. Later, a video was sent to the Facebook page for SlutWalk Hamilton. An MRA had found their poster covered with ours. He zoomed in on the poster, and without showing himself, talked about how SlutWalk is clearly full of "misandrists" who support the abuse of men. Obviously, we were saddened by this—SlutWalk stands for people of all genders. We publicly acknowledge that men are hurt by rape culture and patriarchy, and we welcome male survivors and allies to march with us. I felt like I had made a mistake: I think we should have put our poster right next to theirs and let people make up their own mind. Censoring a group, no matter how much I disagree with them, is something I never want to do. The next year, I made sure not to cover any MRA posters. In one of their threatening messages in 2013, they let us know that they were planning to come to the march to disrupt as much as possible, so we put a message on our Facebook page to suggest that people avoid interacting with the MRAs, as they tend to provoke emotionally volatile responses in order to "prove" that feminists hate men and free speech. The day of the 2013 march, the MRAs stood across the street from city hall holding signs with messages along the lines of "What if she got HIM drunk?" During the march, as we went past the MRAs, a female attendee pointed at that sign and started yelling, "Then it was rape!" A few more voices joined in until the whole crowd was yelling about how the male would have been the one who was raped. I could see that the MRAs looked shocked. After the march, when we returned to city hall, they came up to some of the organizers to tell us that they were impressed by the protest. They thought we had done a good job and had tackled some important issues. This was probably supported by the fact that we had male speakers. The one lasting problem they had with us, they said, was the use of the word feminism. While we wanted to spit back "Yeah, we'll get right on that," we did not take the bait. The thing that bothers me most is that if the MRAs are truly for men's rights, they would be feminists and would work with us, because we *are* for men's rights! We are for the rights of everyone who is touched by the patriarchy—and therefore for the rights of every human on the planet. That is what is misunderstood about feminism, and especially about SlutWalk. We are here for all survivors.

During my second year at York University, a very close friend introduced me to the concept of fat feminism. That friend, also fat, was so confident in herself that I couldn't help but be drastically impacted both by her confidence and the concept of fat feminism. Before SlutWalk, I had been unable to identify my experiences of sexual assault. They had always felt like weird little experiences that made me ashamed and I tried not to think about them. Fat feminism drastically changed my feelings of self-worth. It strengthened me; I felt like a whole, worthy person. By the time SlutWalk first came around in 2011, I had developed a self-image that was full of self-love and acceptance. This outlook allowed me to examine what I was learning from SlutWalk. I realized that the "weird little experiences" were indeed assaults, and it was powerful to be able to name them. Because I had formerly believed that I was too fat to be worthy of positive sexual attention, I had latched onto any sexual attention. There was one person on my floor in residence at York University who had a hard time understanding boundaries in general, and most certainly sexual boundaries. I was attracted to him, and we spent a lot of time hanging out together. Once in awhile, he would touch my body in a sexual manner without my consent. Because I had so much self-loathing, I interpreted this as flirting, which encouraged me to hang out with him more. Occasionally he would do something that caused me to freak out, but not stop hanging out with him: He would come up behind me, put his hand between my legs, and then run his hand down my body, down the centre of my vagina and ass. He usually did this when we were drunk. I would yell at him and he would shrug it off and not do it for awhile. One night, at a party at a friend's house, he was wasted and I was sober. He grabbed my arm, pulled me into a bedroom, and touched me in that way. When I yelled at him he said, "You like it." I got up in his face, looked in his eyes, and growled at him, "Never do that again." He looked startled—although I think I was more surprised than he was—and said ok. He never did. He is now out of my life, but it took a long time for me to understand that he had problems, not me.

This experience was the catalyst for my testimony at SlutWalk Hamilton 2013. I talked about how there is a belief that fat people are not capable of being sexually assaulted because no one would want to touch them, and if they had in fact been assaulted, they should feel grateful to be touched. I talked about how I have been fat from the moment I was born, and how I had suffered much abuse, misguided advice, and sexual misconduct because of it. I shared how in the past, I too believed that no one would want to touch a fat person. Because of that, as a teenager and young adult, I had consented to many things that I did not actually want to do because I figured the chance to be touched might never come again and that I might as well take what I could get even if it didn't feel good. Each time I did something like that, in the moment I felt like I was doing myself a favour—that now I would be more desirable, and would always have the knowledge that there was someone out there who did not find me repulsive. As an adult looking back on those situations, I don't feel dirty or damaged or like used goods, because those are all aspects of rape culture. Instead, I prefer to learn from them. I shared with the crowd that by the time I left York University, I felt beautiful not in spite of my body, but because of it. I have these amazing, wonderful curves, a squishy lap that my niblings (the gender neutral word for nieces and nephews) love to sit in, and a soft, strong body that people love to hug and kiss and caress. The crowd cheered when I said these things, and I realized that not only were they cheering for what I was saying, they were cheering for my body too! This was the first time I had been privy to such an outpouring of support for fat bodies, and it was overwhelming to realize that I was the medium. Afterwards, some of the fat-identified women in the crowd came up to congratulate me on being so brave and for saying things that they had been feeling but didn't know how to express. This was the best part, knowing that I had touched fellow fat-identified people, who now knew that they were not alone in their thinking and that they are beautiful no matter what anyone says. I am often overwhelmed by the fact that I have gone from a child who hated myself and other fat people so much that I thought fat people should not be allowed to wear shorts in the summer so they could suffer for being fat, to a women who loves her body, goes topless at feminist events, and inspires others to thoroughly love their fat, gorgeous bodies. While protesting rape culture was my goal, I ended up feeling triumphant in these matters of body image and fat positivity.

When it came time to start planning for SlutWalk Hamilton 2014, I was struck by the fact that even though we knew how to go about the planning, it was still stressful, time consuming, and emotionally draining. We also learned from a major mistake: the previous year, we had often left the organizing meetings feeling depressed, angry, and alone. It is difficult to know that the onus is on you to create a safe, strong, feminist environment for over one hundred people. This difficulty was compounded by the fact that all of the organizers were there for personal reasons, many of us being survivors. That year, we made sure to spend some time after the meetings just hanging out as friends, at the very least to ensure that no one felt alone. We also started a tradition: watching silly YouTube videos of baby animals. It may sound unnecessary, but I firmly believe that without those videos we would have all burnt out faster and lost focus and passion. Instead, we felt rejuvenated. It is amazing what group laughter can do for people. We also spent time doing group guerrilla postering for the event after the meetings, and that made us feel powerful and accomplished. There's nothing quite like walking around your city and seeing posters for your protest. From the first Toronto SlutWalk in 2011, we had become increasingly aware of criticism, both local and global, that the name SlutWalk was not inclusive of all survivors of sexualized violence. In an attempt to respond to this concern, we decided to re-name our annual event. Eventually, we decided on "The Walk of No Shame" in order to highlight our main goal, which is to end the shaming and blaming of survivors of sexualized violence. We had observed that the conversations around SlutWalk were getting bogged down in the use of the word slut. While the organizers of the event still choose to identify as The SlutWalk Hamilton Collective, we changed the protest name in an attempt to redirect conversation towards support and solidarity for survivors.

In 2014, there was more media coverage than in 2013, and I believe some of that can be attributed to the name change. A few hours after the march, an online article was published about the march. We were still enjoying our after-party when one of us showed the article to everyone, choking out through tears, "They finally got it." It seemed that a journalist had finally understood that we were not trying to be provocative or looking for an excuse to be scantily clad in public; we were doing this in solidarity, to educate, to support, and indeed to save lives. This was one of the most fulfilling moments of this journey.

At the 2014 march my voice again grew hoarse before the half-way mark, and yet again, I continued chanting and yelling and screaming. At one point, one of the organizers took a turn on the bullhorn. Although my voice was already thick and gravelly, I surprised myself by still yelling without the horn, and in fact being the loudest voice, as attested by some of the volunteers. It just felt so good to chant with all my might, all my power. Marching through the city, literally screaming at the top of my lungs, throat aching, I have never felt better. That year, I decided to perform a spoken word piece about being fat. It addressed the names fat people are called, and how they are actually complimentary: thunder thighs—thunder is powerful and in many cultures is attributed to the anger of gods; muffin tops—everyone knows that the top of the muffin is the most delicious part and often the only part people eat! I talked about my own body, and how I used to hate it but now love and cherish it. The crowd roared with cheers for me, for my body, something that as a child I covered and hid and hated and harmed, and would never have imagined as worthy of cheers. The cheers were so loud and so unending that I had pause my performance where I had not intended, in order to be heard. I don't really know how to sum this up, other than to note that I cried a lot, both from happiness for myself, and sorrow for child-me who so deeply hated herself. I never thought I would love my body, let alone that a crowd full of people would love my body too! This experience is something for which I am completely grateful, and one that I think about if I am feeling bad about my body. Those cheers gave me power—power to keep on wholly loving myself.

One of the bands at the after-party had written a song inspired by the Hamilton SlutWalkers in 2013. It was pretty cool to see them on stage, singing about how we all have the right to be safe and decrying the notion that women are pieces of meat to be hunted. One of the lingering aspects of my personal body hatred was that I have always been too ashamed to dance. I have a couple of friends who are amazing dancers, who just do their own thing and don't worry about looking silly. I realized that I, too, have the right to dance! I danced my fucking ass off that night, flab jiggling, fat flying, twirling and stomping and feeling stronger with each movement. It was strange to say goodbye to my co-organizers that night. Even though we are all friends, which means we would see each other again soon, it felt like a forever-goodbye. As I write this, just a few weeks after that night, I still miss our weekly Sunday meetings. There is something so special about organizing with like-minded people who have survived similar things. It is therapeutic and encouraging, and we are excited to bring the hammer to rape culture together.

In organizing SlutWalk I have felt a sense of being truly, intimately connected with others, and have felt the power of support run through us all. It is a feeling that I so rarely experience that I cannot aptly describe it. It is the stuff you look back on and think "Yup, I was doing the right thing, and I am still proud." It feels like being a part of change. SlutWalk provides an opportunity for dialogue. It changes the conversation from the actions of survivors to the choices of perpetrators. We touch the lives of survivors and we all feel strong, if for only fleeting seconds. We hear others' stories and know that we are not alone, and because we hear these stories over and over, we gain strength. It is the sharing of stories that makes us feel less isolated and completely enraged—enraged that this has happened before and that it keeps happening again. In sharing stories we learn we are not alone, and that is why we are so compelled to support survivors and to never, ever stop talking about rape culture. To stop talking about rape culture is to bury our fears; it is to never go anywhere alone, and never be comfortable in our own skins. SlutWalk is our lifeline to each other. Only together can we raise awareness about rape culture in order to annihilate it.

Contributor Biographies

Raushan (Raisa) Bhuiyan is a writer from Dhaka, Bangladesh. She has been writing professionally since she was sixteen, producing works published in many publications and winning the 2008 Stephen Leacock Medal for Humour from the Stephen Leacock Foundation. Raisa is passionate about issues of access and equity for marginalized peoples.

Tracy B. Citeroni is an Associate Professor of Sociology at the University of Mary Washington in Fredericksburg, VA. She is a feminist scholar with a PhD from the University of Texas at Austin and specializes in the study of gender and health using qualitative research methods.

Nancy Effinger Wilson, PhD, is an Assistant Professor of English at Texas State University. Her publications include "Bias in the Writing Center: Tutor Perceptions of African American Language" and "Stocking the Bodega: Towards a New Writing Center Paradigm." Nancy's research focuses on countering (hetero)sexism and racism, especially in the composition classroom.

May Friedman teaches at Ryerson University in the School of Social Work and the Graduate Program in Communication and Culture. She is absolutely passionate about popular culture and has published extensively on the topics of motherhood, fat, and digital technologies.

Daniel Garrett is a PhD Student in the Department of Applied Social Sciences, City University of Hong Kong. He utilizes visual methods to investigate moral panic and enemy image processes underlying identity politics, image wars, international relations, and visual representation(s) of social movements. He is a SlutWalk Hong Kong supporter.

Nish Israni is a crazy/beautiful brown femme who loves to make art in its many mediums as well as riot in her everyday life. She is a writer first and foremost and has been published in many zines (*Pink Ink, Forum Magazine, Shameless*). She has also published her own zines (*Revolver, Pussy Manifesto*). She loves to meet new people, build community, and heal through solidarity. You can follow her blog at shebleeds.wordpress.com.

Norah Jones is a recent graduate of Middlebury College Sociology and Anthropology Department, and is currently working in museum education and children's media in New York City. She studied Slutwalk commentary as her senior thesis project.

Corinne L. Mason is an Assistant Professor in Gender and Women's Studies and Sociology at Brandon University in Manitoba. She conducts transnational critical race feminist analyses of development discourses and popular news media, focusing specifically on representations of global LGBT rights, violence against women, reproductive justice, and foreign aid. Her work has been published in *Feminist Formations, International Feminist Journal of Politics, Critical Studies in Media Communication,* and *Surveillance & Society.*

Clementine Morrigan is a multidisciplinary artist, writer, essayist, zinester, and community organizer. Her first book, *Rupture*, was published in 2012. She produced a short film entitled *Resurrection* in 2013. She writes a zine called *seawitch* and also works on other zine projects. Her work is concerned with a bottom-up approach to knowledge production, undermining the authority of meaning-makers such as medicine, psychiatry, law, and academia. More of her work can be found at clementinemorrigan.com.

Margaret K. Nelson is the Hepburn Professor of Sociology at Middlebury College. She advised Norah Jones on her senior project on Slutwalk. With Anita Ilta Garey and Rosanna Hertz she recently edited *Open to Disruption: Time and Craft in the Practice of Slow Sociology.*

Angie Ng is a PhD Candidate at Durham University (UK). She is the initiator of the local SlutWalk in Hong Kong, which has held an annual march for the past four years. Her research interests include the sex trade, violence against women, social movements and the media, and general health.

Andrea O'Reilly, PhD, is Professor in the School of Gender, Sexuality, and Women's Studies at York University. O'Reilly is founder and director of *The Motherhood Initiative for Research and Community Involvement,* founder and editor-in-chief of the *Journal of the Motherhood Initiative* and founder and editor of Demeter Press, the first feminist press on motherhood. She is editor and author of 19 books, including most recently *Mothers, Mothering and Motherhood across Cultural Differences: A Reader* (2014) and *Academic Motherhood in a Post Second Wave Context: Challenges, Strategies, Possibilities* (2012). She is editor of the first encyclopedia on Motherhood (2010). She is a recipient of the CAUT Sarah Shorten Award for outstanding achievements in the promotion of the advancement of women in Canadian universities and colleges, is twice the recipient of York University's "Professor of the Year Award" for teaching excellence, and in 2015 was the first inductee into the Museum of Motherhood Hall of Fame. She and her partner are the parents of three fabulous and feminist adult children.

Nicole Pietsch is Coordinator of the Ontario Coalition of Rape Crisis Centres. Her written work has appeared in *Canadian Woman Studies, the Journal of the Association for Research on Mothering,* and the University of Toronto's *Women's Health and Urban Life.* Her considerations of sex, race, gender, and the legal system are published in *Reena Virk: Critical Perspectives on a Canadian Murder* (Canadian Scholars Press) and *Sideshow of Merit* (Namelos).

Shannon Salisbury parents, teaches, and studies in Toronto. On the odd occasion that she has some downtime, she slowly works on curating and developing Ontario-based teacher resources to promote issues of consent, body autonomy, and resistance against rape culture from kindergarten to Grade 12.

Jacqueline Schiappa earned her PhD in Rhetoric, Scientific and Technical Communication from the University of Minnesota. After discovering intense debates in the feminist blogosphere on the Slutwalk movement, she travelled to Toronto to interview Slutwalk's original founders. Her interviews led to unique insights about the intentions of the organizers and how to better interpret controversies regarding Slutwalk's name. Her current research examines how the Black Twitter community functions as an effectively anti-racist counterpublic.

Erika Jane Scholz is a social worker who operates from a feminist, critical theory lens. She is a social justice advocate who is passionate and committed to working with women and those living with mental health challenges. She has a broad range of front-line community experience with various organizations including the TRCC-MWAR, Planned Parenthood, SlutWalk and CAMH. She currently resides in the heart of the Rockies in Calgary, Alberta, working as a Mental Health Clinician in the area of concurrent disorders. She holds a MSW from the Factor-Inwentash Faculty of Social Work.

Morrisa Silvert has an honours degree from York University in Professional Writing and Creative Writing. She is a proud, loud-mouthed feminist, fat activist, and Aunty. She enjoys cooking, hiking, and reading, as well as conversing about the foolishness of gender norms with her five-year-old neicey-nephew.

Alyssa Teekah is a ponderer, a question asker, and a perpetual laugher invested in the ongoing journey of knowledge-making and knowledge-breaking. Alyssa organized heavily at York University preceding her co-creation of the original SlutWalk. She has organized in community and academic research spaces since, including working with queer Asian-Canadian filmmaker Richard Fung, the

Centre for Women and Trans People at York University, and Masala Militia, a collective of 'brown'identified diasporic feminists. She holds a Master's in Gender Studies from the University of Toronto.

Amanda D. Watson is a PhD candidate at the Institute of Feminist and Gender Studies at the University of Ottawa. Her dissertation examines how contemporary mothers in the United States and Canada are responsibilized toward multiple, incoherent labours simultaneously according to new, empirical measures of responsible motherhood and work. She examines a range of mediated sites—from popular culture to biomedical research—where mothers are seen coming undone to cure social ills outside of their control. Amanda is also a writer with bylines in the *Toronto Star, National Post, Ottawa Citizen*, and *Humber Literary Review.*